International Guide to Drinks

International Guide to

DRINKS

Compiled by the United Kingdom Bartenders Guild

CENTURY

LONDON MELBOURNE AUCKLAND JOHANNESBURG

First published by Hutchinson & Co. (Publishers) Ltd
Reprinted in 1986 by Century, an imprint of Century Hutchinson Ltd,
Brookmount House, 62-65 Chandos Place, London WC2N 4NW

Century Hutchinson South Africa (Pty) Ltd
PO Box 337, Bergvlei 2012, South Africa

Century Hutchinson Australia (Pty) Ltd
PO Box 496, 16-22 Church Street, Hawthorn, Victoria 3122, Australia

Century Hutchinson New Zealand Ltd
PO Box 40-086, Glenfield, Auckland 10, New Zealand

First published 1953
Second edition 1955
Third edition 1960
Fourth edition 1965
Fifth edition 1971
Sixth edition 1976
Seventh edition 1978
Eighth edition 1981
Ninth edition 1986

Compiled and produced under the auspices of the United Kingdom Bartenders Guild
© United Kingdom Bartenders Guild

Colour separation by Sotographics Ltd
Set in VIP Candida by Phoenix Photosetting,
Chatham, Kent
Printed and bound in Great Britain by
Anchor Brendon Ltd, Tiptree, Essex

ISBN 0 7126 1704 3

Cover photograph by Robert Dowling
Cover design by Ewing Paddock

CONTENTS

FOREWORD

The worldwide revival of interest in the cocktail and the appearance of new products have meant that a new edition of the *International Guide to Drinks* is needed to keep pace with current trends and the Council of the UKBG has taken advantage of this opportunity to revise the book completely. The format has remained the same but some chapters have been expanded so that there are now over 700 recipes for cocktails and mixed drinks. Many of these are so famous that few bartenders need to refer to any book for the recipes, but others are new creations that are rising stars on the cocktail scene or regional specialities of general interest. The chapters on wines, spirits and aperitifs have been written as general introductions and if they should kindle an interest in a particular subject the reader is referred to the bibliography, which contains the titles of in-depth studies of most beverages.

Cocktail drinking is now a thoroughly acceptable social habit and it is not unusual to see American truckers drinking Daiquiris in roadside cafés or the local British publican cheerfully mixing a Harvey Wallbanger, while many a harassed businessman has retired to the bar for a Dry Martini and a relaxing chat with the bartender. The cocktail bar has also become a meeting place for younger people, which is one reason for the increased interest in long drinks, and the advent of the bar blender or liquidizer has introduced a new range of drinks that appeal particularly to women. A natural development of this trend is the increasing number of people who are keen to mix cocktails at home. Although this is essentially a reference book for working bartenders, the interested amateur will find much of interest.

The committee appointed by the Council to compile this ninth edition of the Guide has included two Councillors of the Guild, James McQuade and Brian Page, both holders of the coveted Advanced Bartender's Certificate, who have drawn on their wealth of experience in cocktail bars and have given unstintingly of their time. The Guide also owes much to the expertise and knowledge that have gone into producing previous editions and to the trade support that has made it possible.

Marilyn Harvey BA, ATCL
Editor

INTRODUCTION

In 1933 a small committee of bartenders founded the United Kingdom Bartenders' Guild which has grown into a national organization large enough to be divided into twelve regional areas as well as having branches overseas. The UKBG is a non-political trade association for male and female cocktail bartenders and it has an active associate membership mostly drawn from kindred trades. The Council is the governing body and it consists of a President, Vice-President, Councillors and one Representative from each of the regional areas. All officers are elected by secret ballot of full members and the Guild's finances are controlled by independent trustees.

The UKBG's primary function is the advancement of the bartending trade by promoting a high standard of workmanship, encouraging participation and maintaining a code of ethics applicable to a craft dedicated to quick efficient service and customer satisfaction. The Guild is also pledged to a policy of furthering goodwill and understanding between members and management and since its inception the organization has proved a valuable link between the two.

Education is recognized as being of prime importance and two scholarships are awarded each year to enable promising young people to attend a training course in Stresa, Italy, which is conducted by the International Bartenders' Association. The Guild is also responsible for organizing the Advanced Bartender's Course which is held every second year and is open to experienced working bartenders who have been members of the Guild for a minimum of five years. This course, which is recognized by the government, includes both theoretical and practical examinations and successful candidates are recognized as extremely skilled 'Master' bartenders. The UKBG also maintains a reference file of cocktails and mixed drinks that has been built up over many years and must represent the largest collection of recipes of this nature anywhere in the world.

An important aspect of the Guild's activity over the years has been to set up a channel of communication between its members and the wine and spirit trades because a thorough understanding of the products he is selling is a great advantage to a bartender, enabling him to mix drinks with confidence and to advise customers correctly, so increasing his ability as a salesman, which in turn contributes substantially to the profitability of the bar. The UKBG is keen to increase public awareness of the role of a bartender and to this end the National Demonstration Team attends Trade Exhibitions to mount a display that attracts thousands of people each year. At the same time commercially sponsored cocktail competitions are organized on a regional as well as a national basis, to test the skill and ingenuity of bartenders and increase consumer interest in cocktails.

The United Kingdom Bartenders' Guild has always been committed to promoting the highest principles of bartending and its members are noted for their skill, salesmanship and initiative so that a customer can feel confident of efficient, knowledgeable service in any cocktail bar that displays the pennant of the UKBG.

THE COCKTAIL
BAR

HISTORY OF THE COCKTAIL

It is strange that the origin of the famous and mysterious word 'cocktail' as a term for a mixed drink cannot be precisely established. Mixed drinks have been drunk since the dawn of civilization. Some claim that the first recipe for a cocktail was lemon juice and powdered adders, praised by the Emperor Commodus in the second century AD as a fine aperitif. The first 'cocktail book' might be said to be the seventeenth-century publication by the Distillers' Company of London (whose charter was granted by Charles I) which describes many spirituous drinks of singular complexity. These were medicinal in intention – but do we not claim therapeutic value for some of our modern mixes?

The word 'cocktail' was first defined in print as a mixture of spirits, sugar, water (ice?) and bitters, in an American magazine in 1806. The term was certainly not then in common use, nor does this reference preclude its prior regional usage.

Earlier, it was common for horses of mixed stock – in Yorkshire, particularly – to have their tails docked, to distinguish them from thoroughbreds; such horses were said to be 'cocktailed', and maybe mixed drinks took their name from the practice.

One popular notion is that during the American War of Independence a tavern-keeper called Betsy Flanagan, whose premises were frequented by Lafayette's as well as Washington's officers, once prepared a meal of chickens she filched from a pro-British neighbour. To celebrate this minor victory she decorated glasses used at the feast with feathers from the birds. Her French customers toasted her with cries of 'Vive le cocktail!'

If you think that's far-fetched, read on! Another inn story of the same period concerns a patriotic host who owned a celebrated fighting cock called Washington. One day it disappeared and he offered the hand of his daughter, Bessie, to any man finding it. In fact the man who returned the bird was a suitor whom Bessie's father had previously spurned – which looked like a put-up job if ever there was one. However, the host held a betrothal dinner and the happily confused Bessie muddled up the drinks. The guests liked them, none the less, and, in honour of the bird which was the cause of it all, they named the concoctions 'cock tails'.

It is said that at Campeche, on the Gulf of Mexico, visiting British sailors drank local punches called 'dracs' – possibly a corruption of Drake – which were stirred with a wooden spoon so shaped that it was known locally as 'cola de gallo' ('cock's tail'). This name was later applied to the drinks themselves.

Mexico is the source of another charming legend. After a successful visit to a local overlord by American naval officers, exotic drinks were offered the guests by the chief's lovely daughter, X-octl. The senior American said that they would never forget her or her drinks, which in her honour they called 'cock-tails' – that being the nearest they could get to pronouncing her name.

In eighteenth-century England a spirituous 'cock ale' was given to fighting cocks. Sometimes victorious birds were toasted in a mixture containing as many ingredients as the survivor had tail feathers; such drinks might easily have attracted the name of 'cocktail'.

French influence is conspicuous in the two other suggestions: first, that 'cocktail' derives from the traditional name of the mixed wine cup, *'coquetel'*, of the Bordeaux region; secondly, that an eccentric French physician in New Orleans served drinks in double-ended egg-cups known as *'coquetiers'* which his American friends pronounced 'cock tails'.

Far-fetched as it may sound, the final story in this list is supported by an illustration to a ballad of 1871 entitled 'An American Cock-Tale'. It appears that on old-time Mississippi river steamers, to while away the tedium, a well-heeled toper would sometimes call for a tub to be filled with every liquor on board. The glasses from which this horrible mixture was drunk were traditionally shaped roughly in the form of a cock's breast and stirred with rods approximating to a cock's tail. The implications are obvious.

In English literature both Hughes' *Tom Brown's Schooldays* and Thackeray's *The Newcomes* mentioned cocktails, in the sense of mixed drinks. The first true book of cocktails was by Jerry Thomas, who published in 1862 *The Bon Vivant's Guide, or How to Mix Drinks*. Twenty years later came Harry Johnson's *Bartenders' Manual, or How to Mix Drinks of the Present Style*. Many others were to follow, with American influence very strong, though any imbalance was corrected by the first edition of the authoritative *UKBG International Guide to Drinks* in 1953.

Cocktails as we know them first gained popularity in the United States. They were originally as much pre-mixed stimulant mixtures for taking on sporting occasions and picnics as they were bar drinks. The first American (i.e. cocktail) bar did not open in London until the first decade of the present century. The great stimulus to universal interest in cocktails came with the Roaring Twenties, when Prohibition in the USA changed everyone's drinking habits. If their usual tipple was not available, people would try to put together acceptable concoctions from whatever they could find. If the initial result was unpalatable, they would seek to improve matters by means of additives – often very successfully.

Generally, the term 'cocktail' is accepted today as a generic name for all mixed drinks. The cocktail bartender, however, understands a cocktail to be a short drink of approximately $3\frac{1}{2}$–4 ounces, and anything larger than this he would call a 'mixed drink' or 'long drink'.

The 1970s and '80s have brought about not only a widespread appreciation of the long-established 'classic' mixes but sufficient change in consumer tastes to promote active and professional experimentation in the esoteric world of the cocktail. All the more pity, then, that we shall never know its true origin.

DESIGN

Cocktail bars are governed by certain legal requirements regarding space, storage and hygiene. Equipment may include ice machines, refrigerated cupboards, bottle skips, liquidizers, fruit squeezers, automatic cash registers and calculators, as well as a range of glasses, shakers, utensils, proprietary drinks and other obvious necessities. Bars vary widely according to their location, size and function, so not all these amenities can be regarded as standard. However, there are certain considerations affecting all bars where some standardization is desirable.

Space

There should be sufficient room behind the bar counter for the bartender to move about when his bar is busy. However, too much space is as undesirable as too little. The ideal distance between the back of the bar counter and the back cupboards is 100–125 cm. The length must depend on the number of persons required to work behind the counter, but preferably each should have his own station, that is to say his own ice sink, wash-up and draining area and space for his glasses and equipment; he should also be able to reach containers of the standard drinks easily, without crossing the working areas of his colleagues. Each station should also incorporate an empty-bottle skip. Usually placed under the sink, this can be made of plastic, glass fibre or woven cane and ideally should be set on wheels. Crown cork bottle openers should be fixed beneath the bar counter or working surface at convenient intervals.

The Service Area

This will vary according to the type of business that the bar is expected to attract. In addition to the requirements of each station, described above, there should be a firm horizontal surface, below the bar counter and extending from it, for preparing drinks and cutting fruit. Also, bottle racks should be sited where the most regularly needed bottles can be stored and used quickly without the bartender having to turn his back on his customer.

Plumbing

In an ideal bar the wash-up area is set aside from the service area, and if there is space for this in a back room so much the better. However, if this is not possible then a plentiful supply of hot and cold water at the bar is essential. All bars now require at least two sinks. Taps should be of the swivelling kind so that they can be pushed back out of the way when not in use (many glasses have been broken on overhanging taps).

The ice sinks or wells should have drain plugs so that melting ice can drain away and also to facilitate cleaning. It also helps if the bottom of the ice sink contains a drainer tray to prevent the ice from touching the bottom, which considerably reduces the effect of condensation on the outside of the sink. All sinks should be of stainless steel. Complete units can be made to order.

Refrigeration

A refrigerator, or fan-controlled refrigerated cupboards, should be part of every bar. Cold shelves are an adequate alternative providing care is taken to ensure that they are not used just for general storage. Stock should be rotated at regular intervals so that ice does not form on the base of the bottles. Regular defrosting is essential for cold shelves. Sometimes, when the bar area adjoins a storeroom, refrigerated units have doors on both sides so that they may be filled from the rear. This makes stock rotation much easier.

Storage

The storeroom, containing ample reserve stock, is best sited adjacent to the bar. However, where this is not possible it is important that sufficient cupboard space is available to house the stock required for daily business. Drawers are necessary for items that require safe keeping, such as order books, documents and petty cash. Ice storage, and the question of where to site an ice machine, need careful consideration. All too often ice machines are placed in a hot kitchen with insufficient ventilation to enable them to work efficiently; the bar area itself is unsuitable, too, mainly because the machines themselves are unsightly and often noisy. If there is a room behind the bar, that will usually be the ideal place.

Electricity

As so many electric machines, such as cash registers, ice crushers and liquidizers, are now used in cocktail bars, a plentiful supply of power points is essential. Power points are best sited in the area above the working surfaces and below the bar counter, but well away from water. If they are positioned near the floor, there will be a treacherous network of cables trailing over the working area.

The Bar Counter

The bar counter itself should be neither too high nor too wide. The recommended height is approximately 110 cm and no wider than 60 cm. The surface should be of a material that is easy to clean and resistant to stains. A padded front to the counter and a foot rail contribute to the comfort of customers. A place for ladies to put their handbags might also help in keeping the counter-top clear.

In most cocktail bars the bartender also serves to the tables, and provision must be made for a flap to be incorporated in the counter. As this will remain open during service hours, it should be so placed as to cause no inconvenience to customers at the bar counter. This area should be designated the service area and be kept separate from the customer area.

Flooring

However careful a bartender is, it is inevitable that there will be some spillage behind the bar. The best material for the floor is one that is easily sponge-mopped dry and is as slip-resistant as possible.

EQUIPMENT

The Cocktail Shaker
This is the ideal utensil for mixing ingredients that stirring will not normally blend properly. To use it, insert the ice and mix, secure all parts together and, using both hands, place the forefinger of one hand over the top of the shaker and the thumb of the other hand under the bottom. Grasp the shaker fully around the body crossing little fingers to ensure the connection remains sealed. Move the wrist and forearm together, shake sharply and briefly for a few seconds.
There are two basic types of cocktail shaker, the Boston and the Standard.

The Boston Shaker Consisting of two cones, this shaker is perhaps the one most favoured by professionals as it can be used quickly and strained with the aid of a Hawthorn. Some have one cone made of glass, the other of stainless steel; others consist of two cones of plated silver. One cone overlaps the other.

The Standard Shaker This three-piece utensil is usually made entirely of stainless steel or plated silver. It has a cone-shaped base and a dumpy top with a built-in strainer and fitted cap. Although service is slower, this type of strainer is ideal for the home. Many bartenders who prefer to use the Standard strain the drink from the cone through a Hawthorn.

The Mixing Glass
This is like a jug without a handle, or in some cases like a very large brandy balloon. It is used for mixing clear drinks which do not contain juices or cream.

The Strainer
There are many types of strainers, the most popular being the Hawthorn. This is a flat, spoon-like utensil with a spring coiled round its head. It is used in conjunction with the cocktail shaker and mixing glass to hold back the ice after the drink has been prepared. A large-headed strainer with lugs and a short handle is available specifically for use with liquidizers and mixers.

Bar Spoon This is a long-handled spoon with a twisted shaft and a flat muddler end. The muddler is used for crushing sugar and mint in certain drinks.

Bar Liquidizer or Blender Although there are many types, with various speeds, perhaps the most efficient is the Hamilton-Beach. Liquidizers are used for making drinks that require puréed fruit.

Drink Mixer This machine is used for drinks that do not need liquidizing, especially those containing cream or ice cream. Where ice is required, use only crushed or cracked ice.

Other Bar Utensils

'Waiter's friend' corkscrew
Ice buckets or trough
Ice pick
Ice scoop or tongs
Fruit tongs or fork
Plastic buckets for transporting ice
Bottle skip or empty cases
Crown cork bottle openers
Broken cork extractor
Bitters bottles
Electric drinks mixer
Electric juice extractor or hand squeezer
Stainless steel or plastic pourers
Spirit measures
Stainless steel fruit knife
Straws, stirrers and cherry sticks
Champagne mossers and swizzle sticks
Champagne cooler, stopper and tongs
Port strainer, muslin and funnel
Good supply of practical glassware
Glass cloths and serviettes
Cocktail napkins and coasters

Kitchen Supplies

Olives
Pearl onions
Maraschino cherries
Worcestershire sauce
Ketchup
Tabasco sauce
Salt and pepper
Celery salt
Cinnamon
Nutmeg
Cloves
Orange flower water
Angostura bitters
Vanilla essence
Beef bouillon
Tomato juice
Coffee beans
Cube sugar
Caster sugar
Demerara sugar
Eggs
Cream
Mint
Cucumber rind
Oranges
Lemons
Limes
Bananas
Strawberries
Coconut cream
Pineapple juice

Glassware

Glass has a special affinity for liquid and so enhances its appearance that the name of the substance (the constituents of which are sand, soda ash and limestone) has been adopted as the name of the utensil most commonly used to hold liquid: the glass. Choosing the right glassware is a vital element when preparing a drink if it is to be invitingly presented and give satisfaction to the consumer. Well-designed glassware combines elegance, strength and stability. Most drinks are enhanced by being served in fine-rimmed clear glass, which should be clean and well polished. Examples of glassware may be found on pages 24–5

Hamilton Beach
electric ice crusher

three piece standard
silver plated cocktail
shaker

'Boston' shaker wit
bar spoon and strair
in stainless steel

stainless steel
ice bucket
and scoop

stain
ste
serv
tra

straws and
bitters bottle

stainless steel
ice tongs

stainless steel shaker
and spirit measures

bottle pourer

Hamilton Beach
electric drinks
mixer

Hamilton Beach bar blender
with graduated 'see-through'
or stainless steel top

mixing glass with
bar spoon and
'Hawthorn' strainer
in silver plate

champagne
ork extractors

cigar cutters

champagne
stopper

fruit knife

waiter's friend
or knife

plastic, glass
and wooden
muddlers

champagne
flute

double cocktail
glass

liqueur
glass

hot drink
glass

highball or
beer glass

white wine, sour or general purpose glass

standard cocktail glass

large goblet suitable for red wine or fruit daiquiris

brandy balloon

old fashioned or whisky glass

GUIDE FOR BEGINNERS

Always be clean, tidy and diplomatic.

Remember your hands are in constant view, so pay special attention to your fingernails.

Smoking or drinking behind the bar is unsightly and in some countries is also illegal.

Ice is essential for all cocktail bars. See that you have a plentiful supply and that it is always clean and clear.

Always keep your glasses and equipment clean and polished. See that where necessary glasses are chilled before serving.

Always handle glasses by the stem or base and never put your fingers inside a glass or near to the rim.

Remember that a broken glass kills the profit on four drinks.

It is bad taste, bad for the wine and dangerous to allow a champagne cork to 'pop' on removal.

When serving drinks or wine at a table always serve, where practicable, from the right of each person.

Handle a glass soda syphon by the plastic or metal part only. Glass is a poor conductor of heat and cannot stand sudden changes in temperature. The heat of the hand could cause the glass to burst – with disastrous consequences.

You will extract considerably more juice from citrus fruit if you warm it, by soaking in hot water, before squeezing.

Sugar of all kinds is necessary in all cocktail bars. Ensure it is dry and uncaked.

A supply of egg white and some egg yolks is also essential. Always break an egg in a separate glass to test its freshness.

Remember that a bartender should always carry the tools of his trade. Just as you would not think highly of a plumber who does not have a wrench, blow-lamp, etc., you will not be highly thought of as a bartender if you do not have such things as a cigarette lighter or matches, a 'waiter's friend' knife, a cigar cutter and a pen or pencil.

Always use good-quality products. Poor-quality ones are a false economy.

It is acceptable in a busy bar to use your own pre-mixes, i.e., a ready-seasoned tomato juice for Bloody Marys and tomato-juice cocktails, or a sour premix of lemon juice, gomme syrup and egg white.

Never put an effervescent ingredient into your shaker, mixing glass or liquidizer.

In a mixed order of drinks, always make the cocktails last so that they can be served fresh – 'whilst they are smiling at you'. Remember that a cocktail is a mixture and will separate if left too long.

Do not rock your cocktail to sleep. A short, sharp, snappy action is sufficient. Shake – do not rock.

Decoration of a cocktail or mixed drink is a matter for the individual. Normally, it will either complement the flavour of the drink, as does the twist of orange in an 'Adonis', or contrast the colour; sometimes it will do both, as can be seen in the practice of many bartenders of serving a stick of celery with a 'Bloody Mary'. This does not mean that you should make your drink into a fruit salad. Apart from being expensive, this makes it look ludicrous. Remember that when you please the eye you invariably please the palate.

Pour the cheapest ingredient into the mixing glass or cocktail shaker first. Then, if you make a mistake, you will have wasted only the cheapest ingredient, not the expensive spirits.

Never fill a glass to the brim. Spillage will result in a messy counter or table, and spoilt clothes.

Try to lay out your bar so that it is both attractive to the eye and efficient to work in, and keep it that way by returning bottles to their rightful positions after use.

Remember that a good bartender is invariably a good salesman. 'Sell' cocktails you know you make well. This will ensure that your customers return again.

DRINKS AT HOME

Served in moderation, alcohol is a useful aid to relaxation, especially in the home. A simple mixed drink can soothe tangled nerves after a hard day at the office, a cocktail with friends can enliven lagging conversation, a glass of wine can be the difference between eating and dining and a slowly sipped post-prandial drink in good company gives immense satisfaction.

However, a little organization can save a lot of panic, even in the context of serving drinks at home. Guests can be embarrassed if they hear a noisy clanging of bottles, frantic washing-up of glasses or sounds of dismay as their hosts realize there is no ice in the freezer; at least, they will get the impression that they are putting their hosts to a great deal of trouble. It is best to have stock and equipment properly stored so that drinks can be dispensed easily, and preferably without interrupting the flow of conversation.

The Home Bar
One of the most attractive and useful assets you can have for home entertainment is a well-equipped bar for mixing and serving drinks. Such bars can be very elaborate or very simple, and can occupy either

Some mixed drinks for different occasions

Pre-dinner drinks	After-dinner drinks	Party drinks
Martini	Sidecar	Harvey Wallbang
Champagne drinks	Frappés	Tequila Sunrise
White Lady	B & B	Tidal Wave
Manhattan	Stinger	Moscow Mule
Old-fashioned	Golden Cadillac	Cuba Libre
Sours	Black Russian	Salty Dog
Screwdriver	Silver Bullet	Cups
Bloody Mary	Rusty Nail	Punches
Negroni	Grasshopper	Horse's Neck
Gibson	Godmother	Highballs
	Alexander	
	Irish Coffee	

an area set aside for the purpose or merely a small cabinet or table in a corner of the room. The type you choose will depend on the amount of space you have available and the amount of entertaining you do. Should you have sufficient time, enthusiasm and skill, you can build your own bar; otherwise they can be bought from large department stores. There are many kinds available, but basically those sold through the shops fall into three categories.

The first of these, the mobile bar, is perhaps the most versatile and useful. The fact that it can be readily moved from place to place is its greatest asset; mounted on a trolley, for example, your equipment, glasses and bottles can be moved as a unit for the easy serving of drinks, whether it be in the living room or out on the patio.

Of the semi-permanent bars, the most familiar type is the cocktail cabinet. Here the equipment, glasses and spirits can be conveniently and attractively displayed. Take into account proximity to washing-up facilities when deciding where to position your cocktail cabinet.

The most ambitious of the three types, the permanent bar, forms an integral part of the interior decoration. Its design is of the greatest importance and care must be taken that the bar, while being an

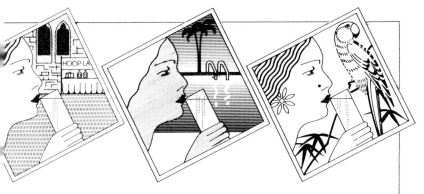

ss potent drinks	Hot-weather drinks	More exotic drinks
r	Coolers	Mai Tai
nericano	Cups	Zombie
ritzer	Collins	Margarita
uit Daiquiris	Planter's Punch	Scorpion
na Colada	Juleps	Silk Stockings
aterloo	Buck's Fizz	Bleu-Do-It
owball	Long Island Tea	Brandy Crusta
ngria	Rickeys	Pousse Café
rawberry Dawn		
aster		
nms		

eye-catching showpiece, enhances but does not overwhelm the room. Lighting here plays a vital part; ideally it should be indirect, for this will highlight the bar in a way that is understated yet highly effective. Should you decide to make your own bar, remember that it should be of a height that is comfortable to sit at while one's drink rests on top of the bar.

Equipment
Whether it is a mobile bar, a cocktail cabinet or a separate piece of furniture, the area used for storing stock and equipment must be stable, accessible and easily cleaned. There is no need for much of the intricate equipment of a professional bar as most kitchens have many items that can be used in the preparation of drinks. These are the more useful pieces of equipment:

Three-piece cocktail shaker with built-in strainer
Mixing glass or large jug
Hawthorn strainer
Bar spoon or long-handled spoon
Cutting board and sharp stainless steel knife
Corkscrew and bottle opener
Fruit squeezer
Ice bucket or large bowl with ice tongs
Liquidizer
Stirrers, straws and cherry sticks
Mineral maker

Glassware
The essentials of fine glassware are brilliant clarity, good balance and a fine rim. Remember when wiping glasses to use a clean dry glass cloth and rinse well to remove all traces of detergent (which flattens beer and sparkling wines, and detrimentally flavours delicate drinks). Glassware should be repolished just before use and stored out of the reach of small children. A wide variety of styles of glassware is available. The following is a guide to capacity only.

2–3-oz glass for liqueurs, schnapps and chilled vodka
4-oz stemmed glass for cocktails, port and sherry
8-oz all-purpose glass such as a Paris goblet, for wine, spirits or mixed drinks
10–12-oz Highball glass, for long drinks, cups and beers. (Glasses for mixed drinks must be large enough to contain plenty of ice plus additives.)
Snifter glass for brandy or cognac.

Basic Stock
A little imagination and thought can turn home stock into delightful drinks. The recipes later in the book will provide specific instructions for mixing, but the following list is offered as a guide to home provisions.

Brandy	Limes or lemons
Gin	Oranges
Vodka	Maraschino cherries
Rum – light and dark	Small cocktail olives
Tequila	Celery salt
Scotch whisky	Cubed sugar
Bourbon whiskey	Grenadine syrup
Vermouth – dry and sweet	Gomme syrup
Sherry	Club soda
Tawny Port	Tonic water
Cointreau or Triple Sec	Dry ginger ale
Crème de menthe	Bitter lemon
Kahlua or Tia Maria	Cola
Crème de Cacao	Lemonade or 7-Up
Kummel	Grated nutmeg
Advocaat	Tomato juice
Crème de cassis	Pineapple juice
Peppermint cordial	Coconut cream
Lime juice cordial	Angostura bitters

Giving a Party

Few people are fortunate enough to have at their disposal the amount of working space and range of equipment and drinks that are available to the professional bartender. But if you throw a sizeable party, the pressure of 'business' on you is going to be almost as great, even without your other duties. One way out – unfortunately one which is all too often taken – is to cut down on the variety and quantity of what you offer. This is a shame, and sometimes means serving a single concoction, prepared long in advance, which is topped up from time to time (this can cause wild and sometimes treacherous fluctuations in its content).

For the more ambitious, advance preparation is still the key. The following hints will, if followed, do much to guarantee an enjoyable party.

Fruit Juice should be squeezed and oranges and lemons required for garnishing sliced fairly thickly.

When cutting peel for a twist, take only the coloured rind, not the bitter pith. Fruit cut into slices and twists will keep fresh if covered by a damp cloth or plastic wrap and stored in the refrigerator.

Ice Make plenty, well in advance. A spare sink or a bath can be a good place to store it, as the ice keeps cold there and the mess caused by melting is avoided.

Sugar If you are planning drinks containing sugar, a good tip is to make up a sugar syrup in the proportions of 1 cup of sugar to 1 cup of water. Bring to the boil and simmer until the sugar is dissolved. This can be bottled and refrigerated and will keep indefinitely. Also, gomme syrup is available in most good liquor stores.

Glasses Have in store a good supply, ideally twice as many as the number of your guests.

Non-alcoholic Drinks Provide a good choice for the teetotallers at the party.

Advance Preparation Drinks made of liquor and wine may be prepared in quantity in advance, but drinks containing fruit juices and sugar will separate unless mixed just before drinking.

Equipment Check that you have in your bar everything else you are likely to need: serving trays, water jugs, soda syphon, bar tools, knife and board for cutting and preparing fruit, oranges and lemons, cucumber, maraschino cherries, mint, toothpicks, glass cloths and sponge for mopping up.

COCKTAILS
AND MIXED DRINKS

Blend   Put ingredients into electric blender, add crushed ice if required by recipe, blend until required consistency is achieved – pour unstrained into suitable glass.

Build   Pour necessary ingredients directly into suitable glass without any premixing, add ice only if required by recipe. Mixed drinks made in this way are usually served with a muddler.

Mix   Put ingredients into the cone of electric drink mixer, add crushed ice if specified, mix until drink reaches required consistency, then pour or strain into glass.

Shake   Put ice into the cocktail shaker, pour in the necessary ingredients, shake shortly and sharply unless otherwise instructed, strain into required glass.

Stir   Put ice into mixing glass, pour in the necessary ingredients, stir until cold, strain into required glass.

Stir in   When topping with final ingredient use barspoon to stir as it is added.

Zest   A small thin piece of citrus peel with as little pith as possible. The essential oil is squeezed on top of the drink and it is optional whether the zest is then dropped into the drink.

Twist   A long zest twisted in the centre and normally dropped into the drink.

Spiral   Complete peel of fruit cut in spiral fashion.

Unless otherwise stated the normal 3–4 oz cocktail glass should be used for these recipes.

RECIPES

A

A1
⅓ Grand Marnier
⅔ gin
1 dash lemon juice
Shake. Add a twist of lemon.

Adonis
⅓ sweet vermouth
⅔ dry sherry
1 dash orange bitters
Stir. Add a twist of orange peel.

Ad-Vo-Tizer
1 fl oz advocaat
2 fl oz dry vermouth
Tizer
Build the advocaat and
vermouth into an ice-filled
highball glass. Stir in the Tizer.
Add a slice of orange.

Affinity
⅔ Scotch whisky
⅓ sweet vermouth
2 dashes Angostura bitters
Stir.

After Dinner
⅓ prunelle brandy
⅓ cherry brandy
⅓ lemon juice
Shake.

Alaska
¾ gin
¼ yellow Chartreuse
Shake.

Alexander (Brandy)
⅓ brandy
⅓ brown crème de cacao
⅓ cream
Shake. Sprinkle nutmeg on top.

Alexander (Gin)
*sometimes known as Princess
Mary*
⅓ gin
⅓ brown crème de cacao
⅓ cream
Shake.

American Beauty
¼ brandy
¼ grenadine
¼ dry vermouth
¼ orange juice
1 dash white crème de menthe
Port wine
Shake together all but the port
wine. Pour into a double
cocktail glass. Top with a little
port wine.

Americano
1½ fl oz Campari
1½ fl oz sweet vermouth
Soda water
Build the Campari and
vermouth into a large ice-filled
glass. Top with soda water. Add
a twist of lemon or slice of
orange.

Angel's Tip
¾ brown crème de cacao
¼ cream
Float the cream on top of the
crème de cacao in a liqueur
glass.

Angel Face
⅓ gin
⅓ apricot brandy
⅓ calvados
Shake.

Angers Rose
⅓ Cointreau
⅓ bourbon whiskey
⅓ pineapple juice
1 dash Campari
1 dash egg white
Shake. Decorate with a small
slice of orange and a cherry.

Aurum
¼ Aurum
¼ gin
½ sweet vermouth
Stir.

B

Bacardi
¾ Bacardi rum
¼ fresh lime or lemon juice
½ barspoon grenadine
Shake.

Balalaika
⅓ vodka
⅓ Cointreau
⅓ lemon juice
Shake.

Bamboo
½ dry sherry
½ dry vermouth
1 dash orange bitters
Stir. Decorate with a twist of
lemon peel.

Banana Bliss
½ brandy
½ banana liqueur
Stir.

Barbican
⁷⁄₁₀ Scotch whisky
¹⁄₁₀ Drambuie
²⁄₁₀ passion fruit juice
Shake.

Baronial
⁷⁄₁₀ Lillet
³⁄₁₀ lemon gin
2 dashes Angostura bitters
2 dashes Cointreau
Stir.

Barracuda
1 fl oz golden rum
½ fl oz Galliano
1 fl oz pineapple juice
2 dashes gomme syrup
¼ fl oz fresh lime juice
Shake. Strain into pineapple
shell. Top with champagne.
Decorate with a slice of lime
and cherry.

Bartender
¼ gin
¼ sherry
¼ Dubonnet
¼ dry vermouth
1 dash Grand Marnier
Stir.

Bentley
½ Dubonnet
½ applejack brandy
Stir.

Bermudiana Rose
⅖ dry gin
⅕ apricot brandy
⅕ grenadine
⅕ lemon juice
Shake.

Between-the-Sheets
⅓ brandy
⅓ white rum
⅓ Cointreau
1 dash lemon juice
Shake.

Billy Hamilton
⅓ brandy
⅓ orange curaçao
⅓ brown crème de cacao
1 dash egg white
Shake.

Black Magic
Juice of 2 grapes
2 dashes Mandarine Napoléon
Dry sparkling wine
Pour grape juice and Mandarine Napoléon into a champagne glass. Top up with wine. Decorate with 2 black grapes one submerged and one on side of glass.

Black Russian
⅔ vodka
⅓ Kahlua
Build into an ice-filled old-fashioned glass.

Blackthorn
⅔ sloe gin
⅓ sweet vermouth
1 dash orange bitters
Stir. Add a twist of lemon peel.

Block and Fall
⅓ Cointreau
⅓ apricot brandy
⅙ anisette
⅙ applejack brandy
Stir.

Bloodshot
1 fl oz vodka
2 fl oz beef bouillon or condensed consommé
2 fl oz tomato juice
1 dash fresh lemon juice
2 dashes Worcestershire sauce
Celery salt
Shake. Strain into a large glass.

Bloody Mary
1 fl oz vodka
4 fl oz tomato juice
2 dashes Worcestershire sauce
1 dash fresh lemon juice
Celery salt
Add Tabasco sauce and pepper to taste. Shake, stir or build.

Blue Bottle
½ gin
¼ blue curaçao
¼ passion fruit
Stir.

Blue Jacket
½ gin
¼ blue curaçao
¼ orange bitters
Stir.

Blue Lady
½ blue curaçao
¼ gin
¼ fresh lemon juice
1 dash egg white
Shake.

Blue Lagoon
½ fl oz vodka
½ fl oz blue curaçao
Lemonade
Pour the vodka and curaçao over ice in a highball glass. Top up with lemonade.

Blue Riband
⅖ gin
⅖ white curaçao
⅕ blue curaçao
Stir.

Blue Star
⅙ Lillet
⅙ orange juice
⅓ gin
⅓ blue curaçao
Shake.

Bobby Burns
½ Scotch whisky
½ sweet vermouth
3 dashes Bénédictine
Stir.

Bombay
½ brandy
¼ dry vermouth
¼ sweet vermouth
1 dash pastis
2 dashes orange curaçao
Stir.

Bosom Caresser
⅔ brandy
⅓ orange curaçao
1 egg yolk
1 barspoon grenadine
Shake. Serve in a double
cocktail glass.

Bossa Nova Special
1 fl oz Galliano
1 fl oz white rum
¼ fl oz apricot brandy
2 fl oz pineapple juice
¼ fl oz lemon juice
1 dash egg white
Shake. Serve in a tall glass with
ice. Decorate with fruit.

Bourbonella
½ bourbon whiskey
¼ dry vermouth
¼ orange curaçao
1 dash grenadine
Stir.

Brandy (1)
⅘ brandy
⅕ sweet vermouth
1 dash Angostura bitters
Stir.

Brandy (2)
⅘ brandy
⅕ orange curaçao
2 dashes Angostura bitters
Stir. Add a cherry.

Brandy Gump
½ brandy
½ lemon juice
2 dashes grenadine
Shake.

Brave Bull
½ tequila
½ Kahlua
Build into an ice-filled
old-fashioned glass.

Brazil
½ dry sherry
½ dry vermouth
1 dash Angostura bitters
1 dash pastis
Stir. Add a twist of lemon peel.

Breakfast
½ ruby port
¼ crème de cacao
¼ fresh lemon juice
2 dashes golden rum
1 dash egg white
Shake. Strain into a cocktail
glass. Sprinkle nutmeg on top.

Brewer Street Rascal
4 fl oz pure grapefruit juice
1 fl oz Mandarine Napoléon
⅓ fl oz vodka
1 dash egg white
Shake. Serve in a 6–8-oz wine
glass. Decorate with wedge of
grapefruit.

Bronx
½ gin
⅙ dry vermouth
⅙ sweet vermouth
⅙ fresh orange juice
Shake.

Bronx Terrace
⅔ gin
⅓ dry vermouth
1 dash lime cordial
Stir. Add a cherry.

Brooklyn
½ rye
½ sweet vermouth
1 dash maraschino
1 dash Amer Picon
Stir.

Bullshot
1 fl oz vodka
4 fl oz beef bouillon or
  condensed consommé
1 dash fresh lemon juice
2 dashes Worcestershire sauce
Celery salt
Shake. Strain into a large glass.

Byrrh Special
½ Byrrh
½ gin
Stir.

C

Calvados
⅓ calvados
⅓ orange juice
⅙ Cointreau
⅙ orange bitters
Shake.

Cardinale
½ fl oz crème de cassis
Dry red wine
Add the wine to the crème de
cassis in a wine goblet.

Caribbean Sunset
⅕ gin
⅕ crème de banane
⅕ fresh cream
⅕ blue curaçao
⅕ fresh lemon juice
1 dash grenadine
Shake all but the grenadine.
Strain into a large cocktail
glass. Add the grenadine.

Carnival
⅓ brandy
⅓ apricot brandy
⅓ Lillet
1 dash kirsch
1 dash orange juice
Shake.

Caruso
⅓ gin
⅓ dry vermouth
⅓ green crème de menthe
Stir.

Casino
½ gin
¼ lemon juice
¼ maraschino
1 dash orange bitters
Shake. Add a cherry.

Champs Elysées
⅗ brandy
⅕ yellow Chartreuse
⅕ lemon juice
1 dash Angostura bitters
Shake.

Cherry Blossom
⅗ cherry brandy
⅖ brandy
1 dash lemon juice
1 dash grenadine
1 dash curaçao
Shake.

Chocolate Soldier
⅓ brandy
⅓ dry vermouth
⅓ crème de cacao
2 dashes orange bitters
Shake.

Chop Nut
1 fl oz vodka
½ fl oz coconut liqueur
½ fl oz crème de banane
1 fl oz orange juice
1 dash egg white
Shake.

Claridge
⅓ gin
⅓ dry vermouth
⅙ Cointreau
⅙ apricot brandy
Stir.

Classic
½ brandy
⅙ lemon juice
⅙ orange curaçao
⅙ maraschino
Shake. Strain into a
sugar-rimmed medium goblet.
Add a twist of lemon.

Clover Club
1½ fl oz gin
½ fl oz grenadine
¼ fl oz fresh lemon juice
1 dash egg white
Shake. Strain into a medium
goblet.

Clover Club (Royal)
½ gin
¼ lemon juice
¼ grenadine
1 egg yolk
Shake. Serve in a double
cocktail glass.

Clover Leaf
1½ fl oz gin
½ fl oz grenadine
¼ fl oz fresh lemon juice
1 dash egg white
Shake. Strain into a medium
goblet. Decorate with sprig of
mint.

Coaster
Put several dashes of Angostura
bitters into a spirit glass. Swirl
and discard. Add 1 measure gin.
Serve with soda water.

Combination
½ gin
¼ dry vermouth
¼ Amer Picon
6 dashes lemon juice
6 dashes orange curaçao
Shake. Sprinkle grated nutmeg
on top.

Commodore
⅘ rye
⅕ fresh lime juice
2 dashes orange bitters
Add sugar to taste. Shake.

Conca d'Ora
⅝ gin
⅛ cherry brandy
⅛ triple sec
⅛ maraschino
Orange peel
Stir.

Cool Banana
1 fl oz crème de banane
¾ fl oz triple sec
¼ fl oz grenadine
1 fl oz double cream
1 dash egg white
Shake.

Copperino
⅓ Galliano
⅓ Kahlua
⅓ fresh cream
Shake. Add grated nutmeg on
top.

Corpse-reviver
1 fl oz brandy
½ fl oz calvados
½ fl oz sweet vermouth
Stir. Add a twist of lemon.

Crème de Rhum
⅓ white rum
⅓ crème de banane
⅓ orange squash
1 dash cream
Shake. Add a cherry and a slice
of orange.

Cross Bow
⅓ gin
⅓ Cointreau
⅓ crème de cacao
Shake.

Cuban
½ brandy
¼ apricot brandy
¼ fresh lime juice
Shake.

Cupid's Bow
¼ gin
¼ Forbidden Fruit liqueur
¼ Aurum
¼ passion fruit juice
Shake.

Czarine
½ vodka
¼ dry vermouth
¼ apricot brandy
1 dash Angostura bitters
Stir.

Daily Mail
⅓ rye whisky
⅓ Amer Picon
⅓ orange squash
3 dashes orange bitters
Shake.

Dandy
½ rye whisky
½ Dubonnet
1 dash Angostura bitters
3 dashes Cointreau
Stir. Add a piece each of orange peel and lemon peel.

Dean's Gate
½ light rum
¼ lime juice cordial
¼ Drambuie
Stir. Add a twist of orange.

Derby
2 fl oz gin
2 dashes peach bitters
2 sprigs fresh mint
Shake.

Diki-Diki
⅔ calvados
⅙ Swedish punsch
⅙ grapefruit juice
Shake.

Doctor
⅔ Swedish punsch
⅓ fresh lemon or lime juice
Shake.

Dubonnet
½ gin
½ Dubonnet
Stir. Add a twist of lemon peel.

Dubonnet Royal
⅔ Dubonnet
⅓ gin
2 dashes Angostura bitters
2 dashes orange curaçao
1 dash pastis
Stir together all but the pastis.
Add the pastis and a cherry.

Duchess
⅓ sweet vermouth
⅓ dry vermouth
⅓ pastis
Stir.

Duke
½ Drambuie
¼ orange juice
¼ lemon juice
1 egg
1 dash champagne
Shake together all but the champagne. Strain into a wine glass. Add the champagne.

Dunhill '71
⅓ brandy
⅓ Royal Orange Chocolate
  liqueur
⅓ crème de banane
Shake. Float cream on top.

Dunhill '74
½ gin
²⁄₁₀ apricot brandy
¹⁄₁₀ peach brandy
¹⁄₁₀ orange squash
¹⁄₁₀ lemon barley water
1 egg white
Shake. Add a ¼ slice of orange
and a cherry.

East India
¾ brandy
⅛ orange curaçao
⅛ pineapple juice
1 dash Angostura bitters
Shake. Add a twist of lemon
peel. Add a cherry.

Ed's Baby
⁵⁄₁₀ rum
²⁄₁₀ cherry brandy
²⁄₁₀ curaçao
¹⁄₁₀ banana liqueur
Juice of 1 lime
Shake.

Eight Bells
½ Jamaican rum
⅙ Van der Hum
⅙ dry vermouth
⅙ orange and lemon squash
Shake. Add a little grated
nutmeg on top.

Embassy Royal
½ bourbon whiskey
¼ Drambuie
¼ sweet vermouth
2 dashes orange squash
Shake.

Empire Glory
½ rye whisky
¼ ginger wine
¼ fresh lemon juice
2 dashes grenadine
Shake.

Evans
2 fl oz rye whisky
1 dash apricot brandy
1 dash curaçao
Stir.

Fairy Belle
¾ gin
¼ apricot brandy
1 egg white
1 barspoon grenadine
Shake.

Fallen Angel
¾ gin
¼ fresh lemon or lime juice
2 dashes crème de menthe
Dash Angostura bitters
Shake.

Fernet
½ brandy
½ Fernet Branca
1 dash Angostura bitters
2 dashes gomme syrup
Stir. Add a twist of lemon peel.

Fino Mac
2 fl oz dry sherry
1 fl oz ginger wine
Stir.

First Night
½ brandy
¼ Van der Hum
¼ Tia Maria
1 barspoon cream
Shake.

Fixer
½ brandy
¼ crème de noyeau
⅛ prunelle
⅛ cream
Shake.

Foresters' Delight
1½ fl oz bourbon whiskey
1½ fl oz Cointreau
2 dashes blue curaçao
2 dashes fresh lemon juice
Shake. Sugar-rim the glass. Add
a cherry.

Forty Eight
2/5 gin
1/5 apricot brandy
1/5 orange curaçao
1/5 dry vermouth
1 dash lemon juice
Shake.

Fourth Degree
1/3 gin
1/3 dry vermouth
1/3 sweet vermouth
2 dashes pastis
Stir.

French Connection
1½ fl oz brandy
1½ fl oz amaretto
Build into ice-filled
old-fashioned glass.

Frosty Dawn
1/3 white rum
1/6 maraschino
1/6 falernum syrup
1/3 orange juice
Shake.

Furore
2/5 Aurum
3/10 brandy
2/10 Lillet
1/10 orange juice
Shake.

Futurity
½ sloe gin
½ sweet vermouth
2 dashes Angostura bitters
Stir.

G

Gimlet
2/3 gin
1/3 lime juice cordial
Soda water (optional)
Stir together all but the soda
water. Serve on the rocks,
splash of soda water if desired.

Gin Aurum
4/10 gin
3/10 Aurum
3/10 lemon juice
1 dash grenadine
Shake.

Gin and It
½ gin
½ sweet vermouth
Build into a cocktail glass. Add
a cherry.

Ginger Square
1 fl oz ginger brandy
Stir in ginger ale. Build into an
ice-filled highball glass.

Gloom Chaser
¼ Grand Marnier
¼ white curaçao
¼ grenadine
¼ lemon juice
Shake.

Godfather
1½ fl oz Scotch or bourbon
¾ fl oz amaretto
Build into an ice-filled
old-fashioned glass.

Godmother
1½ fl oz vodka
¾ fl oz amaretto
Build into an ice-filled
old-fashioned glass.

Golden Cadillac
1 fl oz Galliano
1 fl oz white crème de cacao
1 fl oz fresh cream
Shake or mix. Strain into a
saucer-type glass.

Golden Dawn
¼ gin
¼ calvados
¼ apricot brandy
¼ orange juice
1 dash grenadine
Shake together all but the
grenadine. Add the grenadine
after the cocktail has been
poured.

Golden Dream
¼ Galliano
¼ Cointreau
¼ orange juice
¼ cream
Shake.

Golden Gleam
⅓ brandy
⅓ Grand Marnier
⅙ lemon juice
⅙ orange juice
Shake.

Golden Medallion
⅓ Galliano
⅓ cognac
⅓ fresh orange juice
1 dash egg white
Shake. Add zest of orange.

Golden Slipper
1 fl oz yellow Chartreuse
1 fl oz apricot brandy
1 egg yolk
Shake.

Golden Tang
½ vodka
¼ Strega
⅛ crème de banane
⅛ orange squash
Shake. Add a cherry.

Grand Slam
¼ dry vermouth
¼ sweet vermouth
½ Swedish punsch
Stir.

Grapefruit
½ gin
½ grapefruit juice
1 dash gomme syrup
Shake.

Grasshopper
⅓ white crème de cacao
⅓ green crème de menthe
⅓ cream
Shake.

Greenbriar
⅔ dry sherry
⅓ dry vermouth
1 dash peach bitters
Stir. Add a sprig of mint.

Green Dragon
½ gin
¼ green crème de menthe
⅛ kummel
⅛ lemon juice
Shake.

Green Room
⅓ brandy
⅔ dry vermouth
2 dashes orange curaçao
Stir.

Guards
⅔ gin
⅓ sweet vermouth
3 dashes orange curaçao
Stir.

H

Happy Medium
¼ gin
¼ Pimms No. 1
¼ Cointreau
⅛ Lillet
⅛ orange squash
Shake.

Harvard
½ brandy
½ sweet vermouth
2 dashes Angostura bitters
1 dash gomme syrup
Stir. Add a twist of lemon.

Harvey Cowpuncher
1½ fl oz Galliano
Milk
Pour Galliano into an ice-filled
highball glass. Stir in fresh
milk.

Harvey Wallbanger
1½ fl oz vodka
4 fl oz orange juice
2 barspoons Galliano on top
Build into an ice-filled highball
glass. Serve with straws.

Havana
¼ gin
¼ Swedish punsch
½ apricot brandy
1 dash lemon juice
Shake.

Hawaiian
½ gin
½ orange juice
1 dash orange curaçao
Shake.

Hibernian Special
⅓ dry gin
⅓ Cointreau
⅓ green curaçao
1 dash lemon juice
Shake.

Honeymoon
⅓ Bénédictine
⅓ applejack brandy
⅓ lemon juice
3 dashes orange curaçao
Shake.

Hoopla
¼ brandy
¼ Cointreau
¼ Lillet
¼ lemon juice
Shake.

Hoots Mon
½ Scotch whisky
¼ Lillet
¼ sweet vermouth
Stir.

Hunter
⅔ rye whisky
⅓ cherry brandy
Stir.

I

Inca
¼ gin
¼ dry vermouth
¼ sweet vermouth
¼ dry sherry
1 dash orgeat syrup
1 dash orange bitters
Stir.

Incognito
³⁄₁₀ brandy
⁶⁄₁₀ Lillet
¹⁄₁₀ apricot brandy
1 dash Angostura bitters
Stir.

Ink Street
⅓ rye whisky
⅓ lemon juice
⅓ orange juice
Shake.

Inspiration
¼ gin
¼ dry vermouth
¼ calvados
¼ Grand Marnier
Stir. Add a cherry.

Itza Paramount
½ gin
¼ Drambuie
¼ Cointreau
Stir. Add a cherry.

J

Jack-in-the-Box
½ applejack brandy
½ pineapple juice
1 dash Angostura bitters
Shake.

Jack Rose
¾ applejack brandy
¼ grenadine
Juice of ½ lime
Shake.

Jamaica Joe
⅓ Jamaican rum
⅓ Tia Maria
⅓ advocaat
1 dash grenadine
Shake together all but the
grenadine. Add the grenadine.
Sprinkle nutmeg on top.

Jamaica Rum
⅚ Jamaican rum
⅙ gomme syrup
1 dash Angostura bitters
Stir.

Jerry's Joy
⅓ vodka
⅓ Lillet
⅓ Cointreau
1 dash orange bitters
1 dash egg white
Shake. Add a cherry.

John Simon
¼ gin
¼ Grand Marnier
¼ crème de noyeau
¼ orange squash
1 dash Angostura bitters
Shake.

Julie Marie
⅓ white rum
⅙ Aurum
⅙ Brontë liqueur
⅓ orange squash
1 egg white
Shake.

K

Kelvin 66
¼ aquavit
¼ Grand Marnier
¼ Dubonnet
¼ orange squash
Shake. Add a cherry.

Kentucky Sunset
⅗ bourbon whiskey
⅕ Strega
⅕ anisette
Stir. Add a twist of orange peel.

King Alfonse
¾ Kahlua
¼ cream
Float cream on top. Build into a
liqueur glass.

Kir
½ fl oz crème de cassis
Dry white wine (originally
    Bourgogne Aligoté)
Top the crème de cassis with
chilled dry white wine. Build
into a wine goblet.

Knickerbocker Special
³/₅ dark rum
¹/₁₀ raspberry syrup
¹/₁₀ lemon juice
¹/₁₀ orange juice
¹/₁₀ orange curaçao
1 cube pineapple
Shake liquids. Add the
pineapple.

L

Leviathan
½ brandy
¼ sweet vermouth
¼ orange juice
Shake.

Liberty
²/₃ applejack brandy
¹/₃ white rum
1 dash gomme syrup
Stir.

Limbo
1 fl oz peach brandy
4 fl oz pineapple juice
Serve over ice in a highball
glass.

Linstead
½ Scotch whisky
½ sweetened pineapple juice
1 dash pastis
Shake. Add a twist of lemon
peel.

Little Princess
½ white rum
½ sweet vermouth
Stir.

London Fog
½ white crème de menthe
½ anisette
1 dash Angostura bitters
Shake.

Los Angeles
²/₃ Scotch whisky
¹/₃ lemon juice
1 egg
1 dash sweet vermouth
Shake. Serve in a double
cocktail glass.

Lucky Dip
½ vodka
¼ crème de banane
¼ lemon squash
1 egg white
Shake.

Luxury
¹/₃ gin
¹/₆ Pimm's No. 1
¹/₆ banana liqueur
¹/₆ sweet vermouth
¹/₆ lime juice cordial
1 dash Angostura bitters
Shake.

M

Macaroni
²/₃ pastis
¹/₃ sweet vermouth
Shake.

Magic Trace
⁴/₁₀ bourbon whiskey
³/₁₀ Drambuie
¹/₁₀ dry vermouth
¹/₁₀ orange juice
¹/₁₀ lemon juice
Shake.

Maiden's Prayer
³/₈ gin
³/₈ Cointreau
¹/₈ orange juice
¹/₈ lemon juice
Shake.

Mainbrace
⅓ Cointreau
⅓ gin
⅓ grapefruit juice
shake.

Mai Tai
1 fl oz light rum
1 fl oz golden rum
½ fl oz curaçao
¼ fl oz orgeat syrup
1 dash grenadine
Juice of 1 lime
Build into a large old-fashioned
glass filled with cracked ice.
Decorate with half the spent
shell of lime, a pineapple slice,
a cherry and a sprig of mint.
Serve with straws.

Mallorca
½ white rum
⅙ dry vermouth
⅙ crème de banane
⅙ Drambuie
Stir.

Manhattan
⅔ rye whisky
⅓ sweet vermouth
1 dash Angostura bitters
Stir. Add a cherry.

Manhattan (dry)
⅔ rye whisky
⅓ dry vermouth
1 dash Angostura bitters
Stir. Add a twist of lemon peel.

Manhattan (perfect)
⅔ rye whisky
⅙ dry vermouth
⅙ sweet vermouth
Stir. Serve straight up or on the
rocks. Add a twist of lemon and
a cherry.

Maple Leaf
⅔ bourbon whiskey
⅓ lemon juice
1 barspoon maple syrup
Shake.

Mar del Plata
½ gin
⅜ dry vermouth
⅛ Bénédictine
1 dash Grand Marnier
Stir. Add a twist of lemon.

Margarita
⅖ tequila
⅖ fresh lime juice
⅕ triple sec
Shake. Rub rim of glass with
lemon to moisten, then dip it in
salt.

Mary Pickford
½ white rum
½ unsweetened pineapple juice
1 barspoon grenadine
1 dash maraschino
Shake.

Mediterranean
1 fl oz gin
½ fl oz blue curaçao
Lemonade
Pour gin and curaçao over ice in
a highball glass. Top up with
lemonade.

Merry K
⅔ bourbon whiskey
⅓ orange curaçao
Stir. Add a twist of lemon.

Mikado
⁶⁄₁₀ brandy
¹⁄₁₀ curaçao
¹⁄₁₀ crème de noyeau
¹⁄₁₀ orange curaçao
¹⁄₁₀ orgeat syrup
1 dash Angostura bitters
Shake.

Millionaire No. 1
$7/10$ brandy
$1/10$ crème de noyeau
$1/10$ orange curaçao
$1/10$ orgeat syrup
2 dashes Angostura bitters
Shake.

Millionaire No. 2
$2/3$ rye whisky
$1/3$ grenadine
1 egg white
2 dashes orange curaçao
1 dash pastis
Shake. Serve in a double
cocktail glass.

Million Dollar
$2/3$ gin
$1/3$ sweet vermouth
1 egg white
1 barspoon grenadine
1 barspoon pineapple juice
Shake.

Minnehaha
$1/2$ gin
$1/6$ dry vermouth
$1/6$ sweet vermouth
$1/6$ fresh orange juice
1 dash pastis
Shake.

Mint Royal
$1/3$ brandy
$1/3$ Royal Mint Chocolate liqueur
$1/3$ lemon juice
1 egg white
Shake.

MJ Special
$1/4$ brandy
$1/4$ apricot brandy
$1/4$ Dubonnet
$1/4$ orange squash
1 dash grenadine
1 egg white
Shake.

Mona Lisa
$1/3$ Amer Picon
$1/3$ orange curaçao
$1/3$ Bénédictine
1 barspoon double cream
Shake. Sprinkle cinnamon on
top.

Monkey Gland
$3/5$ gin
$2/5$ orange juice
2 dashes pastis
2 dashes grenadine
Shake.

Montana
$1/2$ brandy
$1/2$ dry vermouth
2 dashes port
2 dashes Angostura bitters
2 dashes anisette
Stir.

Morning Glory
$1/2$ brandy
$1/4$ orange curaçao
$1/4$ lemon juice
2 dashes Angostura bitters
2 dashes pastis
Shake. Add a twist of lemon
peel.

Moscow Mule
1 fl oz vodka
$1/2$ fl oz fresh lime juice
Ginger beer
Build vodka and lime juice into
an ice-filled highball glass. Stir
in ginger beer. Decorate with a
slice of lime and a sprig of mint.
Serve with straws.

Moulin Rouge
$1/2$ fl oz brandy
2 fl oz pineapple juice
Dry sparkling wine
Stir. Pour brandy and pineapple
juice over ice in a highball
glass, topped up with wine.
Decorate with a cherry and a
slice of pineapple and/or orange.

N

Napoleon
$^7/_{10}$ gin
$^1/_{10}$ Dubonnet
$^1/_{10}$ Fernet Branca
$^1/_{10}$ orange curaçao
Stir. Add a twist of lemon peel.

Negroni
$^1/_3$ gin
$^1/_3$ sweet vermouth
$^1/_3$ Campari
Soda water (optional)
Build the gin, vermouth and
Campari into a tall glass over
ice. Add soda water if desired.
Add half a slice of orange. Serve
with a stirrer.

Nevada
$^1/_3$ dark rum
$^1/_3$ grapefruit juice
$^1/_6$ fresh lime juice
$^1/_6$ gomme syrup
Shake.

Night Light
$^2/_3$ white rum
$^1/_3$ orange curaçao
1 egg yolk
Shake. Serve in a double
cocktail glass.

O

Old Etonian
$^1/_2$ gin
$^1/_2$ Lillet
2 dashes orange bitters
2 dashes crème de noyeau
Stir. Add a twist of orange peel.

Old-fashioned
1 small sugar lump
Angostura bitters
1 large measure rye whisky

Place the sugar in an
old-fashioned glass, saturate
with the bitters and add enough
water to dissolve the sugar. Fill
the glass with ice. Add the
whisky. Decorate with half a
slice of orange and a cherry.
Serve with a stirrer.

Old Nick
$^1/_2$ rye whisky
$^1/_4$ Drambuie
$^1/_8$ orange juice
$^1/_8$ lemon juice
2 dashes orange bitters
Shake. Add a cherry.

Old Pal
$^1/_3$ rye whisky
$^1/_3$ dry vermouth
$^1/_3$ Campari
Stir.

Olympic
$^1/_3$ brandy
$^1/_3$ orange curaçao
$^1/_3$ orange juice.
Shake.

Opening
$^1/_2$ rye whisky
$^1/_4$ grenadine
$^1/_4$ sweet vermouth
Stir.

Opera
$^2/_3$ gin
$^1/_6$ Dubonnet
$^1/_6$ maraschino
Stir. Add a twist of orange peel.

Orange Bloom
$^1/_2$ gin
$^1/_4$ Cointreau
$^1/_4$ sweet vermouth
Stir. Add a cherry.

Orange Blossom
$^1/_2$ gin
$^1/_2$ orange juice
Shake.

Oriental
⅖ rye whisky
⅕ sweet vermouth
⅕ white curaçao
⅕ fresh lime juice
Shake.

P

Pall Mall
⅓ gin
⅓ sweet vermouth
⅓ dry vermouth
1 barspoon white crème de
    menthe
2 dashes orange bitters
Stir.

Palm Breeze
½ dark rum
⅓ yellow Chartreuse
⅙ crème de cacao
Juice ½ fresh lime
1 dash grenadine
Shake.

Paradise
½ gin
¼ apricot brandy
¼ orange juice
Shake.

Parisian
⅖ dry gin
⅖ dry vermouth
⅕ crème de cassis
Stir.

Patricia
⅓ vodka
⅓ sweet vermouth
⅓ orange curaçao
Stir. Add a twist of lemon.

Pefect Lady
½ gin
¼ peach brandy
¼ lemon juice
1 egg white
Shake.

Petake Cocktail
2 fl oz golden rum
1 fl oz Cointreau
1 dash Van der Hum
1 dash pineapple juice
1 dash papaya juice
1 dash lime juice
Shake. Strain into a large
cocktail glass.

Petite Fleur
⅓ white rum
⅓ Cointreau
⅓ fresh grapefruit juice
Shake.

Picca
1 fl oz Scotch whisky
½ fl oz Galliano
½ fl oz Punt-e-Mes
Stir. Decorate with a cherry.

Piccadilly
⅔ gin
⅓ dry vermouth
1 dash pastis
1 dash grenadine
Stir.

Picon
½ Amer Picon
½ sweet vermouth
Stir.

Pink Lady
⅘ gin
⅕ grenadine
1 egg white
Shake.

Pink Pussy
1 fl oz Campari
½ fl oz peach brandy
1 dash egg white
Shake. Strain into an ice-filled
highball glass. Top with bitter
lemon.

Planters
½ golden rum
½ fresh orange juice
1 dash fresh lemon juice
Shake.

Playmate
¼ brandy
¼ apricot brandy
¼ Grand Marnier
¼ orange squash
1 egg white
1 dash Angostura bitters
Shake. Add a twist of orange peel.

Port Wine
⅘ port wine
⅕ brandy
Stir. Add a twist of orange peel.

Prince Charles
⅓ cognac
⅓ Drambuie
⅓ fresh lemon juice
Shake.

Princeton
⅔ gin
⅓ port wine
1 dash orange bitters
Stir. Add a twist of lemon peel.

Quarter Deck
⅔ dark rum
⅓ dry sherry
1 dash lime juice cordial
Stir.

Queens
¼ gin
¼ dry vermouth
¼ sweet vermouth
¼ pineapple juice
Shake.

Quiet Sunday
1 fl oz vodka
½ fl oz amaretto
4 fl oz fresh orange juice
Few dashes grenadine
Shake together all but the grenadine. Strain into an ice-filled highball glass. Add a few dashes grenadine.

RAC
½ gin
¼ dry vermouth
¼ sweet vermouth
1 dash grenadine
1 dash orange bitters
Stir. Add a twist of orange peel and a cherry.

Red Hackle
½ brandy
¼ Dubonnet
¼ grenadine
Shake.

Red Lion
⅓ gin
⅓ Grand Marnier
⅙ orange juice
⅙ lemon juice
Shake. Frost rim of glass with sugar.

Regent Star
½ gin
¼ orange curaçao
⅛ dry vermouth
⅛ passion fruit juice
Shake.

Resolute
½ gin
¼ lemon juice
¼ apricot brandy
Shake.

The Road Runner
1 fl oz vodka
½ fl oz amaretto
¼ fl oz coconut milk
Shake. Sprinkle with nutmeg.

Roadster
⅓ gin
⅓ Grand Marnier
⅓ orange juice
Shake. Add a twist of lemon peel.

Roberta May
⅓ vodka
⅓ Aurum
⅓ orange squash
1 dash egg white
Shake.

Rob Roy
½ Scotch whisky
½ sweet vermouth
1 dash Angostura bitters
Stir. Add a cherry.

Rolls-Royce
⅓ brandy
⅓ Cointreau
⅓ orange juice
Shake.

Rose
⅓ kirsch
⅔ dry vermouth
1 barspoon rose syrup
Stir. Add a cherry.

Ross Royal
⅓ brandy
⅓ crème de banane
⅓ Royal Mint Chocolate liqueur
Shake.

Royalist
½ dry vermouth
¼ bourbon whiskey
¼ Bénédictine
1 dash peach bitters
Stir.

Royal Mail
¼ sloe gin
¼ Van der Hum
¼ orange juice
¼ lemon juice
1 dash pastis
Shake.

Royal Romance
½ gin
¼ Grand Marnier .
¼ dry passion fruit juice
1 dash grenadine
Shake.

Royal Smile
⅔ gin
⅓ calvados
3 dashes grenadine
3 dashes lemon juice
Shake.

Royal Victor
⅓ lemon gin
⅓ Liqueur d'Or
⅙ Cointreau
⅙ lemon squash
1 dash fresh lemon juice
Shake. Add a cherry.

Rusty Nail
⅔ Scotch whisky
⅓ Drambuie
Serve in an old-fashioned glass, on the rocks. Add a twist of lemon.

Rye Lane
⅓ rye whisky
⅓ white curaçao
⅓ orange juice
2 dashes crème de noyeau
Shake.

S

Salome
⅓ gin
⅓ Dubonnet
⅓ dry vermouth
Stir.

Salty Dog
1½ fl oz vodka
3½ fl oz fresh grapefruit juice
Salt the rim of a large glass. Fill
with ice. Build.

Satan's Whiskers
⅕ gin
⅕ Grand Marnier
⅕ dry vermouth
⅕ sweet vermouth
⅕ orange juice
1 dash orange bitters
Shake.

Sazerac
1 large measure rye whisky
2 dashes Peychaud or Angostura
bitters
3 drops pastis
2 dashes gomme syrup
Stir. Strain into an
old-fashioned glass. Serve on
the rocks or straight up. Add a
twist of lemon.

Scotch Frog
½ vodka
¼ Galliano
¼ Cointreau
Juice of 1 lime
1 dash Angostura bitters
1 barspoon maraschino cherry
   juice
Shake.

Screwdriver
1 fl oz vodka
4 fl oz fresh orange juice
Build into a large ice-filled
glass.

Sea Breeze
½ vodka
⅙ dry vermouth
⅙ blue curaçao
⅙ Galliano
Stir. Strain into an ice-filled
goblet or old-fashioned glass.
Add a twist of orange.

Shamrock
½ Irish whiskey
½ dry vermouth
3 dashes green Chartreuse
3 dashes green crème de
   menthe
Stir.

Shanghai
½ dark rum
⅛ pastis
⅜ lemon juice
2 dashes grenadine
Shake.

Shannon Shandy
1 fl oz Irish Mist
1 dash Angostura bitters
Dry ginger ale
Pour the Irish Mist and bitters
over ice in a highball glass. Top
with dry ginger ale.

Sherry Twist
⅖ dry sherry
⅖ orange juice
⅕ Scotch whisky
2 dashes Cointreau
Shake.

Sidecar
½ brandy
¼ Cointreau
¼ lemon juice
Shake.

Silent Third
⅓ Scotch whisky
⅓ Cointreau
⅓ lemon juice
Shake.

Silver Bullet
1½ fl oz vodka
1 fl oz kummel
Stir or build on the rocks.

Silver Jubilee
½ gin
¼ crème de banane
¼ cream
Shake.

Silver Streak
1½ fl oz dry gin
1 fl oz kummel
Stir or build on the rocks.

Silver Sunset
1 fl oz vodka
½ fl oz apricot brandy
½ fl oz lemon juice
3 fl oz orange juice
1 dash Campari
1 dash egg white
Shake. Strain into an ice-filled
highball glass. Decorate with an
orange slice and a cherry. Serve
with straws.

Six Bells
½ dark rum
¼ orange curaçao
¼ fresh lime juice
2 dashes Angostura bitters
1 dash gomme syrup
Shake.

Slipstream
¼ brandy
¼ Grand Marnier
¼ Lillet
¼ orange juice
2 dashes Angostura bitters
1 egg white
Shake.

Sloe Comfortable Screw
1 fl oz vodka
½ fl oz sloe gin
½ fl oz Southern Comfort
4 fl oz fresh orange juice
Build into an ice-filled highball
glass.

Sloe Gin
½ sloe gin
¼ dry vermouth
¼ sweet vermouth
Stir.

Starboard Light
½ sloe gin
¼ green crème de menthe
¼ lemon juice
Shake.

Stinger
⅔ brandy
⅓ white crème de menthe
Stir. Serve straight up or on the
rocks.

Stone Fence
1 measure Scotch or bourbon
Dry cider
Build the spirit into an ice-
filled highball glass. Stir in the
dry cider. Add a twist of lemon.

Suissesse
½ pastis
½ lemon juice
1 egg white
Soda water
Shake together all but the soda
water. Strain into a small
tumbler. Add a splash of soda
water.

Sunrise
⅖ tequila
⅕ Galliano
⅕ crème de banane
⅕ cream
1 dash grenadine
1 dash lemon juice
Shake.

Scotch Sour   Bobby Burns   Old-fashioned   49

St Germain
⅓ green Chartreuse
⅓ lemon juice
⅓ grapefruit juice
1 egg white
Shake.

Smiling Duchess
⅓ gin
⅓ Lillet
⅙ apricot brandy
⅙ crème de noyeau
Stir. Add a cherry.

Smiling Ivy
⅓ dark rum
⅓ peach liqueur
⅓ pineapple juice
1 dash fresh lemon juice
1 egg white
Shake.

Smiling Through
⅓ rum
⅓ Grand Marnier
⅓ maraschino
1 dash fresh lemon juice
1 dash grenadine
Shake. Add a cherry.

Snake-in-the-Grass
¼ gin
¼ Cointreau
¼ dry vermouth
¼ lemon juice
Shake.

Sweet Memories
⅓ white rum
⅓ dry vermouth
⅓ orange curaçao
Stir.

SW1
⅓ vodka
⅓ Campari
⅓ fresh orange juice
1 dash egg white
Shake.

T

Tango
½ gin
¼ sweet vermouth
¼ dry vermouth
2 dashes orange curaçao
1 dash orange juice
Shake.

Temptation
⁷⁄₁₀ rye whisky
¹⁄₁₀ orange curaçao
¹⁄₁₀ pastis
¹⁄₁₀ Dubonnet
Shake. Add a twist each of
orange peel and lemon peel.

Tempter
½ port wine
½ apricot liqueur
Stir.

Tequila Sunrise
1 fl oz tequila
4 fl oz fresh orange juice
2 dashes grenadine
Build tequila and orange juice
into ice-filled pils glass. Stir.
Splash in grenadine. Decorate
with orange slice and cherry.
Add straws.

The Clubman
1 fl oz Irish Mist
4 fl oz orange juice
1 dash egg white
Shake. Pour over ice in a
highball glass. Trickle blue
curaçao down inside of glass to
make green patterns.

Three Miler
⅔ brandy
⅓ white rum
1 dash lemon juice
1 barspoon grenadine
Shake.

Tidal Wave
1 fl oz Mandarine Napoléon
1 dash fresh lemon juice
Build into an ice-filled highball
glass. Stir in bitter lemon.
Decorate with a lemon slice.

Tiger Lillet
⅓ Lillet
⅓ Van der Hum
⅙ dry vermouth
⅙ maraschino
Stir. Add a twist of orange peel.

Tiger's Tail
⅓ pastis
⅔ fresh orange juice
Build into an ice-filled
old-fashioned glass. Add a slice
of orange.

Trinity
⅓ gin
⅓ sweet vermouth
⅓ dry vermouth
Stir.

Tropical Dawn
⅖ dry gin
⅖ fresh orange juice
⅕ Campari
Shake gin and orange juice.
Pour over a ball of crushed ice
in an 8-oz goblet. Splash with
Campari. Serve with short
straws.

TNT
⅔ brandy
⅓ orange curaçao
1 dash Angostura bitters
1 dash pastis
Stir.

Twentieth Century
⅖ gin
⅕ crème de cacao
⅕ Lillet
⅕ lemon juice
Shake.

U

Up-to-Date
⅖ rye whisky
⅖ dry vermouth
⅕ Grand Marnier
1 dash Angostura bitters
Stir. Add a twist of lemon peel.

V

Valencia
⅔ apricot brandy
⅓ orange juice
4 dashes orange bitters
Shake.

Vanderbilt
½ brandy
½ cherry brandy
2 dashes Angostura bitters
2 dashes gomme syrup
Stir. Add a twist of lemon and a
cherry.

Velvet Hammer
⅓ Cointreau
⅓ Tia Maria
⅓ fresh cream
Shake.

Venetian Sunset
⅖ dry gin
⅕ Grand Marnier
⅕ Campari
⅕ dry vermouth
Stir. Add a cherry.

The Visitor
⅓ gin
⅓ Cointreau
⅓ crème de banane
1 dash orange juice
1 egg white
Shake.

W

Ward Eight
½ rye whisky
¼ orange juice
¼ lemon juice
1 barspoon grenadine
Shake.

Waterloo
1 fl oz Mandarine Napoléon
4 fl oz fresh orange juice
Build into an ice-filled highball
glass.

Wax
½ gin
½ pastis
3 dashes gomme syrup
1 egg white
Shake.

Wembley
⅓ Scotch whisky
⅓ dry vermouth
⅓ pineapple juice
Shake.

Western Rose
½ gin
¼ apricot brandy
¼ dry vermouth
1 dash lemon juice
Shake.

Whip
¼ brandy
¼ pastis
¼ dry vermouth
¼ curaçao
Shake.

Whisky
⅘ Scotch whisky
⅕ orange curaçao
2 dashes Angostura bitters
Stir. Add a cherry.

Whisky Mac
1½ fl oz Scotch whisky
1 fl oz ginger wine
Build straight into an
old-fashioned glass.

White Lady
½ gin
¼ lemon juice
¼ Cointreau
1 dash egg white
Shake.

White Lily
⅓ Cointreau
⅓ white rum
⅓ gin
1 dash pastis
Stir.

White Russian
½ fl oz vodka
¾ fl oz Kahlua
Build into an ice-filled
old-fashioned glass.
Float cream on top.

White Satin
³⁄₁₀ gin
⁶⁄₁₀ white curaçao
¹⁄₁₀ lemon juice
Shake.

Whizz Bang
⅔ Scotch whisky
⅓ dry vermouth
2 dashes pastis
2 dashes grenadine
2 dashes orange bitters
Stir.

X

Xanthia
⅓ gin
⅓ yellow Chartreuse
⅓ cherry brandy
Stir.

XYZ
½ golden rum
¼ Cointreau
¼ lemon juice
Shake.

Y

Yellow Bird
1½ fl oz white rum
½ fl oz Galliano
½ fl oz Cointreau
½ fl oz fresh lime juice
Shake with cracked ice and
pour unstrained into a stemmed
glass. Decorate with a slice of
lime.

Yellow Daisy
⅖ gin
⅖ dry vermouth
⅕ Gand Marnier
Stir.

Yellow Parrot
⅓ pastis
⅓ yellow Chartreuse
⅓ apricot brandy
Stir.

Z

ZaZa
½ gin
½ Dubonnet
1 dash Angostura bitters
Stir.

Zombie
1 fl oz light rum
1 fl oz golden rum
1 fl oz dark rum
¾ fl oz lime juice
¾ fl oz pineapple juice
½ fl oz apricot liqueur
1 dash gomme syrup
1 dash 151-proof Demararan
    rum
Shake together all but the 151-
proof rum. Strain into a 12-oz
highball glass filled with
crushed ice. Splash the rum on
top. Decorate with a slice of
orange and a sprig of mint.
Serve with straws.

Zoom
1 barspoon honey
1 barspoon cream
1 measure desired spirit
Dissolve the honey in a little hot
water. Add the cream and spirit.
Shake. Strain into a medium
goblet.

CLASSIC STYLES

BLENDED DRINKS

The liquidizer is now standard equipment in most cocktail bars, for it increases the variety of drinks the bartender can offer his customers and enables him to meet the demand for a wide range of long drinks. The actual liquidizing, or blending, time is short and, if preparation is done in advance, blended drinks can be made in multiples very quickly. Certain machines have toughened blades to cope with cubed ice, but crushed ice is preferable because it saves on wear and tear and keeps blending time to a minimum. Overblending will result in a diluted, thin-bodied drink. Presentation of blended drinks offers much scope: a variety of glassware and garnishes can be used, including novelty containers such as coconut and pineapple shells.

Apricot Lady
1 fl oz golden rum
1 fl oz apricot brandy
3 dashes orange curaçao
½ fl oz fresh lime juice
2 dashes egg white
Blend with a half-scoop of crushed ice. Pour into a small wineglass.

Banshee
1 fl oz cream
¾ fl oz white crème de cacao
¾ fl oz crème de banane
1 dash gomme syrup
Blend with a half-scoop of crushed ice. Pour into a small wineglass.

Blue Hawaiian
1 fl oz white rum
½ fl oz blue curaçao
2 fl oz pineapple juice
1 fl oz coconut cream
1 scoop crushed ice
Blend. Pour into a large-bowled glass.

Casablanca
1½ fl oz white rum
2 fl oz pineapple juice
1 fl oz coconut cream
2 dashes grenadine
2 scoops crushed ice
Blend. Pour into a large bowled glass.

Chi Chi
1½ fl oz vodka
1 fl oz coconut cream
4 fl oz unsweetened pineapple juice
Blend with two scoops of crushed ice. Serve in a large glass. Decorate with a slice of pineapple and a cherry. Serve with straws.

Frozen Steppes
1 fl oz vodka
1 scoop vanilla ice cream
½ fl oz brown crème de cacao
Blend. Serve in a small goblet with short straws.

Orange Cadillac
1 fl oz Galliano
¾ fl oz white crème de cacao
¼ fl oz fresh orange juice
1 fl oz cream
1 scoop cracked ice
Blend. Serve in a small goblet.

Pina Colada
1½ fl oz white rum
2 fl oz pineapple juice
1 fl oz coconut cream
2 scoops crushed ice

Blend. Pour into a large-bowled glass. Decorate with a slice of pineapple and a cherry. Serve with short straws.

Scorpion
1½ fl oz golden rum
1 fl oz fresh orange juice
1 fl oz fresh lemon juice
½ fl oz brandy
2 dashes orgeat syrup
Blend with a scoop of crushed ice. Pour into a large old-fashioned or bowl glass filled with ice cubes. Decorate with a slice of orange and a sprig of mint. Serve with short straws.

Silk Stockings
1½ fl oz tequila
1 fl oz white crème de cacao
1 dash grenadine
1½ fl oz fresh cream
Blend with a scoop of crushed ice. Serve in a tulip glass. Decorate with a cherry. Sprinkle cinnamon on top. Serve with straws.

Strawberry Dawn
1 fl oz dry gin
1 fl oz coconut cream
2–3 fresh strawberries
2 scoops crushed ice
Blend. Serve in a large, saucer-type glass. Decorate with a strawberry. Serve with short straws.

Sunny Dream
1 fl oz apricot brandy
½ fl oz Cointreau
3 fl oz orange juice
1 scoop soft vanilla ice cream
Blend. Decorate with an orange slice.

CHAMPAGNE COCKTAILS

Alfonso
1 lump sugar
2 dashes Angostura bitters
1 fl oz Dubonnet
Champagne
Place sugar in a champagne glass, shake bitters on to sugar. Add Dubonnet. Fill glass with iced champagne. Stir slightly. Add a twist of lemon.

Bellini
Peach juice
Champagne
Fill a champagne glass one-third full with peach juice. Top with iced champagne.

Black Velvet
½ chilled Guinness
½ chilled champagne
Build into a beer glass or tankard.

Buck's Fizz
Orange juice
Champagne
Fill a champagne glass one-third full with fresh orange juice. Top with iced champagne.

Champagne Cocktail
1 lump sugar
Angostura bitters
2 dashes brandy
Champagne
Place sugar in a champagne glass, saturate with bitters and add the brandy. Fill with iced champagne. Add a slice of orange and a cherry.

Champagne Napoleon
1 fl oz Mandarine Napoléon
1 dash orange juice
Champagne
Pour into a champagne glass.
Top with iced champagne.

Fraise Royale
2 fresh strawberries
1 dash fraise liqueur
Champagne
Blend the strawberries with the
liqueur. Pour into a champagne
glass. Top with iced
champagne.

French 75
¾ fl oz gin
¾ fl oz fresh lemon juice
2 dashes gomme syrup
Shake. Strain into an ice-filled
highball glass. Top with iced
champagne.

Happy Youth
1 lump sugar
½ fl oz cherry brandy
1½ fl oz fresh orange juice
Champagne
Place sugar in a champagne
glass. Add the brandy. Top with
iced champagne.

Kir Royale
2 dashes crème de cassis
Champagne
Place the crème de cassis in a
champagne glass. Top with iced
champagne.

Mimosa
Fresh orange juice
1 dash orange curaçao
Champagne
Fill a champagne glass
one-third full with orange juice.
Add curaçao. Top with iced
champagne.

Ritz Fizz
1 dash amaretto
1 dash blue curaçao
1 dash clear lemon juice (PLJ)
Champagne
Place amaretto, curaçao and
lemon juice in a champagne
glass. Top with iced
champagne. Decorate with a
rose petal.

Valencia Smile
⅔ apricot brandy
⅓ orange juice
4 dashes orange bitters
Shake. Strain into a champagne
glass. Top with iced
champagne.

COBBLERS

The Cobbler, a drink of
American origin, is now an
established favourite,
particularly in warm climates. It
is simple to make and attractive
to both the eye and the palate,
by virtue of its fruit and mint
decoration.

To make a Cobbler, fill a
glass with ice and pour the
necessary ingredients over the
top. Stir well. Cobblers are
usually served with straws.

Wine Cobblers
Burgundy, claret, port, Rhine
  wine or sherry
4 dashes orange curaçao
1 barspoon gomme syrup
Fill a medium-sized wineglass
with ice. Half-fill with the
required wine. Add the curaçao
and gomme syrup. Stir.
Decorate with fruit. Add a sprig
of mint. Serve with straws.

SMIRNOFF
1886
1882
1877
1896
PURVEYORS TO
THE IMPERIAL RUSSIAN COURT
PIERRE SMIRNOFF
EST. 1818 MOSCOW
1886-1917
Ste Pierre Smirnoff
VODKA
PRODUCED IN ENGLAND
International Distillers & Vintners
1 York Gate London N W 1
75 cl
SMIRNOFF
65.5° Pro

Spirit Cobblers
Rum, whisky, brandy or gin
1 barspoon sugar
4 dashes orange curaçao
Fill a medium-sized wineglass
with ice. Add the required
spirit, sugar and curaçao. Stir.
Decorate with fruit. Add a sprig
of mint. Serve with straws.

COLLINS

These are normally summer or
hot-weather drinks, long and
refreshing and made with
plenty of ice. There is some
doubt as to their origin, though
they are often claimed to be
American and may have been
derived from the Gin Sling.
However, as gin was widely
drunk in the British Isles long
before it gained popularity in
the United States, it is quite
probable that the drinks
originated in Britain.
Supporting evidence for this
view is contained in a book
called *Drinks of the World*,
published in 1892, in which a
celebrated waiter of the time is
immortalized in verse:
'My name is John Collins,
   head-waiter at Limmer's,
Corner of Conduit Street,
   Hanover Square.
My chief occupation is filling
   brimmers
For all the young gentlemen
   frequenters there.'
   The book states that the
ingredients of the drink
dispensed by Mr Collins were
gin, soda, lemon and sugar.
   There is no doubt that the
Collins has spawned a large
family since the early days.
Among its cousins are the Gin
Coolers and Gin Rickeys.

In the late 1930s and before, a
John Collins was made with
Dutch gin, and Tom Collins
with 'Old Tom' gin. It is now
accepted, however, that both
drinks should be made with
London Dry gin and are
therefore identical.

John or Tom Collins
Juice of 1 lemon
1 barspoon gomme syrup
1 measure of gin
Soda water
Place some ice in a highball
glass, add the lemon juice,
syrup and gin. Fill with soda
water. Stir and serve with a
slice of lemon Serve with
straws.

Brandy, Rum or Whisky Collins
As above, substituting an
alternative spirit for the gin.

Note A Collins may also be
shaken with the addition of a
little egg white, then topped up
with soda.

COOLERS

These are almost identical to
the Collins but usually contain
the peel of the fruit cut into a
spiral.

Apricot Cooler
Juice of 1 lemon or lime
2 dashes grenadine
1 liqueur glass apricot brandy
1 dash Angostura bitters
Shake together all but the
bitters. Strain into a highball
glass. Fill up with soda water.
Add the bitters.

Harvard Cooler

Juice of 1 lemon or lime
1 barspoon gomme syrup
1 measure applejack brandy
Soda water
Shake together all but the soda
water. Strain into a highball
glass. Fill up with soda water.

Limbo Cooler

1 fl oz dark rum
¾ fl oz Amer Picon
2 fl oz lemon juice
1 barspoon grenadine
7-Up
Shake all but the 7-Up with an
orange slice. Strain into a goblet
filled with crushed ice. Stir in
the 7-Up. Decorate with an
orange slice, a cherry and a
stirrer.

Misty Cooler

1 fl oz Irish Mist
2 fl oz lemon juice
1 dash grenadine
1 dash egg white
Soda water
Shake all but the soda water.
Serve in a highball glass with
ice, topped with soda water.

Rum Cooler

Juice of 1 lemon or lime
4 dashes of grenadine
1 measure dark rum
Soda water
Shake all but the soda water.
Strain into a highball glass. Add
ice. Fill up with soda water.

Shady Grove Cooler

1 barspoon gomme syrup
Juice of 1 lemon
1 measure gin
Ginger beer
Place the gomme syrup, lemon
juice and gin in a highball
glass. Fill with ginger beer. Add
ice. Stir slightly.

Wine Cooler

1 measure red or white wine
4 dashes of grenadine
Soda water
Add ice to the wine and
grenadine in a highball glass.
Fill with soda water.

CRUSTAS

A crusta can be made with any
spirit, the most popular being
brandy.
  To prepare the glass, rub the
rim of a large goblet with a slice
of lemon, dip the edge in
powdered sugar, fit a spiral of
orange into glass and fill with
cracked ice.

Brandy Crusta

1 dash Angostura bitters
3 dashes maraschino
1 measure brandy
1 dash fresh lemon juice
½ fl oz orange curaçao
Shake or stir. Strain into a
prepared glass. Add a
maraschino cherry.

CUPS

Cups are of English origin, the
most famous being the Stirrup
Cup, served to members of a
hunting party about to set off or
to travellers in need of hasty
refreshment. A special glass
was used which had a long stem
and a knob instead of a flat
base, so that the contents –
usually sloe gin – had to be
finished before the glass could
be put on the tray, upside down.
The phrase 'in his cups' was a
common euphemism meaning
'under the influence of alcohol'.

Today, cups are regarded as hot-weather drinks with a wine base. They are normally made in large quantities.

Chablis Cup (4–6 glasses)
1 bottle chablis
2–3 fl oz sherry
Rind of a lemon
1 tablespoon gomme syrup
Mix all the ingredients in a large jug. Add ice.

Champagne Cup
1 tablespoon powdered sugar
4 fl oz brandy
3 fl oz orange curaçao
1 fl oz maraschino
1 bottle champagne
Stir together in a jug or bowl. Add ice. Garnish with sliced fruit.

Claret Cup (10 glasses)
3 oz sugar
¼ pint water
Juice of 2 oranges
Juice of 2 lemons
2 bottles claret
Orange and lemon rind
Soda water
Boil the sugar and water with the orange and lemon rind. Add the fruit juices and claret. Keep refrigerated until ready to serve. Put ice in a bowl, add the wine mixture and soda water. Float slices of cucumber, apple and orange and a sprig of mint on top.

Coronation Crystal (18 glasses)
1 bottle white wine
3 glasses marsala or madeira
1 slice lemon
1 large bottle soda water
Sprig of borage
Mix all the ingredients together and leave for about 2 hours. Sweeten to taste. Serve well iced.

Dry White Wine Cup (32 glasses)
3 bottles dry white wine
1 bottle bianco vermouth
1 large bottle lemonade
Slices of orange and lemon
Chill the ingredients in the refrigerator. Mix together. Add fruit and a sprig of mint.

Hock Sparkler (24–30 glasses)
3 bottles hock
1 bottle sekt
1 liqueur glass brandy
1 melon or other fresh fruit
Sugar to taste
Cube the melon or slice the other fruit and place in a large bowl with the sugar and the still wine. Leave for one hour, then add the sparkling wine and other ingredients. Serve slightly iced, decorated with more fruit.

Peace Cup (8–10 glasses)
2 dozen strawberries
2 slices chopped fresh pineapple
2 tablespoons caster sugar
2 fl oz water
2 fl oz maraschino
1 bottle dry sparkling wine
Soda water
Blend the fruit, sugar and water into a purée. Pour into a large jug with ice. Add the maraschino, wine and soda water. Stir well.

Pimm's No.1

The original and best known of the cups marketed as Pimm's has a gin base. Prepare by pouring the Pimm's into an ice-filled highball glass then topping with lemonade, ginger ale or 7-Up. Decorate with slice of lemon or orange and rind of cucumber or mint.
Note There is also a vodka-based Pimm's.

Riesling Cup (10 glasses)
1 bottle Yugoslav Riesling
½ bottle dry cider
1 small bottle lemonade
Slices of orange and lemon
Chill the ingredients in the
refrigerator. Stir together and
add the fruit and a sprig of mint.

DAIQUIRIS

The origin of this drink is
unknown but it was given this
name early in the 1900s when
American engineers were
developing the Daiquiri iron
mines in Cuba. As they
emerged from the pits they were
handed an iced drink made
with rum, lime and sugar.
Daiquiris are very refreshing
but should be drunk
immediately as they tend to
separate if allowed to stand.

Daiquiri
¾ white rum
¼ fresh lime juice
3 dashes gomme syrup
Shake.

Daiquiri Blossom
½ white rum
½ fresh orange juice
1 dash maraschino
Shake.

Daiquiri Liberal
⅔ white rum
⅓ sweet vermouth
1 dash Amer Picon
Stir.

Coconut Daiquiri
½ fl oz white rum
1 fl oz coconut liqueur
2 fl oz fresh lime juice
1 dash egg white
Shake.

King's Daiquiri
½ fl oz fresh lime juice
½ fl oz Parfait Amour
1½ fl oz white rum
¼ barspoon sugar
1 dash egg white
Blend. Serve in a champagne
glass.

FROZEN DAIQUIRIS
These blended variations of the
Daiquiri cocktail are very
popular. Make them with plenty
of dry crushed ice: if made
correctly, the finished drink
should be of the consistency of a
sorbet and may be piled above
the rim of a large goblet.

By using fresh fruit and an
appropriate liqueur, a whole
range of frozen-fruit daiquiris
may be made.

Frozen Daiquiri
1½ fl oz white rum
1 dash maraschino
Juice of ½ lime
1 dash gomme syrup
Blend on high speed with two
scoops crushed ice. Pour
unstrained into a glass. Serve
with short, thick straws.

Banana Daiquiri
1½ fl oz white rum
½ fl oz crème de banane
Juice of ½ lime
½ banana
Prepare and serve as for Frozen
Daiquiri.

Peach Daiquiri
1½ fl oz white rum
½ fl oz peach brandy
Juice of ½ lime
⅓ of a fresh peach (skinned)
Prepare and serve as for Frozen
Daiquiri. Decorate with a
wedge of peach.

Strawberry Daiquiri
1½ fl oz white rum
½ fl oz fraise liqueur
Juice of ½ lime
3 strawberries
Prepare and serve as for Frozen
Daiquiri. Decorate with a fresh
strawberry.

DAISIES

These may be made with any
spirit and are usually served in
tankards or wineglasses filled
with cracked ice. They must be
served very cold, which makes
hard, vigorous shaking
necessary.

1 measure desired spirit
½ fl oz lemon juice
2 dashes grenadine
Soda water (optional)
Shake together the spirit, lemon
juice and grenadine. Add soda
water if desired. Decorate with
sprigs of mint and fruit.

Star Daisy
1 fl oz gin
½ fl oz fresh lemon juice
½ barspoon powdered sugar
1 fl oz calvados
2 dashes grenadine
Soda water
Shake together all but the soda
water. Add the soda water.
Decorate with fruit.

EGG NOGGS

The traditional Christmas
morning drink, these may be
made in bulk and ladled into
small wine goblets at time of
serving, as long as the
proportions stated for individual

drinks are maintained. If you
prefer a thicker consistency, use
more egg yolk, and cream
instead of milk.

Egg Nogg.
1 egg
1 tablespoon gomme syrup
1 measure brandy
1 measure dark rum
3 fl oz milk
Shake together all but the milk.
Strain into a goblet. Stir in the
milk. Sprinkle grated nutmeg
on top.

Baltimore Egg Nogg
1 egg
1 barspoon gomme syrup
1 measure brandy
½ measure dark rum
1 measure madeira
3 fl oz milk
Shake. Strain into a large
goblet. Sprinkle grated nutmeg
on top.

Breakfast Nogg
1 egg
1 measure orange curaçao
1 measure brandy
3 fl oz milk
Shake. Strain into a medium
goblet. Sprinkle grated nutmeg
on top.

Nashville Egg Nogg (20–25
glasses)
1 pint brandy
1 pint golden rum
1 quart bourbon
18 eggs
3 quarts double cream
1 lb sugar
Blend. Serve in small goblets.
Garnish with cloves and
nutmeg.

Rum Nogg
1 egg
1 measure dark rum
1 barspoon gomme syrup
3 fl oz milk
Shake. Strain into a goblet.
Sprinkle grated nutmeg on top.

FIXES

A fix is a short drink made by pouring any spirit over crushed ice. It is usually decorated with fruit and served with short straws.

Brandy Fix
1½ fl oz brandy
½ fl oz cherry brandy
4 fl oz fresh lemon juice
1 barspoon gomme syrup
Build into a goblet filled with crushed ice. Stir gently. Add slices of lemon and orange, and a cherry. Serve with straws.

Gin Fix
2½ fl oz gin
1 fl oz fresh lemon juice
1 barspoon gomme syrup
Build into a goblet filled with crushed ice. Stir gently. Add a slice of lemon. Serve with straws.

FIZZES

The Fizz is a close cousin of the Collins, but is always shaken. It is served in a tall highball or 'Collins' glass with ice, straws and a muddler. Fizzes are very good morning drinks but they should be drunk as soon as they are ready because they lose their flavour very quickly.

Clark and Randolph Fizz
1 large measure gin
1½ fl oz pineapple juice
1 egg white
Soda water
Shake together all but the soda water. Top up with soda water.

Dubonnet Fizz
1 measure Dubonnet
½ measure cherry brandy
1 fl oz fresh lemon juice
1 fl oz fresh orange juice
1 egg white
Soda water
Shake together all but the soda water. Top up with soda water.

Gin Fizz
1 measure gin
1 fl oz fresh lemon juice
1 barspoon gomme syrup
Soda water
Shake together all but the soda water. Top up with soda water.

Golden Fizz
As Gin Fizz, plus an egg yolk.

May Blossom Fizz
2 fl oz Swedish punsch
¾ fl oz lemon juice
2 dashes grenadine
Soda water
Shake togther all but the soda water. Top up with soda water.

Merry Widow Fizz
1 large measure Dubonnet
1 fl oz fresh lemon juice
1 fl oz fresh orange juice
1 egg white
Soda water.
Shake together all but the soda water. Top up with soda water.

Morning Glory Fizz

1 large measure whisky
1 dash anisette
1 fl oz fresh lemon juice
1 egg white
1 barspoon gomme syrup
Soda water
Shake together all but the soda
water. Top up with soda water.

New Orleans Fizz

1 large measure gin
½ fl oz fresh lime juice
½ fl oz fresh lemon juice
2 dashes gomme syrup
3 dashes orange flower water
1 dessertspoon cream
Soda water
Shake or mix all but soda water.
Top up with soda water.

Pineapple Fizz

1 large measure light rum
1½ fl oz pineapple juice
1 barspoon gomme syrup
Soda water
Lemonade
Shake togther rum, pineapple
juice and gomme syrup. Top up
with half soda water, half
lemonade.

Ramos Fizz

1 large measure gin
1 fl oz fresh lemon juice
1 dash gomme syrup
3 dashes orange flower water
1 dessertspoon cream
1 egg white
Soda water (optional)
Shake together all but soda
water. Add soda water if
desired.

Royal Fizz

As Gin Fizz, using a whole egg.

Silver Fizz

As Gin Fizz, plus an egg white.

Texas Fizz

1 large measure gin
½ fl oz fresh lemon juice
½ fl oz fresh orange juice
2 dashes gomme syrup
1 dash egg white
Soda water
Shake together all but soda
water. Stir in the soda water.

FLIPS

Flips belong to the same family
of drinks as egg noggs. They
contain the yolk of a fresh egg
but never any milk. They can be
made with any of the following
spirits or wines: gin, whisky,
brandy, rum, port, sherry or
claret.
   Serve in a medium-sized
wineglass.

Ale Flip

2 pints ale
Grated rind of 1 lemon
3 eggs
½ barspoon ground ginger
8 oz brown sugar
4 fl oz brandy
Heat the ale and lemon rind.
Beat the rest of the ingredients
together in separate bowl. Pour
the heated ale into the egg
mixture. Blend and pour back
and forth from bowl to saucepan
until mixture is creamy and
smooth. Grate nutmeg on top.

Boston Flip

½ rye whisky
½ madeira
1 egg yolk
1 barspoon gomme syrup
Shake.

Brandy Flip

1 measure brandy
1 egg
1 barspoon gomme syrup
Shake well with ice. Sprinkle grated nutmeg on top

Champagne Flip

1 fl oz fresh orange juice
3 dashes orange curaçao
1 barspoon gomme syrup
1 egg yolk
Champagne
Shake together all but the champagne. Strain into a large goblet. Top up with champagne.

Nightcap Flip

1 fl oz anisette
1 fl oz orange curaçao
1 fl oz brandy
1 egg yolk
Shake.

Sifi Flip

1 fl oz gin
½ fl oz Cointreau
½ fl oz grenadine
½ fl oz fresh lemon juice
1 egg yolk
Shake.

FRAPPES

The word Frappé should not be confused with 'glacé' (chilled) or 'on the rocks' (with ice cubes); it means 'served with finely crushed ice'.

Liqueur Frappés

All kinds of liqueurs may be used for these. Fill a medium-sized stemmed glass (or large cocktail glass) with crushed ice. Then pour a measure of the desired liqueur on to the ice. Serve with short straws.

The most commonly requested frappé is made with crème de menthe.

Frappés may also be prepared with more than one ingredient, as demonstrated in two of the examples below.

Nap Frappé

⅓ kummel
⅓ green chartreuse
⅓ brandy

Ward's Frappé

Rind of lemon in glass
½ green chartreuse
½ brandy
Pour the brandy in last. Do not mix the ingredients.

Scotch Mist

1 measure Scotch whisky
Shake the whisky with crushed ice. Pour unstrained into an old-fashioned glass. Add a twist of lemon.

HIGHBALLS

This famous American contribution to the terminology of drinking is said to have originated in the nineteenth century. On some US railroads, a ball would be raised on a pole to indicate to a locoman passing through a station that he was behind schedule and should speed up. Hence the term 'high ball' became associated with a simple drink, quickly prepared.

Cuba Libre

1 fl oz white rum
Juice of ½ fresh lime
Cola

Build the rum and lime juice into an ice-filled highball glass. Drop in the spent lime shell. Stir in cola. Serve with straws.

Horse's Neck
1 measure brandy
Dry ginger ale
1 dash Angostura bitters
  (optional)
Peel the rind of a lemon in one spiral. Place the end of the spiral over the edge of a highball glass, allowing the remainder to curl inside and anchor with the ice at the bottom of the glass. Add brandy. Fill with dry ginger. Add bitters if desired.

Rye Highball
1 measure rye whisky
Dry ginger ale or soda water
Pour whisky into an ice-filled highball glass. Stir in dry ginger ale or soda water. Add a twist of lemon.

Spritzer
½ dry white wine
½ soda water
Build into a large ice-filled glass. Add a twist of lemon.

Stone Fence
1 measure whisky
2 dashes, Angostura bitters
Cider
Pour whisky and bitters into an ice-filled highball glass. Stir in cider.

HOT DRINKS

Black Stripe
2 fl oz dark rum
1 tablespoon honey
Mix rum with honey in a silver tankard. Fill with boiling water.

Stir. Pour into a stemmed glass. Add a twist of lemon.

Blue Blazer
2 fl oz Scotch whisky
2 fl oz boiling water
1 barspoon powdered sugar
Use 2 large silver mugs with handles. Heat the whisky and put into one mug. Put the boiling water in the other mug. Ignite whisky. While blazing, mix both ingredients by pouring them four or five times from one mug to the other. If done well, the liquid will resemble a continuous stream of liquid fire. Sweeten with the sugar. Serve in an old-fasioned glass. Add a twist of lemon.

Glühwein
This is a German hot toddy.
2 lumps sugar
1 slice lemon
1 piece cinnamon
½ pint red wine
Boil and serve as hot as possible.

Grog
1 measure dark rum
1 lump of sugar
2 cloves
Lemon juice
1 small stick cinnamon
Place in an old-fashioned glass. Fill with boiling water. Stir.

Hot Buttered Rum
1 measure dark rum
1 lump sugar
1 slice butter
4 cloves
Place in an old-fashioned glass. Fill with boiling water. Stir.

Hot Egg Nogg
1 barspoon sugar
1 egg
1 measure brandy
1 measure rum
Place in a highball glass. Fill
with hot milk. Stir. Grate
nutmeg on top.

Tom and Jerry
1 egg
1 barspoon sugar
1 measure dark rum
2 dashes brandy
Beat up egg yolk and white
separately, then mix them
together in an old-fashioned
glass. Fill with boiling water.
Add brandy. Grate nutmeg on
top.

Irish Coffee
Coffee
2 barspoons Demerara sugar
1 measure Irish whiskey
Cream
Stir the sugar and whiskey into
an 8-oz Paris goblet or special
Irish Coffee glass containing hot
coffee. Float the cream on top
by pouring over the back of a
warmed spoon. Do not stir.

Some liqueurs and spirits
marry so well with black coffee
and cream that special names
are given to the combinations:

Aquavit	– Scandinavian coffee
Bénédictine	– Monks' coffee
Calvados	– Normandy coffee
Cognac	– Royale coffee
Drambuie	– Prince Charles coffee
Elixir d'Anvers	– Belgian coffee
Genever	– Dutch coffee
Kahlua	– Mexican coffee
Kirsch	– German coffee
Strega	– Italian coffee
Royal Mint Chocolate Liqueur	– Royal Mint coffee
Rum	– Caribbean coffee
Scotch whisky	– Gaelic coffee
Tia Maria	– Calypso coffee

Mulled Wines
A mull is basically hot wine
with sugar and spices added.
Brandy, a liqueur or a fortified
wine can also be added to give
it extra strength. But it is a
mistake to use expensive wines:
the inexpensive ones are very
good, and far more economical.

It is important to serve mulls
really hot – but never boiled, or
the alcohol will evaporate. If
you do not want to spend all
evening in the kitchen
concocting the brew, keep it
reasonably simple.

Apart from the ingredients,
you will need a 6–8-pint
saucepan, a plastic funnel and
ordinary wineglasses. To
prevent the glasses from
cracking, warm them first or
place a spoon in them while
pouring in the hot wine.

Christmas Cheer (30 glasses)
4 bottles red wine
1 pint of water
¼ bottle dark rum
1 lemon
12 cloves
½ teaspoon ground cinnamon
Nutmeg
Heat the wine, water and rum
together.
Stick lemon with cloves and
bake in the oven for 15 minutes
at 350° F/Gas 4. Add the
cinnamon and a little grated
nutmeg to the wine mixture.
Float the hot lemon in it.

Firecracker (8 glasses)
1 bottle full red wine
1 pint water
8 oz granulated sugar
2 lemons
4 small sticks cinnamon
4 cloves
Boil water with sugar, lemon juice, cinnamon and cloves for 5 minutes. Add wine and heat slowly to boiling point.

Mistletoe Mull (8 glasses)
1 bottle Burgundy
1 pint water
8 oz granulated sugar
1 stick cinnamon
4 cloves
2 lemons
Boil water with sugar, cinnamon and cloves for 5 minutes. Add lemon thinly sliced and allow to stand for ten minutes. Add wine and heat slowly but do not allow to boil. Serve very hot.

Mulled Claret (8 glasses)
1 bottle claret
1 wineglass port
¼ pint of water
1 tablespoon sugar
Rind of ½ lemon
12 whole cloves
A pinch grated nutmeg
Put spices into a saucepan with ¼ pint water and simmer gently for ½ hour. Strain. Pour claret into a pan Add spiced water. Add port and sugar and bring almost to the boil. Serve very hot with thin slices of lemon rind. A small stick of cinnamon can be used with, or instead of, the lemon.

Negus (18 glasses)
1 bottle sherry
2 pints boiling water
1 lemon, sliced
2½ fl oz brandy
Nutmeg
Sugar
Warm the sherry in a saucepan very slowly. Add the lemon. Pour in the boiling water. Add a little grated nutmeg, sugar to taste, then the brandy.

Twelfth Night (8 glasses)
1 bottle red wine
1 apple
Cloves
Hot water
Stick an apple full of cloves and float in a bowl filled with the heated red wine. Add hot water to dilute according to taste.

JULEPS

Captain Marryat was the first Englishman to write about this famous American drink, in the year 1815, when he was entertained by one of the wealthiest planters in the southern states of America. There were many varieties of juleps, he wrote, such as those made of claret, madeira, etc., but the one on which he lavished the most praise was the Mint Julep, for which he gave a recipe:

'Put into a tumbler about a dozen sprigs of the tender shoots of mint, upon them put a spoonful of white sugar, equal proportion of peach or common brandy so as to fill it up to one-third or a trifle less. Then take pounded ice and fill up the tumbler. Epicures wet the lip of the tumbler with a piece of fresh pineapple and the tumbler itself is very often encrusted with ice. When the ice melts, you drink.'

After the Civil War, bourbon whiskey became the accepted spirit base.

Mint Julep
Fresh mint
1 tablespoonfull fine sugar
1 tablespoonful water
1 measure bourbon whiskey
Place 4–5 leaves of mint in a highball glass. Crush the mint, sugar and water together until the sugar is dissolved and the flavour of the mint extracted. Add bourbon and fill tumbler with crushed ice. Stir until the outside of the glass is frosted. Decorate with a sprig of mint. Serve with straws.

Champagne Julep
1 lump sugar
Fresh mint
Champagne
Place the sugar in a champagne glass. Add 2 leaves of mint and muddle gently with a barspoon to extract the flavour. Add iced champagne. Stir gently. Decorate with a sprig of mint and an orange slice.

Old Georgia Julep
1 lump sugar
4 leaves mint
1 measure peach or apricot
    brandy
Place the sugar in a highball glass. Dissolve the sugar in a little water. Add the mint. Muddle together. Add the brandy. Fill with ice. Stir carefully.

Martinis

The martini is the most famous of all cocktails, but its origins are unclear. In the 1860s a drink known as the Matinez Cocktail contained gin, vermouth, maraschino and bitters. If this is the original recipe then it was much altered by the time it became the Martini Cocktail of pre-World War I, when the mixture is said to have consisted of two parts gin to one part vermouth. After World War II it was being served four parts gin to one part vermouth and became progressively drier, to the extent that there is even a recipe for a Naked Martini, which is simply gin on the rocks.

Dry Martini Cocktail
2½ fl oz gin
2 dashes dry vermouth
Stir. Serve straight up or on the rocks. Add a twist of lemon or an olive.

Sweet Martini Cocktail
⅔ gin
⅓ sweet vermouth
Stir. Add a cherry.

Perfect Martini
⅔ gin
⅙ dry vermouth
⅙ sweet vermouth
Stir. Add a twist of lemon.

Other variations are:

Vodkatini
2½ fl oz vodka
2 dashes dry vermouth
Stir. Serve straight up or on the rocks. Add a twist of lemon.

Gibson

2½ fl oz gin
1 dash dry vermouth
Stir. Serve straight up or on the
rocks. Add a pearl onion.

Sakini

3 parts gin
1 part saké
Stir. Serve straight up or on the
rocks. Add an olive.

NON-ALCOHOLIC DRINKS

Cinderella

⅓ lemon juice
⅓ orange juice
⅓ pineapple juice
Shake and strain into a
medium-sized glass.

Creole Cooler

1 pint milk
8 oz crushed pineapple
2 fl oz fresh orange juice
1 fl oz fresh lime juice
Sugar
Combine the pineapple with the
juices in a jug. Add sugar to
taste. Add milk. Mix well.
Refrigerate. Serve straight up.

Florida Cocktail

3½ fl oz grapefruit juice
1½ fl oz orange juice
2 dashes lemon juice
2 fl oz gomme syrup
Soda water
Salt
Combine everything except the
soda water with ice. Shake.
Strain into a highball glass
filled with crushed ice. Top with
soda water. Decorate with mint.

Iced Mint Tea

1 dozen sprigs fresh mint
2 cups boiling water
2 pints cold water
Granulated sugar
Combine mint and boiling
water and steep over hot water
in a double boiler for at least 30
minutes. Strain the minted
water clean and allow to cool.
Combine with cold water in a
large jug. Add granulated sugar
to taste and stir until completely
dissolved. Serve in a tall glass
with ice. Garnish with a spiral
of lemon peel and sprigs of
mint.

Keelplate

2 fl oz tomato juice
1 fl oz clam juice
2 dashes Worcestershire sauce
2 dashes celery salt or ordinary
   salt
Shake.

Lemonade

2 fl oz lemon juice
1½ barspoons sugar
Half-fill a large tumbler with
cracked ice. Stir. Fill up with
plain water. Add a slice of
lemon on top. Serve with straws.

Non-alcoholic Egg Nogg

1 egg
1 barspoon soft sugar
½ pint milk
Shake well. Serve in a 12-oz
tumbler. Grate nutmeg on top.

Parson's Special

4 dashes grenadine
2 fl oz orange juice
1 egg yolk
1 dash soda water
Shake all but soda water and
strain into a medium-sized
glass. Add soda water.

Pussyfoot

⅓ fresh orange juice
⅓ fresh lemon juice
⅓ lime juice
1 dash grenadine
1 egg yolk
Shake well. Serve in a double
cocktail glass.

Shirley Temple

Ginger ale
Grenadine
Top ice-filled highball glass
with ginger ale. Add grenadine.
Stir gently. Decorate with
cherries.

Surfer's Paradise

3 dashes Angostura bitters
1 fl oz lime juice
Lemonade
Build the bitters and lime juice
into an ice-filled highball glass.
Stir in the lemonade. Decorate
with a slice of orange.

Tomato Juice Cocktail (Virgin Mary)

4 fl oz tomato juice
½ fl oz lemon juice
2 dashes Worcestershire sauce
2 dashes celery salt
Shake. Strain into a 6-oz goblet
or an ice-filled highball glass.

Yellow Dwarf

1 egg yolk
½ cream
½ orgeat syrup
1 dash soda water
Shake together all but the soda
water. Strain. Fill up with soda
water.

PICK-ME-UPS

Bars should have a supply of
aspirin, Alka-seltzer or other
such useful aids to recovery.

Fernet Branca and Underberg
are recognized as possessing
restorative powers. However,
some digestive relief can be
gained simply by taking a few
drops of Angostura bitters or
peppermint in a glass of soda
water.

Pick-me-up No. 1

⅓ cognac
⅓ dry vermouth
⅓ pastis
Stir and strain.

Pick-me-up No. 2

1 measure brandy
4 fl oz milk
1 dash Angostura bitters
1 barspoon sugar
Soda water
Shake together all but the soda
water. Strain into a highball
glass. Add soda water.

Prairie Hen

2 dashes vinegar
2 barspoons Worcestershire
sauce
1 whole egg (do not break yolk)
2 dashes Tabasco sauce
Scant salt and pepper
Pour into a small wine glass.

Prairie Oyster

1 barspoon Worcestershire
    sauce
1 barspoon tomato sauce
1 egg yolk (do not break yolk)
2 dashes vinegar and a dash of
    pepper
Pour into a small wine glass.

Fernet Menthe

⅔ Fernet Branca
⅓ green crème de menthe
Stir.

POUSSE-CAFE

The various liqueurs in a Pousse Café must remain strictly separated one above the other. What makes it possible to prepare the drink in this way is the fact that each liqueur has a different specific weight or density. Basically, syrups are heavier than liqueurs and spirits are lighter. Formulas differ between manufacturers and consequently densities vary slightly, so it is necessary to be certain of your recipe before starting to prepare the drink.

To make a Pousse Café, pour each liqueur carefully into a small, straight-sided glass over the back of a spoon, held so that it touches the inner edge of the glass. Add the ingredients in the stated order.

Pousse Café 81
⅕ grenadine
⅕ crème de menthe
⅕ Galliano
⅕ kummel
⅕ brandy

French Pousse Café
¼ green Chartreuse
¼ maraschino
¼ cherry brandy
¼ kummel

Rainbow Cocktail
⅙ crème de cacao
⅙ crème de voilette
⅙ yellow Chartreuse
⅙ maraschino
⅙ Bénédictine
⅙ brandy

PUNCHES

Punch in its oldest and simplest form is rum and water, hot or iced, with sugar to taste and orange or lemon juice (for hot punch) or fresh lime juice (for cold punch). It was in 1655 when they took Jamaica from Spain, that the English were first introduced to rum punch. In the eighteenth century this drink became very popular. It was 'brewed' or mixed at the table in a punchbowl by the host, with rum as one of the ingredients but including other spirits as well. Oranges and lemons in thin slices, grated nutmeg and sundry decorations and flavourings were added at the discretion of the mixer.

Brandy Punch
1 measure brandy
4 dashes curaçao
Dry ginger ale
Add the brandy and curaçao to crushed ice in a goblet. Stir. Add mint and fruit.

Brandy Milk Punch
1½ fl oz brandy
2 fl oz milk
1 barspoon sugar
Shake or mix. Strain into a double cocktail glass. Add nutmeg on top.

Claret Punch
4 fl oz of claret
1 fl oz fresh lemon juice
2 dashes orange curaçao
1 barspoon gomme syrup
Dry ginger ale
Stir together in a goblet all but the ginger ale. Add ice. Dress with a slice each of orange and lemon. Add dry ginger ale.

Fiesta Punch (10 glasses)
1 bottle sweet white wine
1 small bottle soda water
Sugar to taste
1 small can unsweetened
    pineapple juice
3 fl oz lemon juice
Dissolve the sugar in the fruit
juices. Add the wine.
Refrigerate. Put ice in the bowl,
add the wine mixture and soda
water. Float sliced fruit on top.

Fish House Punch (40 drinks)
¾ lb sugar
4 pints water
2 pints lemon juice
4 pints Jamaican rum
2 pints cognac
4 fl oz peach brandy
In a large punch bowl, dissolve
the sugar in the water. Stir in
the remaining ingredients. Add
a large block of ice. Allow to
stand for 2 hours. Serve in
punch cups.

M. and M. Punch
⅔ rum
⅙ blackcurrant syrup
⅙ lemon syrup
Add boiling water. Stir. Add a
slice of lemon.

Planter's Punch
1½ fl oz golden or dark rum
1½ fl oz fresh lemon or lime
    juice
1 dash Angostura bitters
2 barspoons grenadine
Soda water
Build all but the soda water into
an ice-filled highball glass. Stir
in the soda water. Decorate with
orange and lemon slices.

St. Charles Punch
1½ fl oz brandy
3 fl oz port wine
4 dashes orange curaçao
1 fl oz fresh lemon juice
Shake and strain into a highball
glass filled with crushed ice.
Add fruit. Serve with straws.

Trinidad Punch
1½ fl oz dark rum
1 fl oz fresh lime juice
1 barspoon gomme syrup
2 dashes Angostura bitters
Shake and strain into a goblet
filled with crushed ice. Grate
nutmeg on top. Add a twist of
lemon.

RICKEYS

The Rickey is a long-drink
cousin of the Collins. Whilst its
origin is somewhat obscure, it
seems pretty clear that the
Rickey is an American drink. To
quote from Jack Townsend's
The Bartenders' Book, 'Not
nearly so obscure is the origin of
the Gin Rickey, a drink which
can be traced not only to the
city – Washington – but also to
the restaurant, Shoemaker's. At
this popular oasis on a dusty
summer's afternoon before the
turn of the century, according to
the most reliable legends, a
bartender squeezed limes into
gin, and hosed the unsweetened
result with a syphon. His first
customer for the potation was
"Colonel Jim" Rickey, a
lobbyist whose first name was
really Joe, and whose military
title probably was of the
honorary Kentucky variety.
Shoemaker's was known as "the
third house of Congress" and
Congressional patrons who

knew the "Cunnel" bestowed
his name upon the drink.'

Gin Rickey
1 large measure gin
Juice of 1 lime
Soda water
Build all but the soda water into
an ice-filled old-fashioned
glass. Drop in the spent lime
shell. Stir in the soda water.

SANGAREES

The Sangaree is a possible
relative of the Rickey. In this
case, however, the drink can be
made not only with the usual
spirits, but also with wines and
other bases. Various views exist
as to its origin; it is very likely
to have come from India, but
other stories say it was used in
the southern states of America
in times of war for the wounded,
and for invalids. The name is
supposed to be derived from
'Singari' meaning 'blood drink'.
    Use an old-fashioned glass,
and serve with straws.

Brandy Sangaree
1 barspoon sugar
Equal parts water and brandy
Fill glass with crushed ice. Stir.
Grate nutmeg on top.

Claret Sangaree
1 barspoon sugar
Juice of 1 lemon
1 measure claret
Fill the glass with crushed ice.
Stir and add a slice of orange.
Grate nutmeg on top.

Port Wine Sangaree
1 barspoon sugar
1 measure port

Fill the glass with crushed ice.
Stir. Grate nutmeg on top. Add
a slice of lemon.

Whisky Sangaree
As for Brandy Sangaree,
substituting whisky for brandy.

SLINGS

Gin Slings are very
old-established, usually
attributed to far-distant places
with a warm climate. The origin
is not too certain, however. It
might well be that the story
quoted in the section on the
Collins also has some
connection with the origin of
the Sling. However, there is
little doubt that the Singapore
Gin Sling had as its original
home the famous Raffles Hotel,
Singapore.

Gin Sling
1 large measure gin
Juice of 1 lemon
2 dashes gomme syrup
Soda water
Build all but the soda water into
an ice-filled highball glass. Stir
in the soda water.

Raffles Bar Sling
2 fl oz gin
1 fl oz cherry brandy
2 dashes Angostura bitters
Juice of ½ lime
Ginger beer
3 dashes Bénédictine
Build the spirits, bitters and
lime juice into an ice-filled
highball glass. Stir in the ginger
beer. Float the Bénédictine on
top. Decorate with the spent
lime shell, mint and a stirrer.

Singapore Sling
1 large measure gin
Juice of 1 lemon
½ fl oz cherry brandy
Soda water
Shake together all but the soda water. Strain into an ice-filled highball glass. Stir in the soda water. Add an orange slice.

Straits Sling
1 fl oz gin
½ fl oz Bénédictine
½ fl oz cherry brandy
Juice of 1 lemon
2 dashes Angostura bitters
2 dashes orange bitters
Soda water
Shake together all but the soda water. Strain into an ice-filled highball glass. Stir in the soda water. Decorate with a slice of lemon.

SMASHES

A smash is a smaller version of a Julep containing sugar, mint and spirit, served with crushed ice.

Brandy Smash
1½ fl oz brandy (or other spirit)
1 barspoon powdered sugar
6 leaves fresh mint
Dissolve the sugar in a little water in an old-fashioned glass. Add mint and bruise to extract flavour. Add the brandy. Fill the glass with crushed ice. Stir until the glass is frosted. Decorate with a lemon slice and short straws.

Mojito
1½ fl oz golden rum
Juice of ½ lime
6 leaves of mint
2 dashes gomme syrup
Sugar
1 dash soda water
Squeeze the lime juice into a highball glass. Add the spent lime shell. Add sugar and mint leaves and muddle. Fill the glass with shaved ice. Add the rum. Stir until the glass frosts. Add the soda water. Decorate with mint. Serve with straws.

SOURS

Sours must be made with fresh juices if they are to have the sharpness necessary to heighten the flavour of the drink. The most popular type is the Whisky Sour, although almost any alcoholic ingredient can be used as a base.

Scotch Sour
1½ fl oz Scotch whisky
1 fl oz fresh lemon juice
½ fl oz gomme syrup
1 dash egg white
Shake. Strain into a double cocktail glass. Decorate with a slice of lemon.

Apricot Sour
1 fl oz apricot brandy
2 fl oz lemon juice
1 dash Angostura bitters
1 dash egg white
1 dash gomme syrup (optional)
Shake. Serve in a champagne tulip. Add wedge of apricot.

Egg Sour

1 barspoon gomme syrup
Lemon juice
1 measure orange curaçao
1 measure brandy
1 egg
Shake. Strain into a goblet.

Fireman's Sour

1½ fl oz golden rum
1 fl oz fresh lime juice
½ fl oz grenadine
2 dashes gomme syrup
Soda water
Shake together all but the soda water. Strain into a double cocktail glass. Splash the soda water on top. Decorate with a slice of orange and a cherry.

Frisco Sour

1½ fl oz bourbon whiskey
½ fl oz Bénédictine
½ fl oz fresh lemon juice
½ fl oz fresh lime juice
Shake. Strain into a double cocktail glass. Decorate with a slice each of lemon and lime.

Mandarine Sour

1½ fl oz Mandarine Napoléon
1½ fl oz fresh lemon juice
2 dashes Angostura bitters
1 dash egg white
Shake. Strain into a wine glass. Decorate with a slice of orange.

Sourteq

2 fl oz tequila
1 fl oz fresh lemon juice
2 dashes gomme syrup
1 dash egg white
Shake. Strain into a double cocktail glass. Decorate with a slice of lemon and a cherry.

SWIZZLES

The Swizzle takes its name from the stick used to stir the drink, which originated in the West Indies. A swizzle stick was originally the dried stem of a tropical plant with a few smaller branches left on the end, and was about two feet long. The stick would be inserted in the jug and rubbed vigorously between the palms of the hands – swizzling the ice and liquor to create a frost on the outside of the glass.

West Indies Swizzle (6 glasses)

½ bottle Jamaican rum
6 fl oz fresh lime juice
6 barspoons sugar
6 sprigs mint
Take a deep glass jug and fill with cracked ice. Set the jug on the floor holding it firmly by the feet. Place the forked end of the stick in the mixture and roll vigorously between the palms until the outside of the jug is completely frosted.

Gin Swizzle

1 fl oz gin
½ fl oz fresh lime juice
2 dashes gomme syrup
2 dashes Angostura bitters
Build into a 12-oz glass filled with crushed ice. Fill the glass with soda water. Serve with a small swizzle stick, allowing the consumer to do the final stirring.

Toddies

In the Victorian era a toddy was a hot drink often taken to soothe the nerves or cure a chill. Today a toddy is a refresher that may be served hot or cold. Toddies usually contain a slice of lemon or some lemon peel and are often made with either cinnamon, cloves or nutmeg.

Hot Toddy
1 barspoon sugar
1 measure desired spirit
Fill a medium-sized goblet with boiling water. Stir. Add a slice of lemon. Dust with grated nutmeg.

Hot Scotch Toddy
2 fl oz Scotch whisky
½ fl oz fresh lemon juice
3 dashes Angostura bitters
1 barspoon powdered sugar or honey
3 fl oz boiling water
Mix the ingredients in a silver tankard. Pour into a 6-oz stemmed glass. Add a slice of lemon. Serve with a napkin.

Toddy
1 barspoon sugar
1 measure desired spirit
Dissolve the sugar with a little water. Add the spirit. Build into an old-fashioned glass. Add a twist of lemon. Serve with a stirrer.

COUNTRIES
& THEIR DRINKS

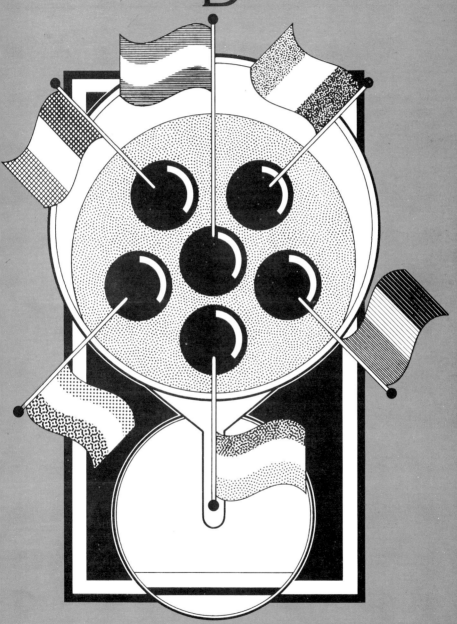

IBA FOREWORD

The International Bartenders' Association came into being in 1951. Delegates from Denmark, France, Great Britain, Holland, Italy, Sweden and Switzerland met in England at Torquay and agreed unanimously that the best interests of bartending would be served by an international organization that had the following aims:

to further and sustain relations among the member guilds;
to enable the member guilds to exchange news, viewpoints and ideas for the benefit of the Association as a whole;
to further the trade interest of the member guilds by encouraging a high standard of qualifications and behaviour;
to sustain customer service and encourage a knowledge of the drinking habits of different countries;
to further the standardization of mixed drinks;
to provide an official administrative body of the Association.

Since its inauguration, the IBA has grown to include twenty-eight member guilds, all of which are committed to the high standards of bartending maintained by the Association. The IBA has a President and four Vice-Presidents for the regions of Europe, North America, South America and Asia-South Pacific, these positions being filled by election every three years. The Annual Congress of the IBA is held in a different country each year, the first one being held in Italy in 1951 while recent hosts have included Switzerland (1981), Italy (1980), Yugoslavia (1979), France (1978) and Brazil (1977). One of the features of the Congress is the cocktail competition, in which the President of each member guild prepares an original recipe on behalf of his country. However, every third year an International Cocktail Competition is held in conjunction with the Congress meeting. This prestigious competition has three sections: Pre-Dinner, After-Dinner and Long Drink, and most countries conduct national competitions to decide which recipes will represent them in the international event.

Education has been a major consideration of the IBA which recognizes the need to train young bartenders thoroughly in the skills of the craft and consolidate their knowledge of beverage products. For this reason the IBA Training Centre was set up in Luxembourg in 1966 and continued there until 1973 when it was moved to Blackpool, England, and came under the guidance of John Whyte. This man's dedication to the education of bartenders was acknowledged when the name of the training programme became the 'John Whyte Course'. The course has been held in Stresa, Italy, since 1977. Every year, each member guild may select two promising young bartenders to attend the two-week course, an in-depth study of all aspects of bartending.

In the interest of standardization it was decided at the 1962 Congress that the UKBG's *Guide to Drinks* should be accepted as the official reference work of the IBA, and a supplement of recipes from member guilds was included to make the book international.

Within thirty years, the IBA has become firmly established as the world authority on cocktail bartending and members of the national guilds actively promote the principles and skills that are the hallmarks of a professional bartender.

ARGENTINA

Association Mutual de Barmen y Afines (AMBA)
Avenue Juan de Garay 1927, Buenos Aires

Argentina has the seventh highest alcohol consumption rate in the world because of its population's love of wine. Vermouth is drunk in huge quantities as an aperitif, being served on the rocks or with a dash of soda and bitters. A local product of interest is *pisco*, which is a brandy made from muscat wine; the Pisco Sour is Argentina's favourite cocktail, widely drunk in the numerous small bars and cafés.

Alvear Palace

⅝ vodka
¼ pineapple juice
⅛ apricot brandy
Shake.

Animador

⅓ sweet vermouth
⅓ gin
⅓ Aperital Delor
Shake.

Gaucho

½ Dutch gin
½ Hesperidina (made from orange and lemon skins – low alcohol content)
1 dash Angostura bitters
Decorate with a slice of orange. Serve in an ice-filled old-fashioned glass.

Pisco Punch

2 fl oz pisco
1 fl oz unsweetened pineapple juice
1 fl oz fresh lime juice
2 dashes maraschino
2 dashes gomme syrup
Shake. Strain into a medium goblet.

Pisco Sour

1½ fl oz pisco
2½ fl oz fresh lime juice
¼ fl oz gomme syrup
1 dash egg white
2 dashes Angostura bitters
Shake together all but the bitters. Strain into a medium goblet. Add the bitters.

Sol de Mayo

½ Scotch whisky
⅕ Cointreau
³/₁₀ orange juice
Shake.

Valeccito

1½ fl oz pisco
1 fl oz dry vermouth
¾ fl oz curaçao
1 fl oz fresh lemon juice
Shake. Strain into an ice-filled highball glass.

AUSTRALIA

Australian Bartenders' Guild (ABG)
c/o Catering Institute of Australia
P.O. Box A.497, Sydney, New South
Wales 2000

Australia is well known as a beer-drinking country, although local wine sales are rising rapidly. This is partly due to the heavy taxation on spirits and the availability of wine by the five-litre cask. These casks have a tap on them which makes them convenient to keep at home. Many Australian restaurants are unlicensed and are therefore referred to as B.Y.Os: patrons may bring their own alcohol at no extra expense and it is served as in a licensed restaurant. Most alcohol is purchased from the drive-in bottle shops and there is a wide range of locally produced spirits and liqueurs. Cocktail bars are located in the central city areas and at the beach resorts.

The popularity of mixed drinks, particularly those served long with plenty of ice, is increasing in Australia.

Barrier Reef

1 fl oz gin
¾ fl oz Cointreau
1 dash Angostura bitters
1 scoop ice cream
Few drops blue curaçao.
Mix together all but the curaçao. Add the curaçao.

Blue Negligée

Winner, National Cocktail Competition, 1975, Frank Clarke
⅓ ouzo
⅓ Parfait Amour
⅓ green Chartreuse
Stir.
Add cherry.

Fluffy Duck

1 fl oz gin
1 fl oz advocaat
½ fl oz Cointreau
¾ fl oz fresh orange juice
Soda water.
Build all but the soda water into an ice-filled highball glass. Stir in the soda water. Add straws and a stirrer.

Fourth of July

Winner, National Cocktail Competition, 1977, Alex Beaumont
⅕ bourbon whiskey
⅕ Galliano
⅕ Kahlua
⅕ orange juice
⅕ cream
Place the whiskey and Galliano in a warm cocktail glass, then flame. Shake ground cinnamon on top whilst flaming. Shake the other ingredients and strain on to the flaming mixture Add a cherry.

Moomba Cocktail

¾ fl oz Bacardi rum
¾ fl oz Grand Marnier
½ fl oz orange juice
¼ fl oz lemon juice
1 dash grenadine
Shake. Add orange peel.

South Pacific

Winner, National Cocktail Competition, Gary Revell
1 fl oz gin
½ fl oz Galliano
½ fl oz blue curaçao
Lemonade
Build the gin and Galliano into a highball glass filled with cracked ice. Top with lemonade. Splash in the curaçao. Decorate with a lemon slice and a cherry. Serve with straws and a swizzle stick.

AUSTRIA

Österreichische Barkeeper Union (OBU)
Tigergasse 6/2, A-1080, Wien 4

Café life thrives in Austria, especially in Vienna. There, outside the tiny inns known as *Heurizes,* green branches are hung to indicate that the hostelry is serving the wine of the new vintage. Austria has her own range of *Obstwassers* or fruit brandies, one of the most widely available being *Wacholderbranntweine,* made from junipers. Enzian, which is distilled from the roots of the gentian plant, is drunk neat, as is schnapps. One of the most popular of the local liqueurs is Wachauer Marillen, made from apricots.

After One

Los Angles, 1973, Reinhold Husar
¼ gin
¼ Galliano
¼ sweet vermouth
¼ Campari
Serve with a cocktail cherry and an orange twist.

Cicero

Toni Stadlbacher
⅓ orange juice
⅓ Honiggoscherl
⅓ dry vermouth
Demi-sec champagne
Shake together all but the champagne. Fill up with champagne.

Emilia

Hans Schinhan
½ Barcardi rum
¼ Grand Marnier
¼ apricot brandy
1 dash orange bitters
Stir.

Sonny Boy

Franz Strobl
½ fl oz peach brandy
½ fl oz orange curaçao
2 dashes Angostura bitters
Champagne
Shake the brandy, curaçao and bitters. Strain into a champagne glass. Fill with iced champagne.

BELGIUM

Union des Barmen de Belgique (UBB)
Rue d'Edimbourg 15, 1050 Bruxelles

The Belgian people are enthusiastic beer-drinkers. Wine is imported from France or Italy and several distilleries make a range of liqueurs although the majority of these are available only within Belgium. The country's most famous liqueur is Mandarine Napoléon, produced from Spanish tangerine peel macerated in a blend of cognacs. There has been an upsurge in the popularity of mixed 'long' drinks, particularly those based on vodka, and although genever is the traditional spirit drink there is increasing interest in pure malt whiskies.

Carine
Geo. Kuypers
½ gin
¼ Dubonnet
¼ Madarine Napoléon
1 dash lemon juice
Stir.

Dry Millenary
*Winner, National Cocktail
Competition to celebrate the
Millenary of the city of Brussels,
1979, Dry Short category,
José Ramos*
⅗ Gilbey's gin
⅕ Cinzano rosé
⅕ Cinzano Americano
1 dash Cinzano Dry
Stir.

Picotin
*Winner, First Benelux
Competition, 1968,
Roland De Bock*
½ Vodka 72
¼ Cinzano bianco
¼ Liquore Santa Vittoria
1 dash fresh lemon juice
Add orange peel.

Stroumf
*Golden Shaker Award, 1980,
Long Drink Competition,
Rochat Roland*
⅖ gin
⅖ apricot brandy
⅕ Amaretto di Saronno
1 dash lemon juice
Orange juice
Shake all but the orange juice. Strain into an ice-filled highball glass. Stir in the orange juice.

Sweet Millenary
*Winner, National Cocktail
Competition to celebrate the
Millenary of the city of Brussels,
1979, Sweet Short category,
Ricardo Rozzi*
⅓ Cinzano rosé
⅓ aperol aperitivo
⅓ Galliano
Stir. Add a twist of orange.

Toio
*Winner, Second Benelux
Competition, 1970, Robert Detry*
⅓ gin
⅓ Bols apricot brandy
⅓ Bols triple-sec
Few drops lemon juice
Add lemon peel.

Yankee-Dutch
*Winner, Belgian Competition,
1969, and awarded membership
in the Bourbon Quaff and Quote
Society, Georges Broucke*
¼ bourbon whiskey
¼ vodka
¼ Bols cherry brandy
¼ Bols triple-sec
Add a twist of orange peel.

Zazie
Jos. Houdmont
⅓ Stock aperitif
⅓ curaçao
⅓ gin
Stir. Add a twist of orange peel.

BRAZIL

Associacao Bradileira de Barmen A.B.B.
Avenida Angelica 845 – C.E.P. 01227 San
Paolo

Brazil is the leading South American producer of *aguadente de cana*, which is distilled from fermented sugar cane. Known as *cachaca*, this is the national drink, and there are over 20,000 registered cachaca distilleries with more than 130 million cases being consumed each year. The cheaper brands can be quite fiery and are often sweetened with sugar syrup; the higher-quality drier versions are drunk neat from one-shot glasses. Brazilians also drink large quantities of vermouth, which is produced locally, although much of the base wine is imported from neighbouring countries. There are also a number of 'whisky' distilleries which produce a range of brands. Wine consumption is high and Brazil is one of the major markets for Chilean wine. Beer consumption has increased dramatically in the last ten years, the most widely available beer being Chopp, which is also exported to other South American countries.

Batida Morango
3 fresh strawberries
2 barspoons sugar
1 measure cachaca
Blend with crushed ice. Serve unstrained in a medium goblet.

Batida Limão (lime)

Batida Abaci (pineapple)

Batida Maracuja (fruit of Brazil)

Batida Goiaba (guava)

Batida Mango (mango)

Batida Caju (cashew)

Caipirinha
1 limão
Sugar
1 measure cachaca
Cut the limão into small pieces. Place in an old-fashioned glass. Sprinkle with sugar. Crush together. Fill with ice. Add the cachaca. Serve with a stirrer.

CANADA

Bartenders' Association of Canada
P.O. Box 1135 Adelaide Street, East
Toronto, Ontario

In Canada vermouths, liqueurs, beers and the well-known brands of spirits are produced locally but Canadian 'rye' is the national spirit and is usually drunk with ginger ale. Southern Ontario, the Niagara region and British Columbia have wine-producing areas that make table and fortified wines, the best-known product being 'Baby Duck', a sparkling wine. Highballs are the most popular mixed drinks, especially those based on vodka and rum, and there has been a significant increase in white wine sales in bars and restaurants.

The Bloody Caesar
1 fl oz vodka
2 dashes Worcestershire sauce
1 dash lemon juice
4 fl oz clamato juice
Shake or stir.

Conroi
Fernando Gomes
²/₆ rye whisky
¹/₆ crème de banane
¹/₆ apricot brandy
²/₆ orange juice
Shake.

'Cool Breeze' Cocktail
1 fl oz cognac
½ fl oz Grand Marnier
3 fl oz cream
1 dash Angostura bitters
2 dashes maraschino cherry
  juice
Shake or mix.

Cougar's Cooler
1st Prize, Oolgaard Blueberry Liqueur Canadian National Competition, 1974, Albert Charlebois
¼ fl oz Oolgaard blueberry
  liqueur
¼ fl oz vodka
½ fl oz lemon juice
Shake. Strain into a 12-oz highball glass filled with crushed ice. Garnish with a red cherry, ½ slice lemon, ½ slice lime, ½ slice orange.

'Heather Mist' Cocktail
1 fl oz Scotch whisky
¼ fl oz Cointreau
2 fl oz lemon mix
1 dash grenadine
Shake. Add a twist of lemon.

Ramcooler
Winner, International Cocktail Competition, St Vincent, Italy, 1976, Fred Falkenburg
1¼ fl oz white rum
½ fl oz Galliano
2 fl oz lime juice
Shake. Strain over ice. Decorate with cherry and slice of lime.

Sunny Dream
Winner, After-Dinner Drink, 14th ICC Competition, Yugoslavia, 1979, Mark Wood
⁸/₁₄ soft ice cream
²/₁₄ fresh orange juice
³/₁₄ apricot brandy
¹/₁₄ Cointreau
Mix. Serve in a large glass bowl. Decorate with orange slices cut in cartwheel fashion and floated on top.

Yellow Sea
1st Prize, Canadian National Cocktail Competition, 1971, Hing Kwok Seto
³/₈ vodka
¼ light rum
¼ Galliano
⅛ maraschino
Juice of 1 lime
1 barspoon sugar
Shake.

DENMARK

Dansk Bartender Laug (DBL)
Postbox 230, DK 1502, Copenhagen

Denmark is the home of *akvavit*, known locally as *snapps*. It is served ice cold, usually with a beer chaser. There is a ritual that accompanies the drinking of snapps: the drinker says 'Skål' (pronounced 'skol'), holds his arm out at a right angle to his body, looks his partner straight in the eye and drinks until the glass is drained completely.

Alcudia
1st Prize, National Cocktail and Long Drink Competition, 1972
²/₅ gin
¹/₅ Galliano
¹/₅ Bols crème de banane
¹/₅ grapefruit juice
Shake. Add a twist of grapefruit peel.

After Eight
¹/₃ J & B Scotch whisky
¹/₃ Royal Mint Chocolate liqueur
¹/₃ cream
Shake. Grate chocolate on top.

Copenheering
²/₃ vodka
¹/₃ Peter Heering
1 dash lemon or lime juice
Stir.

Danish Mary
1 fl oz akvavit
3 fl oz tomato juice
2 dashes fresh lemon juice
2 dashes Worcestershire sauce
1 dash celery salt
Shake or stir. Strain into an ice-filled highball glass.

The Hamlet
¹/₂ Peter Heering
¹/₂ Aalborg akvavit
Stir.

King Peter
¹/₃ Peter Heering
²/₃ tonic water
1 dash lemon juice
Build into an ice-filled highball glass.

Moon River
1st Prize, National Cocktail and Long Drink Competition, 1973
¹/₄ gin
¹/₄ apricot brandy
¹/₄ Cointreau
¹/₈ Galliano
¹/₈ lime juice
Stir. Add a cherry.

FINLAND

Finland Bartenders och Supporters Klubb (FBSK)
Box 150 – 00131 Helsinki 13

The purchasing and marketing of alcoholic drinks in Finland is controlled by the State monopoly Alko, which also manufactures a wide range of beverages. The most famous of these is the excellent Finnish vodka, available in a number of styles. Apart from the dry vodka there is *koskenkorva* (slightly sweeter), and vodkas flavoured with cherry, lemon or chocolate-mint. The Finns are particularly fond of 'Gin Long Drink' a ready-made mixture of gin and grapefruit soft drink, while unique liqueurs are produced from the local cloudberries and Arctic bramble berries which flourish in northern Finland. Other soft fruits used for liqueurs include logonberry (Lapponia), raspberry (Vaapukka), cranberry (Polar), blackcurrant (Herukka), rowanberry (Pihlajanmarja), strawberry (Mansikka), and sea buckthorn berry (Tyrni).

Cincher
1½ fl oz gin
1½ fl oz cherry brandy
Pour over crushed ice into an old-fashioned glass.

Finnor
1st Prize, Scandinavian Long Drink Competition, 1973, Matti Koskinen
1 fl oz rye whisky
1 fl oz Cointreau
Juice of ½ lemon
Schweppes orange tonic
1 dash grenadine
Build the whisky, Cointreau and lemon juice into an ice-filled highball glass. Stir in the orange tonic. Add the grenadine. Garnish with a slice of orange and a cherry.

Garden Party
½ fl oz Vaapukka liqueur
Dry sparkling wine
Pour the liqueur into a champagne glass. Top with iced dry sparkling wine.

Nina
1st Prize, National Bacardi Competition, 1973, Raimo Stenman
1 fl oz Bacardi rum
1 fl oz Vaapukka liqueur
1 fl oz lime juice cordial
Ginger ale
Build the rum, liqueur and cordial into an ice-filled highball glass. Stir in the ginger ale. Garnish with a slice of orange and a cherry.

Polnic
1 fl oz gin
1 fl oz Polar liqueur
Tonic water
Build the gin and liqueur into an ice-filled highball glass. Stir in the tonic water.

Red Sunset
⅖ white rum
⅖ Mansikka liqueur
⅕ fresh lemon juice
Shake.

Scanex
1st Prize, International Wyborowa Competition, Stockholm, 1972, Charles Nyberg
¼ vodka
¼ Polar liqueur
¼ lemon juice
¼ gomme syrup
1 dash grenadine
Shake.

FRANCE

Association des Barmen de France (ABF)
192 Boulevard Haussman, 75008 – Paris

The café plays a large part in French life. Workers may stop at a café on their way home, the family may visit for a friendly chat before dinner or while away a quiet evening over a glass or two. The less alcoholic drinks such as bitters or wine-based aperitifs of the vermouth style are widely drunk in the cafés. Two very popular mixed drinks are vermouth cassis and kir, which is unaccountably referred to as 'rinse cochon' (pig's rinse). France produces such a vast range of spirits, liqueurs and wines that each region has its own particular drinking habits. Pastis is taken with iced water – usually without ice – in most regions and 'le whisky' is a highly regarded evening drink.

Adam and Eve
1st Prize, Short Drink Concours Amaretto di Saronno, 1980, Jean-Claude Hauenstein
$\frac{1}{2}$ gin
$\frac{1}{5}$ Amaretto di Saronno
$\frac{1}{5}$ Drambuie
$\frac{1}{10}$ fresh lemon juice
1 dash gomme syrup
1 dash grenadine
Shake. Decorate with a slice of lemon and a cherry.

Butterfly
1st Prize, Short Drinks Section, National Competition for members of the ABF, 1975, Phil Lacarrière
$\frac{2}{5}$ gin
$\frac{3}{10}$ dry vermouth
$\frac{1}{5}$ Poire Williams
$\frac{1}{10}$ Bols blue curaçao
Shake. Decorate with twists of orange and lemon.

Come Back Marion
Antoine Larocca
$\frac{3}{5}$ gin
$\frac{3}{10}$ grapefruit juice
$\frac{1}{10}$ orgeat syrup
1 dash fraises des bois
Shake.

Crazy Horse
Michel Le Regent
$\frac{1}{2}$ fl oz fraises de boïs
$\frac{1}{2}$ fl oz crème de banane
1 fl oz Scotch whisky
Champagne
Shake. Strain into champagne glass. Top with iced champagne. Decorate with slices of lime and orange, wild strawberry and a sprig of mint.

Dry Melody
Dominique Jacoby
$\frac{4}{5}$ vodka
$\frac{1}{10}$ Mandarine liqueur
$\frac{1}{10}$ fraises de bois
Shake.

Rose de Varsouie
1st Prize, Concours Wyborowa, Angelo Biolato
$\frac{1}{2}$ vodka
$\frac{1}{3}$ cherry cordial
$\frac{1}{6}$ Cointreau
1 dash Angostura bitters
Stir. Add a cherry.

Starico
1st Prize, Concours Ron-Rico, Marc Boccard-Schuster
$\frac{1}{2}$ Puerto Rican rum
$\frac{1}{5}$ Bols apricot brandy
$\frac{1}{10}$ Bols blue cúraçao
$\frac{1}{5}$ pineapple juice
Shake.

Vermouth Cassis
$\frac{1}{2}$ fl oz crème de cassis
$2\frac{1}{2}$ fl oz dry vermouth
Served chilled in a small wine goblet or on the rocks. Add a twist of lemon.

GERMANY

Deutsche Barkeeper-Union e.V. (DBU)
Rentzelstrasse 36 – 40, 2000 Hamburg 13

Germans are beer-drinkers, consuming an average of almost 150 litres per head each year. There are over 1,600 breweries in Germany. Bavaria, with over two-thirds of them, is regarded as the beer-garden of Germany. Many of the beers have a distinctly regional style and are unpasteurized, unless being made for export. The term 'schnapps' is used for vitually all strong drink and in particular for vodka, *Korn*, which is distilled from rye, *Wacholder* and *Steinhager* (juniper-based spirits similar to gin).

Babsi
Egon Grähling
¾ fl oz bourbon whiskey
1 fl oz Grand Marnier
2 dashes orange juice
2 dashes lemon juice
Sekt
Build all but the sekt into a champagne glass. Top with iced sekt.

Flamingo
Hans Günter Zellman
1 fl oz bourbon whiskey
¾ fl oz crème de banane
2 dashes grenadine
2 fl oz orange juice
¾ fl oz lemon juice
1 dash egg white
Shake. Decorate with an orange slice and a cherry. Serve in an old-fashioned glass.

Happy Birithday
Reinhard Skrabal
¾ fl oz Bols dry Johannisberee
¼ fl oz Bacardi rum
2 dashes triple sec
2 dashes peach juice
2 dashes pineapple juice
Champagne
Build all but the champagne into an ice-filled highball glass. Top with champagne. Add a lemon slice and a cherry.

Lucky Summer
Rolf Lautenschlager
¾ fl oz J & B Scotch whisky
¾ fl oz Grand Marnier
¾ fl oz lemon juice
2 dashes grenadine
Shake. Decorate with an orange slice and a cherry.

Meiner
Peter Bohrmann
1 fl oz gin
¾ fl oz Campari
Fresh orange juice
Build the gin and Campari into an ice-filled highball glass. Stir in the orange juice. Decorate with a slice of orange.

William and Robin
Robin Leser
⅓ William Christ
⅓ orange curaçao
⅓ fresh lemon juice
1 dash orange bitters
Shake. Decorate with half a slice of lemon and a cherry.

GREAT BRITAIN

United Kingdom Bartenders' Guild
(UKBG)
70 Brewer Street, London W1R 3PJ

Britain is the home of two of the world's most popular spirits – London Dry Gin and Scotch whisky. The English drink gin and tonic as an aperitif as well as the occasional pink gin. Ten per cent of the total Scotch production is consumed in Scotland. The Scots drink whisky as a beer chaser and also consume large quantities of rum and 'pep' (peppermint cordial). Although ale is the traditional beer there is an increasing trend towards lager-drinking. Real ale, which is unpasteurized ale hand-pumped from the cask, also has a strong following. Cocktails and long drinks are becoming very fashionable amongst younger people and many pubs as well as cocktail bars are offering a variety of mixed drinks.

Black Velvet
½ iced champagne
½ chilled Guinness
Build into a highball glass or tankard.

Blushing Barmaid
Winner, Amaretto di Saronno Competition, London, 1980, G. Glockler
1 fl oz Amaretto di Saronno
1 fl oz Campari
1 dash egg white
Bitter lemon
Shake together all but the bitter lemon. Strain into a large, ice-filled goblet. Stir in the bitter lemon. Decorate with a wedge of apricot.

Bulldog Highball
⅓ gin
⅓ orange juice
Ginger ale
Shake the gin and orange juice. Strain into a highball glass. Top with cold ginger ale. Serve with straws.

The Filby
1st Prize, Golden Shaker Award IBA Congress Meeting, Paris, 1978, P. Brennan
⅖ gin
⅕ Amaretto di Saronno
⅕ Campari
⅕ dry vermouth
Stir. Add a twist of orange.

Glacier Mint
Brian Page
1 fl oz Smirnoff Silver vodka
½ fl oz green crème de menthe
1 dash PLJ
Stir. Strain into a sugar rimmed cocktail glass. Decorate with a sprig of mint.

L'Aird
3rd Prize, Sweet Cocktail Section, International Cocktail Competition, Yugoslavia, 1979, A. Tighe
⅖ Scotch whisky
⅖ Kahlua
1/10 ginger wine
1/10 maraschino
Cream
Stir all but the cream. Float cream on top. Grind coffee beans on top.

Pink Gin
Angostura bitters
1 measure gin
Put several dashes of Angostura bitters into a spirit glass. Swirl and discard. Add the gin. Serve with iced water.

Prince Charles   Rusty Nail   Prince Charles Coffee

Red Azur
*1st Prize, Cointreau
Competition, London, 1980,
M. Boccard-Schuster*
½ Cointreau
¼ kirsch
¼ dry vermouth
1 dash grenadine
Shake.

Rialtococo
*2nd Prize, International Cocktail
Festival, Venice, 1980,
Roger Metcalf*
⅓ Campari
⅓ gin
⅓ coconut cream
1 scoop shaved ice
Blend. Serve in a large glass.

Snowball
1 fl oz advocaat
1 dash lime juice cordial
Lemonade
Stir the lemonade into the
advocaat and cordial. Build into
an ice-filled highball glass or
goblet. Decorate with an orange
slice and a cherry. Serve with a
muddler and straws.

Suspension
*Created to mark the opening of
the Forth Bridge in 1964,
Martin Rowell*
⅓ Scotch whisky
⅓ ginger wine
⅓ orange juice
Shake.

Isabelliter
Brian Page
1½ fl oz amontillado sherry
½ fl oz peach brandy
½ fl oz vodka
Lemonade
Stir the sherry, brandy and
vodka. Strain into an ice-filled
highball glass. Stir in the
lemonade. Add zest of orange.

Stingray
Ray Rastall
⅓ pastis
⅓ apricot brandy
⅓ fresh orange juice
1 dash egg white
Shake.

HOLLAND

Nederlandse Bartenders Club (NBC)
Tollenhof 21, 4041 BH. Kesteren

The cafés, restaurants and hotels in Holland are open almost continuously and are popular meeting places. In the bars long drinks are popular and there has been an increase in wine consumption. The 'bitter hour' may last for two to three hours before dinner and the traditional drink for this time is *oude genever*, drunk neat from a small glass filled to the brim and often followed by a beer chaser. Bitters are drunk in some quantity; the most popular types are berenburg and elskebitter. Beer consumption is second only to genever and Heineken is the most widely available beer in the world. Dutch liqueurs are noted for their high quality and most of the firms are very well established: Bols, for example, was founded in 1575 and has produced a wide range of liqueurs since that time.

Amboina Exotica
1st Prize, Henkes-Betuwe Long Drink Competition, 1980, Jan Opperman
1 fl oz gin
1 fl oz Pisang Ambon Henkes
¼ fl oz lemon juice
Apricot-orange
Build into ice filled highball glass. Fill up with apricot-orange drink.

Angelo
1st Prize, K & B, NBC National Cocktail Competition, 1977, Aart Leenheer
1 fl oz Smirnoff vodka
½ fl oz Galliano
½ fl oz Southern Comfort
1 dash egg white

Orange and pineapple juice
Shake together all but the fruit juices. Strain into an ice-filled highball glass. Top with the fruit juices.

Jungle Juice
2nd Prize, Long Drink Section, International Cocktail Competition, 1979, Ron Busman
1½ fl oz Pisang Ambon Henkes
¾ fl oz gin
½ fl oz Mandarine liqueur
3 dashes lemon juice
3 fl oz orange juice
Serve in a highball glass. Decorate with a slice of pineapple and a cherry.

Kapitein Kok
1st Prize, Dolfi-Long Drink Competition, 1980, Réné Vilé
1½ fl oz fraises de bois Dolfi
¾ fl oz tequila
Bitter orange
Build the fraises de bois and tequila into an ice-filled highball glass. Fill up with bitter orange. Add a slice of orange.

Laguna-Verde
Jan van Hagen
½ vodka
¼ bianco vermouth
¼ Galliano
2 dashes blue curaçao
Stir. Add a cherry.

Mistral Special
1st Prize, Long Drink Section, National Cocktail Competition, 1980, John Engelsman
1½ fl oz cherry whisky liqueur
¾ fl oz liqueur Vieille Curé
¾ fl oz Scotch whisky
1 dash lime juice
Bitter orange
Shake all but the bitter orange. Strain into an ice-filled highball glass. Fill up with bitter orange.

HUNGARY

Section of the Barmen of Hungary (SBH)
Hungarhotels, 1052 Budapest
Petőfi Sándor u.14

Hungarians are wine-drinkers, often drinking white wine with soda water. The spirit most widely consumed is Barack Palinka, a dry unsweetened apricot brandy. There are several other fruit brandies too, made from cherries, plums and pears. Rum, liqueurs and vermouths are produced locally and there is a full range of beers, from the unpasteurized Világos lager to the strong dark Bak beer. Home consumption of beer has increased so rapidly that export has been curtailed to cope with demand.

Winnie-the-Pooh
½ egg flip
⅛ coffee liqueur
⅛ chocolate liqueur
¼ fresh cream
Shake.

Saturnus
½ orange juice
⅛ gin
¼ crème de banane
⅛ bianco vermouth
Champagne
Build all but the champagne into an ice-filled highball glass. Stir. Splash in dry champagne.

ICELAND

Bartenders Club of Iceland (BCI)
P.O. Box 7114 – 127 Reykjavik

Bahamas
⅓ light rum
⅓ Southern Comfort
⅓ fresh lemon juice
1 dash crème de banane
Shake.

Black Jack
1st Prize, Sweet Cocktail Competition, 1976, V. Ottesen
⅓ Scotch whisky
⅓ Kahlua
⅓ Cointreau
1 dash lemon juice
Shake.

Borg Special
⅓ Bacardi rum
⅓ Drambuie
⅓ cherry brandy
Shake.

Frosty Amour
1st Prize, Long Drink Competition, 1974, Daniel Stefánsson
⅓ Southern Comfort
⅓ Smirnoff vodka
⅓ Bols apricot brandy
1 dash Bols parfait amour
1 dash Bols crème de banane
7-Up
Shake all but the 7-Up. Strain into highball glass. Fill with 7-Up. Serve with a straw.

Kina
1st Prize, Dry Cocktail Competition, 1975, B. Olsen
¾ gin
¼ Campari Reed Onion
Stir.

Misty
2nd Prize, Long Drink Competition, 1974, Bjarni Gudjonsson
⅓ vodka
⅓ Cointreau
⅓ apricot brandy
1 dash fresh lemon juice
1 dash crème de banane
Shake. Serve unstrained in highball glass. Decorate with slice of orange, cherry and straws.

Prize Idiot
1 fl oz vodka
1 fl oz crème de banane
1 dash grenadine
2 dashes fresh lemon juice
Sinalco
Build all but the sinalco into an ice-filled highball glass. Stir in the sinalco. Decorate with a wedge of lemon, a green cherry, a stirrer and straws.

Sigtún Special
2nd Prize, Dry Cocktail Competition, 1975, D. Ólafsson Sigtún
⅓ lemon gin
⅓ dry vermouth
⅓ Torres Medium Onion
Stir.

Sweet Blondy
2nd Prize, Sweet Cocktail Competition, 1976, G. R. Sigurösson
⅓ light rum
⅓ Royal Mint Chocolate liqueur
⅓ bianco vermouth
1 dash orange juice
Shake. Add a twist of orange peel.

IRELAND

Bartenders' Association of Ireland (BAI)
Jury's Hotel, Ballsbridge, Dublin 4

Ireland has long been associated with whiskey. Legend has it that St Patrick brought the art of distillation to the country but it is more likely that it was learned from the Spanish monks who visited Ireland. Whatever its origins, distillation was certainly known to the Irish in the twelfth century and poteen is still made today, although potatoes are more likely to be the base ingredient rather than malted barley. Irish liqueurs are based on whiskey and the Irish Coffee is now the classic hot drink served after dinner.

Ireland is the home of the famous dark stout, Guinness, which is widely consumed throughout Ireland and the rest of the world.

'B.A.S.I.L.'
1st Prize, Grand Prix de Paris, 1978, Danny Toland
½ Irish whiskey
¼ Grand Marnier
¼ Tia Maria
Cream
Stir all but the cream. Float the cream on top. Add zest of orange.

The Beefeater
P. McInerney
½ Irish whiskey
¼ Royal Irish Coffee liqueur
¼ Royal Irish Mint Chocolate
   liqueur
Cream
Stir all but the cream. Float the cream on top.

Galway Grey
1st Prize, 16th All-Ireland Cocktail Competition, W. Connaughton
⅓ vodka
⅙ crème de cacao
⅙ Cointreau
⅓ lime juice
Cream
Stir all but the cream. Float the cream on top. Add a twist of orange.

Irish Punch
A great favourite in Ireland during the 'soft' weather.
1 measure Irish whiskey
1 barspoon sugar
Hot water
½ slice lemon studded with
   cloves
Serve in a wine glass.

Kis-Kesay
1st Prize, 15th All-Ireland Cocktail Competition, J. Tyndall
½ white rum
¼ White Bols crème de cacao
⅛ lime juice
⅛ blackcurrant juice
Orange cream
Stir all but the orange cream. Top with orange cream. Add a twist of orange peel.

Mork and Mindy
1st Prize, 17th All-Ireland Cocktail Competition, Vincent Hutchinson
3 parts cognac
2 parts Tia Maria
1 part Royal Irish Chocolate
   Mint liqueur
Cream
Shake all but the cream. Float the cream on top. Sprinkle with chocolate flake.

ITALY

Associazione Italiana Barmen e
Sostenitori (AIBES)
Via Baldissera 2 – 20129 Milan

Italians drink wine at all times of the day and evening. They also consume vast quantities of vermouth, served over ice or with soda water. Bitter aperitif drinks such as Aperol, Amaro, Campari, Cynar, Fernet Branca and Punt-e-Mes are very popular in Italy, too. The favourite spirit is *grappa,* the name being an abbreviation of '*grappolo d'uva*' ('a bunch of grapes'). Italy is widely regarded as the home of liqueurs and literally hundreds are produced; many have gained worldwide recognition.

Danielli
3/5 vodka
3/10 dry vermouth
1/10 Campari
Stir. Add a twist of lemon.

Elisa
St Vincent Competition, 1976, After-Dinner Cocktail, Aldo Ferrier
1/2 light rum
1/8 Amaro
1/8 apricot brandy
1/8 sweet vermouth
Spumante
Stir all but the spumante into a champagne glass. Top with iced spumante. Add zest of orange and a cherry.

Lena
1st Prize, International Cocktail Competition, Tokyo, 1971, Alberto Chirici
5/10 bourbon whiskey
2/10 sweet vermouth
1/10 dry vermouth
1/10 Campari
1/10 Galliano
Shake. Add a cherry.

Maxime
P. L. Didò
3/5 vodka
2/5 cordial Campari
3/20 bianco vermouth
1/20 cherry brandy
Stir. Add a twist of lemon and a cherry.

Roberta
1st Prize, International Cocktail Competition, St Vincent, 1963, Pietro Cuccoli
1/3 vodka
1/3 dry vermouth
1/3 cherry brandy
1 dash Campari
1 dash crème de banane
Shake. Add zest of orange.

Serenissima
1½ fl oz vodka
1½ fl oz fresh grapefruit juice
1 dash Campari
Shake. Strain into an ice-filled goblet.

Roger
Ruggero Caumo, Harry's Bar, Venice
1½ fl oz peach juice
1½ fl oz fresh orange juice
1½ fl oz gin
2 dashes lemon juice
Shake. Strain into an ice-filled highball glass.

Tiziano
1 fl oz freshly squeezed grape juice
Spumante
Top the grape juice with iced spumante. Serve in a champagne flute.

JAPAN

All Nippon Bartenders' Association (ANBA)
Raionzu Mansion Dogenzaka 610,
2-19-3, Dogenzaka, Shibuya-ku,
Tokyo 150, Japan

Japan is a major importer of spirits, particularly whisky, which is now the country's national spirit drink. There are a number of local distilleries producing whisky, including Suntory; this company has spearheaded the industry and its products are now available worldwide. *Saké* is the traditional drink for all ceremonial occasions and there are about 3,500 saké breweries in Japan. Another local product is *shochu* – a white spirit, distilled from rice wine or sweet potato, which resembles vodka. *Umeshu* is a Japanese plum wine often drunk after dinner. In addition, there are several uniquely Japanese liqueurs.

Bridal Cocktail
1st Prize, Hotel Barmen's Club Cocktail Competition, 1977, Ikuo Samejima
5/10 Saké Gozenshu (30°)
3/10 Rosse liqueur
2/10 lemon juice
1 barspoon maraschino
Shake.

Casablanca Collin
1st Prize, Long Drink Section, ANBA Cocktail Competition, 1976, Tetsuji Fujimoto
1¼ fl oz vodka
1 fl oz Bols advocaat
¼ fl oz Galliano
½ fl oz lemon juice
¼ fl oz orange juice
Shake. Strain into a highball glass filled with crushed ice. Add a cherry.

Pearl of Lake
Hiroshi Hashimoto
⅓ whisky
⅓ Bols gold liqueur
⅓ lime juice
Shake.

Pure Love
1st Prize, ANBA Cocktail Competition, 1980, Kazuo Ueda
1½ fl oz gin
¾ fl oz framboise
¾ fl oz lime juice
Ginger ale
Shake all but the ginger ale. Pour into an ice-filled highball glass. Stir in ginger ale. Decorate with a slice of lime.

Scarlet Lady
1st Prize, Hotel Barmens' Club Cocktail Competition, 1976, Yasuo Kuboki
¼ Bacardi white rum
¼ Campari
¼ Mandarine liqueur
¼ lemon juice
2 barspoons maraschino
Shake. Decorate with orange peel on cocktail glass rim.

Slalom
1st Prize, Short Drink Section, ANBA Cocktail Competition, 1977, Yoshitoyo Komiya
½ Bacardi white rum
¼ Cointreau
¼ lime juice
Shake. Add an olive.

Twinkle of the Polestar
1st Prize, Short Drink Section, ANBA Cocktail Competition, 1976, Shuji Kimura
⅓ gin
⅓ green Chartreuse
⅙ Drambuie
⅙ dry vermouth
1 dash orange bitters
Stir.

MALTA

Maltese Bartenders' Guild (MBG)
P.O. Box 368, Valletta, Malta

The popular holiday island of Malta, situated so strategically in the Mediterranean sea, has a wide variety of imported products. Anisette has been made in Malta for thousands of years and there are some very old wineries as well. White wine is drunk in summer. There is one brewery, which makes a range of British-style ales. Malta has an original soft drink called kinnie which is very good as a mixer.

El Cerro
National Long Drink Competition, 1977, Alex Caruana
1 fl oz light rum
1 fl oz dark rum
½ fl oz curaçao
½ fl oz Galliano
2 fl oz pineapple juice
1 dash grenadine
Shake. Fill a sugar-rimmed highball glass with ice. Decorate with a pineapple ring, a fresh strawberry and a straw.

Kinnie Winnie
Kinnie Cocktail Competition, 1979, Edward O'Neill
1 fl oz brandy
1 fl oz Grand Marnier
1 fl oz fresh orange juice
Kinnie
Build the brandy, Grand Marnier and orange juice into an ice-filled highball glass. Top with kinnie.

Mariette
Kinnie Cocktail Competition, 1978, Frank Frenech
1 fl oz light rum
½ fl oz Amaretto di Saronno
½ fl oz Cointreau
Kinnie
Build all but the kinnie into an ice-filled highball glass. Top with kinnie. Decorate with a slice each of orange and apple and a cherry.

Phonicin 47
Mandarine Napoléon Cocktail Competition, 1978, Albert Spiteri
½ vodka
¼ Mandarine Napoléon
¼ sweet vermouth
1 dash lemon juice
Stir. Decorate with slices of lemon and orange and a cherry.

Viva Maria
Tia Maria Cocktail Competition, 1979, Isaac Vella
¼ brandy
¼ Tia Maria
¼ Galliano
¼ blackcurrant juice
Shake. Add a cherry.

KOREA

Korean Bartenders' Association (KBA)
398-1, Jungnung Dong,
Sungbuk-Ku-Seoul

MEXICO

Asociacions Mexicana de Barmen
28,2 Piso-Mexico 1, D.F.

Drinking habits vary considerably from one region of Mexico to another. The poorer people tend to drink beer and *pulque*, a sweet liquor made from the cactus which, if fermented, can be very strong. The middle and upper classes drink the usual international drinks and are especially fond of tequila, which is in great demand both as an aperitif and as a base for cocktails. Tequila as an aperitif is usually consumed as follows: first you take a pinch of salt, then one sip of pure tequila, one of 'Sangrita' (a tomato sauce mixed with Tabasco sauce) and one squeeze of lemon juice directly into the mouth. This ritual is followed until the glass of tequila is finished. Brandy was not produced in Mexico in any great quantity before 1950, but in the past twenty-five years it has become the national spirit drink, surpassing both rum and tequila. Kahlua is served with coffee and with desserts such as ice creams. Among the most popular cocktails is the Margarita – ⅖ tequila, ⅕ triple sec, ⅖ lime juice, shaken with cracked ice. The cocktail glass is prepared by moistening its rim with lemon rind, then dipping it in salt. The cocktail is sipped over the salted edge of the glass.

Blue Margarita
⅖ tequila
⅖ fresh lime juice
⅕ blue curaçao
Shake. Serve in a salt-rimmed cocktail glass.

Mocha Mint
⅓ Kahlua
⅓ white crème de menthe
⅓ white crème de cacao
Shake. Serve on the rocks.

Mockingbird
1 jigger white tequila
3 fl oz grapefruit juice
1 dash lime juice
Fill an old-fashioned glass with ice cubes. Add the ingredients. Stir. Garnish with a cherry

Sunset
½ oz light honey
1 fl oz lemon juice
2 fl oz golden tequila
Stir well. Serve in a cocktail glass with shaved ice.

Tequador
1½ fl oz tequila
2 fl oz pineapple juice
1 dash lime juice
Grenadine
Shake all but the grenadine. Pour over crushed ice in a large goblet. Add a few drops of grenadine. Serve with short straws.

Toreador
⅓ Kahlua
⅔ brandy
1 dash egg white
Shake. Serve straight or on the rocks.

NORWAY

Norsk Bartender Forening (NBF)
P.O. Box 2554, Solli, Oslo 2

Norway has a very strong tradition of home-brewed beer, which is usually made with hops; when juniper berries are used it is called juniper ale. Liquor manufacture and distribution is strictly controlled by the state monopoly. The most famous Norwegian spirit is Linie aquavit which is aquavit that has been shipped to Australia and back by cargo ship. This way it crosses the 'line' – the equator – twice; the journey is said to produce a much smoother softer spirit.

Festrus
1st Prize and team winner, International Cocktail Competition, Los Angeles, 1973, Bjarne Eriksen
⅓ Smirnoff vodka
⅓ Grand Marnier
⅓ Bitter Cinzano
Stir. Add twist of orange peel and cherry.

Green Hope
1st Prize, International Cocktail Competition, Yugoslavia, 1979, Sven-Aage Jonsbråten
½ vodka
¼ Bols green curaçao
⅛ crème de banane
⅛ grape-lemon juice
Shake. Add a cherry.

Orbit
Team winner, International Cocktail Competition, Tokyo, 1971, Arthur Andersen
⅖ rye whisky
⅕ yellow Chartreuse
⅕ Dubonnet
⅕ Cinzano bianco vermouth
Stir. Add a cherry.

Stratos
Team winner, International Cocktail Competition, Tokyo, 1971, Sverre Lunder
⅜ gin
¼ Drambuie
¼ Cinzano dry vermouth
⅛ Bols crème de banane
Stir. Add a cherry and a twist of lemon peel.

Strike
Team winner, International Cocktail Competition, 1973, Sverre Th. Jacobsen
⅓ rye whisky
⅙ Sève Fournier
⅙ Dubonnet
⅙ Cinzano dry vermouth
Stir. Add a twist of orange peel and a red cherry.

Titten Tei
Long Drink team winner, International Cocktail Competition, Los Angeles, 1973, Thorleif Andersen
⅔ Smirnoff vodka
⅓ Bénédictine
Fresh lemon juice
Fresh orange juice
1 dash grenadine
Dry sparkling wine
Shake all but the wine. Strain into tall glass or flute. Fill with iced sparkling wine. Garnish with a slice of orange and a cherry.

VIP
⅓ bitter Cinzano
⅓ rye whisky
⅓ Cointreau
Stir. Add a twist of orange peel.

Sweet Memories
Egil Moum
⅓ dry vermouth
⅓ Bacardi rum
⅓ orange curaçao
Shake.

PORTUGAL

Associação Barmen de Portugal (ABP)
Trav. da Fábrica dos Pentes
27, 1° – 1200 Lisbon

Portugal is the home of port, but although the Portuguese do drink port they are more fond of their wines. From the north comes the *vinho verde*, which froths up as it is poured into the glass; and the more alcoholic red wines come from further south. *Aguadente*, which is distilled from the grape pressings, is the most popular spirit, and there are local specialities such as the *aguadente medrohono*, an eau-de-vie popular in the Algarve.

Alleluia
1st Prize, Long Drink Section, International Cocktail Competition, Yugoslavia, 1979, Antonio Teixeiri de Jesus
1½ fl oz tequila
½ fl oz maraschino
½ fl oz blue caraçao
½ fl oz fresh lemon juice
1 dash egg white
Bitter lemon
Shake all but the bitter lemon. Strain into an ice-filled highball glass. Stir in the bitter lemon. Decorate with a lemon slice, orange peel, a sprig of mint and two cherries.

Caprilia
Felicio Batista-Nogueira
⅗ vodka
⅕ dry port
⅕ cherry brandy
2 dashes grenadine
Stir. Add a cherry.

Cascais
International Cocktail Festival, Venice, 1980, Luis Costa Pereira
⅖ Smirnoff vodka
³⁄₁₀ Campari
³⁄₁₀ dry sherry
Stir. Add a twist of orange.

Damas Do Campo (Country Ladies)
Antero Correia Jacinto
⅓ anis
⅓ Campari
⅓ Bacardi rum
2 dashes grenadine
Stir. Add a slice of orange. Add a cherry.

Luisa
José Dinez M. Pereira
⁴⁄₁₀ Barcardi rum
³⁄₁₀ fresh pineapple juice
³⁄₁₀ Parfait Amour
1 dash egg white
Shake. Serve with a half slice of lemon and green cherry on the rim of the glass.

Marao
Fernando Silva Soares
⅓ advocaat
⅓ anis
⅓ sweet port
Shake.

Michael
Manuel José Rodrigues
⅗ Scotch whisky
⅕ orange juice
⅕ anis
Shake. Decorate with a cherry.

Vilamoura Marina
Tony Fernandes
⁵⁄₁₀ Smirnoff vodka
²⁄₁₀ yellow Charteuse
²⁄₁₀ Bols blue curaçao
¹⁄₁₀ Galliano
2 drops lemon juice
Shake. Add two cherries.

SPAIN

Asociación Barmen Españoles (ABE)
Duque de Medinaceli-2, Madrid

Although Spain's most notable product is sherry, the Spaniards produce more brandy, for they are very fond of their *'coñac'*. This is dark, sweet and highly alcoholic when made for the home market; export brands are lighter and drier. The local *aguadiente* is made from grape pressings but the word is also used for spirits distilled from other ingredients such as fruits or potatoes. Aniseed liqueurs and pastis are very popular and banana liqueurs are the speciality of the Canary Islands. Sangria is made with local wine and is a simple refreshing drink.

Sherry Cobbler
Sherry
4 dashes orange curaçao
1 barspoon gomme syrup
Fill a medium-sized wine glass with ice. Half-fill with the sherry. Stir. Decorate with fruit. Add a sprig of mint. Serve with straws.

Sherry Flip
2 fl oz sherry
1 barspoon sugar
1 egg
Shake. Strain into a small wine goblet. Sprinkle nutmeg on top.

Sherry Sangaree
1 barspoon sugar
1 measure sherry
Fill a glass with crushed ice. Stir. Sprinkle nutmeg on top. Decorate with a slice of lemon.

Sherry Twist
⅖ dry sherry
⅖ orange juice
⅕ Scotch whisky
2 dashes Cointreau
Shake.

Sangria
¼ cup sugar
1 cup water
1 orange, thinly sliced
1 lime, thinly sliced
1 lemon, thinly sliced
1 bottle red or white wine
6 fl oz soda water
Dissolve the sugar in the water in a large jug. Add the fruit and wine. Fill with ice cubes. Stir until cold. Add the soda water. Serve with fruit added to each glass.

Jerez Cocktail
2 fl oz dry sherry
1 dash each orange and peach bitters
Stir well. Add ice.

Sherry Cocktail
2 fl oz medium dry sherry
4 dashes orange bitters
¼ fl oz dry vermouth
Stir well. Add ice.

Springbok
⅓ medium dry sherry
⅓ Lillet
⅓ Van der Hum liqueur
2 dashes orange bitters
Stir well. Add ice.

Syllabub
Sherry is also the prime ingredient of syllabub (half cocktail, half dessert)
2 fl oz sweet sherry
1 fl oz double cream
1 fl oz milk
1 barspoon powdered sugar
Beat well together and serve in a small goblet with a teaspoon.

SWEDEN

Sveriges Bartenders Gille (SBG)
P.O. Box 7579, SE-103 93 Stockholm

The national drink of Sweden is aquavit, which is also known as *brannvin*. The state monopoly makes unflavoured aquavit from potatoes or grain; it can be flavoured with caraway, blackcurrant, fennel, aniseed or bitter orange (there is even an Angostura aquavit). Much illicit aquavit is distilled in Sweden. It is drunk very well chilled with a beer chaser and is usually accompanied by some sort of salty food. Swedish punsch is drunk hot or cold; although it is available commercially, some households still prepare their own to traditional recipes.

Amigo
Richard Bohåll
1 fl oz vodka
½ fl oz apricot brandy
3 fl oz fresh lemon juice
3 dashes Angostura bitters
3 dashes grenadine
Pineapple juice
Shake all but the pineapple juice. Strain into an ice-filled highball glass. Stir in pineapple juice.

Honolulea
Borje Carlsson
½ Irish whiskey
¼ orange curaçao
¼ fresh lemon juice
1 dash gomme syrup
Shake. Decorate with a slice of orange and a cherry.

Linda
Olle Ferm
¼ crème de cassis
¼ gin
¼ crème de banane
¼ fresh lemon juice
Shake.

Nordexpress
Harry Eriksson
⅓ rye whisky
⅓ Cordial Médoc
⅓ Cinzano dry vermouth

Upstairs
Ulf Buhr
⅓ vodka
⅓ port wine
⅙ Lakka liqueur
⅙ fresh lime juice
Shake.

Viking
1½ fl oz Swedish punsch
½ fl oz aquavit
½ fl oz fresh lime juice
Shake. Serve on the rocks.

Volstead
1½ fl oz Swedish punsch
½ fl oz rye whisky
¼ fl oz fresh orange juice
¼ fl oz raspberry syrup
2 dashes anisette
Shake. Serve on the rocks.

SWITZERLAND

Schweizer Barkeeper Union (SBU)
16, Camille Martin, ch. 1203, Genève

Bottom Rose
*1st Prize, SBU Cocktail
Competition, 1975,
Giuseppe Bianchi*
³/₅ genever gin
¹/₅ apricot brandy
¹/₅ Cinzano Rossi

Cinque-Vie
¼ vodka
¼ Kirsch de Zoug
¼ Cointreau
¼ grapefruit juice
Shake. Add a cherry.

Lady Lyssa
*1st Prize, SBU Cocktail
Competition, 1970,
Jean-Claude Schwizer*
5 parts gin
1 part Cointreau
1 part apricot brandy
Shake. Add zest of orange and a
cherry.

Mary Rose
*1st Prize, SBU Cocktail
Competition, 1973,
Jean-Claude Schwizer*
½ Kirsch de Zoug
¼ manzanilla sherry
¼ apricot brandy
Stir. Add zest of orange and a
cherry.

Paradisiaque
*1st Prize, Fancy Drink Cocktail
Competition, 1979,
Gilbert Gaille*
2 fl oz dark rum
1 fl oz Mandarine liqueur
2 fl oz fresh orange juice
1 fl oz fresh lime juice
½ fl oz passion fruit juice
½ fl oz syrup of ginger
1 dash grenadine
Shake. Strain into a 12-oz glass
with ice. Decorate with fresh
mint and two cherries.

Passat
*1st Prize, SBU Champagne
Cocktail Competition, 1979,
Peter Roth*
1 fl oz peach brandy
1 fl oz orange curaçao
2 fl oz passion fruit juice
¼ fl oz lime cordial
¼ fl oz gomme syrup
Champagne
Shake all but the champagne.
Add iced champagne. Strain
into a champagne glass.
Decorate with a cherry.

Salvatore
²/₅ vodka
¹/₅ Cointreau
¹/₅ Kirsch de Zoug
¹/₅ grapefruit juice
Shake. Add a cherry.

Sandro
*1st Prize, SBU Cocktail
Competition, 1979,
Mauro Innocenti*
1½ fl oz Cinzano Rossi
½ fl oz Bacardi light rum
½ fl oz Campari
Stir. Add zest of orange.

St Moritz
⅓ Marc du Valais
⅓ Cointreau
⅓ lemon juice
5 drops pastis
Shake.

Swiss
½ pastis
½ fresh cream
1 barspoon grenadine
Shake.

USA

United States Bartenders' Guild (USBG)
4805 Lindley Avenue, Tarzana, Calif.
91356

The USA has a strong tradition of mixed drinks. During Prohibition the 'bathtub' spirits and moonshine had to be diluted with juices or mixed with flavourings to make them palatable and the American's liking for this style of drink has persisted. The cocktail hour is an American institution and many of the well-known cocktails were invented by US citizens. The USA is such a vast country that drinking trends change from state to state. Long fruity drinks such as Mint Julep, Rickeys and Coolers all come from the South whereas the short cocktails, including the Manhattan and Dry Martini, originated on the east coast.

Antoine's Smile
To be found at Antoine's restaurant, New Orleans
1½ fl oz calvados
½ fl oz fresh lemon juice
½ fl oz gomme syrup
1 dash grenadine
Shake.

Banana's Breeze
José Ruiseco
1 fl oz brandy
¼ fl oz Bols apricot brandy
¾ fl oz Bols crème de banane
1½ fl oz fresh orange juice
½ fl oz sweet and sour lemon
   juice
3 drops of Frothee
Shake.

Bleu-Do-It
*Created in Harper's bar,
Cordon-Bleu Restaurant,
Orlando, Florida*
½ fl oz gin
½ fl oz vodka
½ fl oz tequila
½ fl oz blue curaçao
1 fl oz fresh lemon juice
1 dash egg white
Soda water
Shake or mix all but the soda water. Strain into an ice-filled highball glass. Splash in soda water.

Coconut Breeze
John A. Rettino
1½ fl oz Jamaica rum
¾ fl oz pineapple juice
¾ fl oz coconut milk
1 dash orgeat syrup
1 dash maraschino
Shake.

Hurricane Punch
1½ fl oz dark rum
1½ fl oz fresh lemon juice
2 fl oz passion fruit juice
¼ fl oz gomme syrup
Soda water
Shake all but soda water. Strain into an ice-filled highball glass. Add a splash of soda water. Decorate with a lemon slice. Serve with straws.

Long Island Tea
½ fl oz vodka
½ fl oz gin
½ fl oz light rum
1 fl oz cold weak tea
Cola
Build all but the cola into an ice-filled highball glass. Stir in the cola. Decorate with a slice of lemon and a sprig of mint.

VENEZUELA

Asociación Venezolana de Barmen (AVB)
Nuevo Centro, Piso 11 Office 11b, Av
Libertador Chacao – Carácas

Venezuela is a rum-drinking
country. The light-bodied but
dark-coloured rum is either
drunk neat from a small glass or
is mixed with fruit juice. *Cocui*
is very popular in the interior of
Venezuela: it is a coarse spirit
distilled from the fermented
roots of sisal and is not unlike a
harsh tequila. The region of
Chouao is famous as the home
of the world's finest cacao
beans, and the drink *chouao* is a
chocolate liqueur. Ponche de
Crema is made on a rum base
with milk, eggs and sugar.
Available commercially as a
prepared drink, it is used for the
Tetero.

Tetero

Ponche Crema
1 small spoon grenadine
Put crushed ice in an
old-fashioned glass and fill with
Ponche crema. Do not mix.
Serve with short straws.

Antillano

1 dash Angostura bitters
1 small spoon grenadine
¼ pineapple juice
¼ grapefruit juice
¼ golden rum
¼ light rum
Shake and serve in a highball
glass with crushed ice. Decorate
with pineapple, orange and a
glacé cherry. Serve with large
straws.

Noches de Maquieta

1 barspoon sugar
Lemon peel
1 dash Angostura bitters
1 dash soda water
6 drops crème de cacao
2 fl oz golden rum
Place the sugar, lemon peel,
bitters and soda water in an
old-fashioned glass. Mix well
and add the crème de cacao and
the rum. Stir well. Decorate
with a slice of orange and a
maraschino cherry. Serve with
short straws.

Rom Ponche

1 small spoon sugar
2 dashes Angostura bitters
1 small spoon grenadine
Juice of half lemon
Golden rum
Build the sugar, bitters,
grenadine and lemon juice into
a 12-oz glass containing
crushed ice. Fill the glass with
golden rum. Decorate with
orange, pineapple, lemon and a
cherry.

YUGOSLAVIA

Drustvo Barmanov Slovenije (DBS)
Hotel Lev – Vosnjakova, 1 – 6100
Ljubljana

Five main nationalities merge together in six republics to form the country of Yugoslavia. It has four main languages, three main religions and two alphabets, but only one national spirit – *slivovitz*. Yugoslavia is the world's second largest plum-producer and the dark-blue sliva plums are fermented, then double-distilled, to produce a spirit which is aged in oak. Slivovitz may be colourless or pale gold. If juniper berries have been distilled with the plums the drink is called *klevovka* or *klekovaça*.

Badel 70
⅓ Badel cherry brandy
⅓ Vinjak Cezar
⅓ light vermouth

Brigitt
⅓ Badel vermouth
⅓ Badel whisky
⅓ triple sec
1 dash lemon juice
1 olive

Denisa
1st Prize, International Cocktail Festival, Venice, 1980, Antonjjia Juricev
1½ fl oz lemon vodka
¾ fl oz Galliano
¾ fl oz fresh cream
1 scoop lemon ice cream
Blend or mix. Serve in a large bowl glass.

Palme 70
⅓ extra bitter Badel
⅓ Vinjak Cezar
⅓ Stari Granicar
1 dash strawberry juice
1 cherry.

Wines
OF THE World

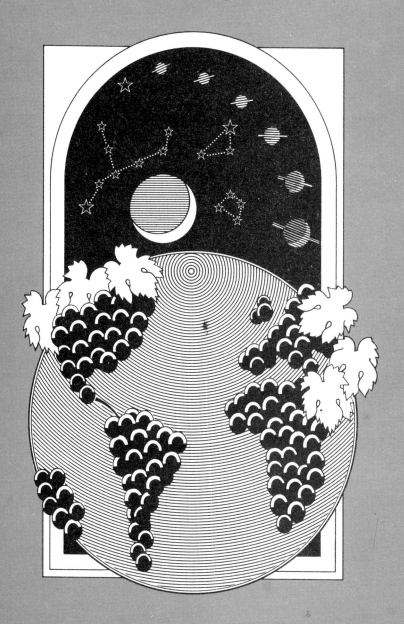

Year	Claret	Sauternes	Red Burgundy	White Burgundy	Rhone	Loire	Rhine & Moselle	Champagne	Port
1945	7†	6†	6†	—	5†	—	4†	4†	7
1947	6†	5†	5†	—	5†	4†	3†	4†	6†
1948	5†	4†	4†	—	4†	—	2†	—	7
1949	6†	6†	5†	—	6†	—	5†	5†	—
1952	4†	5†	5†	3†	6†	—	2†	4†	—
1953	5†	5†	4†	3†	6†	—	4†	3†	—
1955	5	6†	3†	3†	6†	—	1†	5†	7
1957	2†	3†	3†	3†	6†	—	2†	—	—
1958	2†	2†	—	—	4†	—	1†	—	4†
1959	6	6	6	3†	6	—	5†	5†	—
1960	2†	1	0	0	6†	—	—	—	6
1961	7	5†	5	3†	7	—	2†	5†	—
1962	5	6	5	4†	5	—	2†	5†	—
1963	1†	0	1†	2†	2†	—	1†	—	7
1964	3/6	2	6	4†	6	4	5†	6†	—
1966	7	5	5	4†	6	2†	4†	6	6
1967	3†	7	4	4†	6	3†	4†	6	6*
1969	2	4	7	5	6	4†	5†	5	—
1970	7	6	5	3†	6	5	3†	6	7*
1971	5/7	6	7	7	5	6	7	7	—
1972	3	3	5	4	6	2†	2†	—	4*
1973	4	3	3	5	5*	4†	4†	6	—
1974	3	1	3	3	4*	5	2†	—	—
1975	7*	6*	1	5	4*	5	4/6	7	6*
1976	5*	6*	6*	6	5*	6	7	6	—
1977	3	3	4	4	4	3	3	—	7*
1978	6*	3	7*	6*	7*	6	4	6	—
1979	4*	4*	5*	6*	6*	6	5	6*	—

Champagne and Port have been restricted to generally 'declared' vintage years. Certain white wines which do not improve with age have not been evaluated for as far back as 1945: hence the dash.

7 = The best 0 = No good

* Recommended for laying down † Tiring, drink-up

AUSTRALIA

Vines were planted in Australia a few days after the arrival of the first English settlers in 1788. The Governor of the new colony had taken cuttings with him of the 'claret' grape and the wine produced from them during the next ten years was encouraging enough for the settlers to ask the British government to send out someone with technical knowledge of winemaking. Two French prisoners-of-war were duly despatched on the assumption that as they drank wine, they would know how to make it. Unfortunately this was not the case and the settlers had to develop their own winemaking skills. One of the earliest pioneers of viticulture was John Macarthur, better known as the founder of Australia's merino wool industry; he took cuttings of French vines back to the settlement after a trip abroad and by 1827 was selling the wine in Sydney. Another was James Busby, a young Scot who had been sent to Australia to take charge of an orphanage; as part of his teaching post he was required to tend the school's small vineyard. Busby persuaded growers such as Macarthur to distribute their surplus cuttings to other settlers and when he later toured Europe he bought cuttings which were sent back to Sydney and Adelaide. He had great faith in the ability of the land to produce good wine and his enthusiasm, writings and collection of vines contributed greatly to the development of the infant industry.

Vineyards were also planted around the settlement of Port Phillip (now Melbourne) and in the 1850s a group of German Lutheran immigrants settled in the Barossa Valley just north of Adelaide. They had been winemakers in Germany and chose the valley as the best place to establish their new vineyards. From these beginnings viticulture spread to other parts of the country. Expansion was encouraged because there was ample land and Britain provided a ready export market until the turn of the century. However World War I and the Depression reduced the demand and many vines were torn out and the land used for sheep and cattle. In 1925 Britain introduced a preferential tariff for Commonwealth countries and cheap sweet wines of the port and sherry styles were shipped from Australia in great quantity. The high taxation of imported beverages helped the wine industry and local consumption increased steadily. Britain's entry into the EEC terminated the preferential trading terms and the main export market is now North America.

The main wine growing regions of Australia are in the south, and cover the three States of New South Wales, Victoria and South Australia in the east and Western Australia. Some of the very big companies have vineyards in a number of regions and may blend the wines to market under brand names, but quality wine is usually sold under a regional label. Each region has its own style and this is particularly evident in the wines of the smaller family concerns. Australia pioneered the wine cask, which is a cardboard box with a collapsible plastic bag inside it. The cask holds 4.5 litres and has become so popular that about half of the country's wine is now sold either in casks or in flagons. The main red grape varieties are cabernet sauvignon, shiraz and grenache with rhine riesling, sémillon and muscat being widely planted for white wines.

NEW SOUTH WALES

Hunter Valley This quiet rural area, about two hours' drive north of Sydney, is noted for high quality table wine. However, hailstorms are frequent, rain at vintage time is a constant worry and a number of past vintages have been lost to flood or drought. In good years the cabernet and shiraz grapes produce deep-coloured rich red wines. The sémillon grape, used in France for the fine sweet wines of Sauternes, makes delicate, high-acid, dry white wine. Hunter reds mature quite quickly but the whites need time to develop the full bouquet and flavour for which they are famous. Penfolds, McWilliams and Lindemans all have vineyards here and estate wineries include Brokenwood, Draytons, Lake's Folly, Rothbury and Tyrrells.

Mudgee This region is on the same latitude as the Hunter Valley, but is about 130 kilometres further west, and some 600 metres above sea level. When gold was discovered nearby in 1868, the winery boom began in Mudgee. When the gold gave out, so did the wineries, and of thirteen only one survived. The location and ideal soil have, however, once again drawn wine growers to the region and the wines are noted for their rich fruit and longevity. Estate wineries include Augustine, Craigmoor and Huntington.

Riverina This area surrounding the towns of Riverina and Griffith is able to grow grapes because of an extensive irrigation system supplied by the Murrumbidgee River. A great proportion of the everyday drinking wine of New South Wales comes from this area and quality is good as growers have concentrated on planting premium grape varieties. McWilliams, Seppelts and Wynns have interests there.

VICTORIA

Victoria has long hot dry summers and cold winters with frequent frosts. Traditionally wines from this State have been big, dark and alcoholic, but modern winemaking techniques have modified this. Phylloxera, the root-eating insect that devastated most of the world's vineyards late last century, is still a problem in some areas.

Goulburn Valley The region around the town of Nagambie produces quality red and white table wines with distinctive character; the wines of Chateau Tahbilk and Mitchelton are fine examples.

Great Western Although the climate of the small town of Great Western is a harsh one for viticulture, cool temperatures during the ripening period mean the region produces fruit with a high acid content which is well suited to the making of fine quality sparkling wine.

Rutherglen Rutherglen lies some 200 kilometres north-east of Melbourne and is famous for its dessert wines. The liqueur muscats and tokays of Baileys and Morris are fine examples of the luscious sweet wines. The tiny town of Milawa in the foothills of the Australian Alps

WINES OF THE NEW WORLD

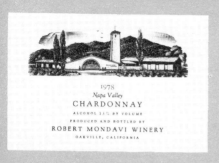

CALIFORNIA

AUSTRALIA

SOUTH AFRICA

has a micro-climate that allows it to produce fine table wine. The Brown family have been winemakers there since 1889.

SOUTH AUSTRALIA

About two-thirds of the country's annual wine production comes from this State and most of the vines are planted within a 200-kilometre radius of Adelaide.

Barossa Valley Climatically similar to Portugal, this beautiful fertile valley produces great quantities of table wine, sparkling wine and brandy. The vines are ungrafted as phylloxera has never struck the valley, and the major problem is the low summer rainfall. The local co-operative markets under the label Kaiser Stuhl, and other firms are Wolf Blass, Leo Buring, Henschke, Orlando, Saltram and Yalumba.

Clare There is little irrigation in the hot dry region around the towns of Clare and Watervale. In good years growers are able to make full rich reds and flavoursome robust white wines. Birks, Quelltaler, Sevenhills, Stanley and Taylors are all situated near Clare.

Coonawarra This is a flat featureless region about 200 kilometres south of Adelaide, with cold summers and wet winters. The *terra rosa* is a strip of red soil about 1 kilometre wide and 9 kilometres long and in good years it produces Australia's premium red grape. Most of the land is owned by big companies such as Wynns and Lindemans but Brand and Redman are two independent winemakers.

McLaren Vale This fertile valley lies just south of Adelaide and has a temperate climate because of its proximity to the sea. Its white wines are good for early drinking and the red wines have a particularly earthy taste with plenty of fruit and oak flavour. Wineries include Hardys, Marienberg, Reynella and Seaview.

Riverland The Murray river is the longest in Australia and its' waters have been dammed to irrigate the large tract of land around the South Australia-Victoria border. Vast quantities of wine and brandy come from around the town of Renmark. Co-operatives such as Berri and Renmano are active in the area.

WESTERN AUSTRALIA

Nearly sixty wineries are concentrated in the 20-kilometre strip of *Swan Valley* just north-east of Perth. However the West Australians are such enthusiastic consumers of the local produce that most wines are not available outside the State. The intense heat and rich soil produce full-bodied, low-acid wines. Legend has it that the bush-ranger Moondyne Joe was captured at Hougton's winery in 1869 after helping himself to the contents of a cask and falling asleep. *Margaret River* and *Mt Barker* are two new areas now under vine.

AUSTRIA

Austria is famous throughout the world for winter sports and fine culture but despite a tradition of over 2,000 years of vine cultivation, her wines are relatively unknown. In the nineteenth century the mighty Austrian Empire covered much of central Europe and her wines then included those which now come from Hungary, the Alto Adige in Italy and northern Yugoslavia. Today much Austrian wine is consumed locally and Germany is the most important export market. The Austrians particularly favour drinking their own reds from the portugieser grape and Italian red from the Alto Adige. Over eighty per cent of production, however, is white wine; the best is made from the local grape variety, grüner veltliner, and there is a system of grading according to sweetness from *kabinett* through to *trockenbeerenauslese* which is very similar to that of Germany. A major contribution to viticulture was made by the Austrian Lenz Moser who developed a method of planting and training vines so that they could be harvested by tractors, even on steep slopes, so reducing labour costs. The standards of quality are high in Austria and strict controls are maintained over all aspects of production. Once a wine has passed a chemical analysis and tasting test, it is officially declared quality wine and awarded the *'Weingutesiegel'* – a red and white goblet on a gold background. These quality wines are in the upper price bracket but some Austrian wine is sold abroad by brand name. All of the wine regions are in the warmer eastern part of the country.

Lower Austria More than sixty per cent of the total wine production comes from the north-east where the Danube flows through the vineyards. The grüner veltliner is widely planted in the Wachau area as are the müller-thurgau and rheinriesling grapes which all make dry fruity wines of good quality. The wine towns of the region are Retz, Krems and Langenlois.

Burgenland This tiny province is situated around the Neusiedlersee on the Hungarian border. Riesling and müller-thurgau grapes flourish in the sandy soil and the lake mists allow development of the noble rot *botrytis* which shrivels the grapes and concentrates the sugar. The town of Rust is the centre for Austria's quality sweet wines, the best known being *Ruster Ausbruch*.

Styria Located along the Yugoslav border, this area has volcanic soil, which suits the traminer grape, producing spicy aromatic wine. There are also pale red and white drinking wines made in this region.

Vienna The vineyards are within the city limits and in the famous Vienna Woods, the best known wine 'suburb' being Grinzig. *Heurige* is the name given both to the local taverns and to the fresh new wine served in them after the harvest. The village of Gumpoldskirchen has given its name to the sweet white wines known abroad.

EAST EUROPE

BULGARIA

Wine production in Bulgaria has been built up since World War II into a modern industry intended to provide valuable currency for the country. The wide flat plains of the Danube and Meritza valleys are easily cultivated mechanically. The farms are run as collectives and the wine is made in about 130 State-owned wineries. Over seventy per cent of Bulgaria's annual production is exported, her major markets being Germany and the other East European countries.

The Balkan Mountains run east-to-west, and the local red grapes mavrud, pamid and gamza are planted north of the range, along the Danube, to produce everyday drinking wine. The valley to the south of the moutains, where musk roses are grown to supply the precious essential oil for the European perfume industry, produces sweet wines as well as a dry Miskat. Eastern Bulgaria, which borders the Black Sea, supplies good dry whites from the local dimiat grape. The success of the Bulgarian wine industry has come from quality wines made from recently planted classic grape varieties. Cabernet, chardonnay and riesling wines are specifically made for export to Western Europe.

GREECE

The Greeks brought civilization to the rest of the Mediterranean and the vine travelled with them. Considering the long historical association between Greece and wine, her production is unexpectedly small, which may be attributed in part to five centuries of Islamic rule. One custom that has survived thousands of years is that of adding pine resin to the must during fermentation. This gives the wine a distinctive bouquet and flavour that is often likened to turpentine. Half the country's wine is treated this way; the white is known as 'Retsina' which is produced in the region of Athens from the savatiano grape. There is also a light red wine named 'Kokkineli'.

Monemvasia on the Pelopennesian peninsula is the original home of the malvasia grape which is now used throughout the world to produce rich sweet wine. 'Mavrodaphne', a sweet red wine fortified with brandy is one of the country's most popular wines. Wine is still made on many of the islands including Samos which produces a sweet luscious 'Muscat'. Most Greek wine is blended and marketed under a brand name but some are allowed to carry the name of their region of origin if they meet approved standards. These wines are sold with a numbered band across the cork.

HUNGARY

Although surrounded by mountains, most of Hungary is a vast flat plain dominated by the largest lake in Europe, Lake Balaton, the holiday mecca of a land-locked country. Both the food and wine of Hungary mirror the essential individuality of the Magyar people. The full-bodied assertive red and white wines complement the rich spicy cuisine, but the star of the wine industry is Tokay. The vineyards are divided amongst over one hundred State Farms and a number of smaller privately run co-operatives which sell their wines to a State-owned wine company. Export is the responsibility of the government organization Monimpex.

The sandy soil of the Great Plain of the Danube is ideal for vine cultivation and produces about half the wine of Hungary. The red 'Kadarka' and white 'Olaz Riesling' are everyday drinking wines. Most Hungarian wine is marketed with a regional name attached to that of a grape variety as in 'Pecs Olaz Riesling'. Quality wine comes from the hilly terrain in the north-west and around Lake Balaton. The furmint grape is widely planted to produce fragrant dry white. The table wines most seen abroad are from the north near the border with Czechoslovakia. 'Debroi Hárslevelü' is a perfumed sweet white from the Debroi vineyards and 'Egri Leányka' is a light soft white wine from a local grape variety. The wine town of Eger is well known from its association with the full red wine made from the kadarka grape and marked as 'Egri Bikavér' – Bull's Blood of Eger.

Tokay Tokay is a small village in the north-east of Hungary near the Russian border. The volcanic soil, river mist and long dry warm autumns create excellent conditions for ripening the furmint and hárslevelü grapes to full maturity. The 'noble rot' botrytis settles on the fruit, absorbs its water content and leaves the shrivelled berry full of concentrated sugar just as it does in Sauternes. The most shrivelled of all are known as Aszú grapes and these go into a wooden tub called a *puttonyos*. The weight of the fruit squeezes out a viscous sugar-laden juice which ferments very slowly and is known as *essencia*. In former days this precious liquid was given to dying monarchs as it was reputed to have life-giving properties. Very little of it exists today, none of it bottled – it can live in cask for hundreds of years – but a small amount is used to sweeten some aszú wine. The aszú grapes in the puttonyos are crushed to a paste and this added to a barrel of one-year-old wine. The more aszú paste added (up to five puttonyos), the sweeter and more expensive the wine. The Tokay matures in cask for at least six years before being marketed as Tokay Aszú or Tokay Essencia. This is a dessert wine which should be slightly chilled. A glass of Tokay is regarded by many as an excellent tonic.

ROMANIA

Romania has long been the most important wine-producing country in the Balkans and a huge replanting programme over the last twenty years has elevated it to the position of sixth largest producer in Europe with a thriving export market. East Germany, Poland, Czechoslovakia and Austria are her main outlets, but sales to the USA are increasing. The vineyards belong to local co-operative members or private growers although the state does own a small proportion. The Carpathian mountains occupy most of central Romania and the wine regions are located among their foothills. In the north-east are the

'Cotnari' vineyards which produce a white dessert wine a little like the Hungarian Tokay and once just as famous. Focsani, near the Black Sea, is the biggest wine region and grapes grow along the Danube in the south. The quality vineyards are situated around Tirnaveni in the central province of Transylvania and proximity to Hungary means wines from the Banat region are of a similar style. The riesling, muscat and fetcasca white grapes and cabernet, pinot noir, kadarka and babeasca red all produce good quality wine usually named after the grape variety with a regional name attached to it.

USSR

The Soviet Union is the fourth largest wine producer in the world with the amount of land under vine cultivation expanding rapidly. It also import huge quantities from the Balkan countries because the Russian people are enthusiastic wine drinkers. The wine belt follows the Black Sea from the Hungarian border to the Turkish and Iranian borders and covers the republics of Moldavia, Ukraine, Russia, Georgia, Armenia and Azerbaijan. Wines are graded as ordinary table wine, regional wine or selected matured regional wine. These are not bottled at source of origin but transported in bulk to all parts of the USSR. The greatest problem in vine cultivation is the winter climate. The vines are taken off their trellises and buried under a layer of soil to protect them against the freezing weather until the following spring.

Moldavia This region used to belong to Romania and its wine styles are similar to those of its European neighbours. Good reds are made from the cabernet grape and the local fetjaska grape makes a clean dry white wine.

Ukraine This large vineyard area includes the Crimea which produces good quality wine from the muscat grape. The River Don is the centre for sparkling wine.

Southern USSR The republics of Georgia, Armenia and Azerbaijan supply vast quantities of strong sweet red and white wine which is the style most appreciated in the USSR.

YUGOSLAVIA

Yugoslavia is the largest of the Balkan countries and has concentrated recently on exporting wines which grow in four of the six republics that form the country. The peasant growers belong to the many state co-operatives which use modern methods of production to make large volumes of wine. They compete against one another for the domestic and export markets. Yugoslav wines represent good value for money for everyday drinking wines but there is little accent on quality estate-bottled wine. A full range of table, sparkling and dessert wines is made, and the wines are usually named after the grape varieties with a regional name attached, as in 'Lutomer Riesling', with most wines being blends of various years.

Serbia-Macedonia These two provinces stretching down to Greece produce over half of the wines of Yugoslavia. Most of them are consumed locally, being full fruity everyday drinking wines. The white 'Smedervka' and red 'Prokupac' and 'Modri Burgundec' wines are the best known.

Slovenia This region centres on the towns of Ljutomer and Maribor and is noted for its fine white wines. The laski-riesling grape is planted all over the hills to supply the local co-operatives with the country's most exported wine. This part of Yugoslavia once belonged to Austria and other white wines made in the German style are 'Sipon', 'Renski Riesling' and 'Traminer'.

Croatia The Dalmatia coast reaching around the Adriatic Sea to the Italian border is planted with red grape varieties. The hot summers are tempered by sea breezes so that the big full alcoholic wines are made from pinot noir, cabernet, plavac and merlot grapes. 'Opol' is a light red, and whites from the hotter inland areas are also full round wines. 'Vranac' is made from a local red grape in Montenegro and is being exported in two styles.

ENGLAND

Wine has been made in England since the Romans introduced the vine, and the Domesday Book records eighty-three established vineyards, most of which belonged to the religious orders. In the Middle Ages the light delicate native wine was widely drunk until the acquisition of Bordeaux brought French wines to England. In the early eighteenth century a treaty with Portugal brought more rival wines and the English product never regained its popularity. However, a few vineyards continued to flourish in the care of various noblemen.

It was not until 1925 that any scientific research was made into which grape varieties would suit the English climate and ripen enough to produce wine on a commercial basis. The climate in the south of England is not unlike that of parts of Germany and consequently many of the grape varieties and crossings of Germany are suitable for England. The early ripening müller-thurgau does well and in good years makes flowery fruity dry wine that is ready for early drinking. Two varieties now being successfully cultivated are the Seyval Blanc, which is a hybrid produced by the Seyve Villard nurseries in France, and the Schönburger, which is a new variety bred from the muscat grape at the Geisenheim Research Station in Germany. Today the English Vineyard Association has hundreds of members and for small growers the Merrydown winery acts as a co-operative. Most of the vineyards are in the south of England and the better known ones are Kelsale in Suffolk, Pilton Manor in Somerset, Lamberhurst Priory and Biddenden in Kent, Hambledon in Hampshire and Adgestone on the Isle of Wight.

The West Country is famous for its cider which can have a deceptively high alcohol content. The British people have also made wine in their homes for centuries using the fruits of local crops to produce elderberry, apple, pear and gooseberry wines. One of the most successful of this style of wine is made from currants and ginger and has been marketed commercially as ginger wine since the eighteenth century. Dried currants are first steeped in sugar and water; then the yeasts normally present on the skins of the currants begin to work on the sugar and a slow fermentation takes place, producing wine. This is left to mature for about two years; then powdered Jamaican ginger root is added before the wine is filtered and bottled.

Wine is an integral part of life in France. From an early age a French child will drink a little wine in water at meal times, the French housewife uses it as a culinary aid to create the flavours that make the national cuisine so delicious, and Frenchmen sit for hours in small cafés quietly drinking the local product. The truly great wines of France stand unrivalled in the world of fine wine and are made with such loving care and skill that they can be compared with works of art. However, these wines represent a very small proportion of France's production, which covers every style and quality of wine. The small grower who has to store his palettes of new bottles out on the village street is as proud of his simple red wine as the owners of a great château are of their famous wine.

All French wines are graded by quality and the finest of them are described by the name of their place of origin. The Institut National des Appellations d'Origine known as the INAO is the body that authorizes a region to call its wines after their place of origin by granting it the status of *Appellation d'Origine Contrôlée* (name of controlled origin), which is often referred to as an appellation or AC.

To qualify for the use of an AC, wines must be produced from stated grape varieties grown within the authorized area. The INAO sets a maximum yield per hectare and a minimum alcoholic strength for each appellation. Each AC region has a general appellation that can be used for any wine that meets the basic requirements. If that same wine is able to meet even stricter requirements it is entitled to one of the higher classifications within the AC. For example the general appellation for the Rhône Valley is *Côtes du Rhône*. Better wine may have the grading *Côtes du Rhône Villages* and if it is of sufficient quality and grown in the correct locality it is entitled to be labelled *Chateauneuf-du-Pape, Hermitage, Tavel* or the other names listed in the appellations of the Rhône. A winemaker will obviously market his wine with its best possible appellation, so the more specific the *Appellation Controlée* mentioned on the label, the better the wine. The inclusion of a village or vineyard name is an indication of quality.

Certain regions produce good quality wines that are not quite of AC standard and these are given the rating VDQS – *Vins Delimites de Qualité Supérieure*. The vast majority of these come from the Midi. The winemakers hope that their wines will eventually be upgraded to appellations, which provides an incentive for maintaining a good standard and these are given the rating VDQS – *Vins Delimités de* table and comes from about eighty defined areas. The best known come from the Aude, Gard, Herault and Tarn regions in Southern France and are straight-forward flavoursome wines that represent good value. *Vin de Table* is everyday drinking wine, most of which is consumed within France.

ALSACE

The province of Alsace lies in the north-east corner of France, on the German border. For centuries this has been a troubled region of

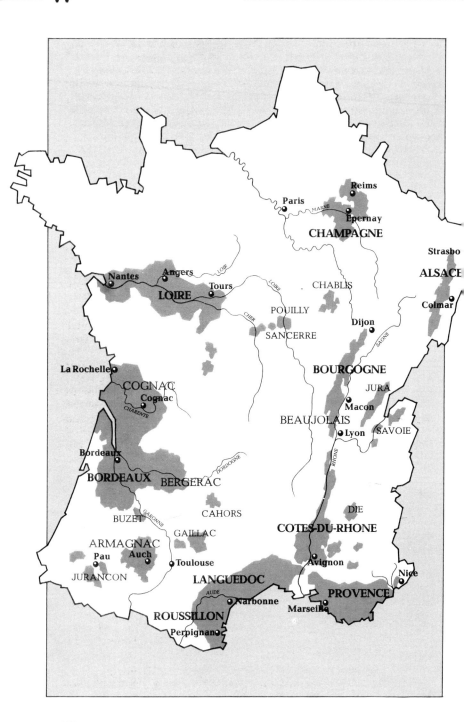

strategic military importance. Its wealth of natural resources caused both France and Germany to regard it as a prize of war.

Alsace has always been wine country and the archives of the city of Colmar include detailed records of over 1,200 vintages. Although famous during the Middle Ages, the wines of Alsace were virtually unknown while the province was under German sovereignty, as they were used for blending with German wines. Since 1945 the growers of Alsace have devoted themselves to re-planting top quality vines and instituting strict controls over all aspects of viticulture and vinification. Today Alsace is one of the world's most consistent producers of good quality white wine and thirty per cent of all appellation contrôlée white wine is produced in Alsace. Germany takes over half of all Alsace wine exports and much of the wine is sold from the 'cellar door' to Germans, Swiss and Belgians who visit this beautiful region.

Climatically, Alsace is near the limit of vine cultivation as it is so far north, but the Vosges mountains which border it on the west form a natural barrier to protect the region from rain and cloud cover. Consequently the sixty mile strip of vineyards nestles on the lower slopes of the mountain range and enjoys warm summers and long sunny autumns. In contrast to other wine-producing areas, Alsace has rich soil, but frost, hail and birds are real dangers. Most vineyards are less than two and a half acres in size so that much of the wine is made by the co-operative wineries or by producer-dealers (*négociants*) who buy grapes to supplement their own vineyard supplies.

The best wines come from the south of Alsace and are much softer and richer than those from north of Barr. There is one single appellation *Alsace* or *'Vin d'Alsace'*. The wine may be sold under a brand name but the vast majority of it is marketed under the name of the grape used to produce the wine. The law requires that if a grape variety or vintage is stated on the label, the wine must be composed entirely of that grape variety or vintage and the label must carry the name and address of the bottler. All Alsace wine must be sold in the tall green flute shaped bottles.

Riesling This variety is considered to produce the best Alsace wine. It makes racy delicate wine with fine grape aroma and fruity flavour. This wine complements fish dishes.

Gewurztraminer This rich spicy wine has an almost overpowering fruitiness and in a good year can have up to 15 per cent alcohol. It is an excellent accompaniment to highly seasoned food and strong cheese. This is the best known of the Alsace wines because of its distinctive spiciness.

Muscat This wine has a very pronounced perfume characteristic of the grape variety. Although it makes sweet wine in other parts of Europe, the Alsace Muscat is bone dry. The best have a gentle delicate flavour and when served chilled make a delicious aperitif.

Tokay d'Alsace This is a full-bodied wine with a subdued fruit flavour. It shows some acidity when young but mellows well with age. Much of this variety is used as the basis for blended wines.

Sylvaner This grape variety is grown predominantly in the north of Alsace. It is good everyday drinking wine.

Edelzwicker This term denotes a blend of several varieties, the most used being tokay d'Alsace, sylvaner and chasselas. Many of these blends are sold under brand names.

Réserve, Cuvée Exceptionelle These terms are used at the discretion of the maker to indicate top quality wines that will repay keeping.

Vendage Tardive This term means that the grapes have been harvested late in the season so that the wine will have a more concentrated sweetness. It is the equivalent of the German term *'spätlese'*.

Eaux-de-vie Orchard fruits and wild berries from the mountain forests are used to produce the many famous *'alcools blancs'* of Alsace.

BORDEAUX

In south-west France, the Dordogne river in the north and the Garonne river from the south converge to become the broad Gironde, which flows to the sea via its long estuary. The whole of the department of the Gironde has been dedicated to vines since Roman times when it was known as Aquitainia. For centuries the Duchy of Aquitaine was almost a mini-kingdom and when Eleanor of Aquitaine married Henry Plantagenet in 1152 this much prized region became English territory. The English took to drinking the pale delicate red wine they named *clairet,* and by the fourteenth century over three-quarters of Bordeaux wine exports went to England. English merchants have lived in Bordeaux ever since and the wine is still referred to as claret.

The most important regions of Bordeaux with their own appellations are as follows:

Médoc	Entre-deux-Mers	St Émilion
Haut Médoc	Premierès Côtes	Pomerol
Graves	Cérons	Fronsac
Barsac	Loupiac	Bourg
Sauternes	Sainte-Croix-du-Mont	Blaye

The châteaux of Bordeaux have been officially classified since 1855 when the local wine brokers drew up a list of the finest wines based on soil, prestige and price. However, only the Médoc and Sauternes regions were recognized to produce quality wines at this time, so that Graves and St Émilion had to wait until 1950s to have an official rating and Pomerol has still not been classified.

Any wine grown within the Bordeaux area is entitled to the AC *'Bordeaux'* or *'Bordeaux Supérieur'* according to the degree of alcohol it contains. Many regions, such as Médoc, Graves, etc, have the right to use their own names as the AC for their wines and some communes (villages) within these regions produce wines of such quality that they can use the village name as the AC for the wine. So, wine from the commune of Pauillac in the Haut Médoc can be labelled *'Appellation*

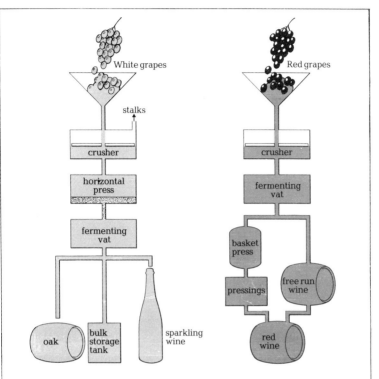

WHITE WINE

Grapes are fed into a
CRUSHER-STEMMER which removes
the stalks. The lightly crushed
fruit is pumped into a HORIZONTAL
PRESS. The plates at either end of
the press move towards each
other, crushing the grapes
between them. The fresh juice
falls into a trough below and is
then channelled into the
FERMENTING VAT. A pure yeast
culture is added and the must is
allowed to ferment for up to six
weeks. The wine is then drained
into clean sterile containers
leaving behind the lees. This
process is known as RACKING and
it ensures that any decomposed
yeasts or bacteria are removed
and sulphur dioxide is often
added as extra insurance against
infection. The wine may be
stabilized by FINING and/or
REFRIGERATION before being
bottled.

RED WINE

Grapes are conveyed to the
CRUSHER-STEMMER which gently
breaks the skins and removes the
stalks. The must is then pumped
into the FERMENTING VATS. Here
the yeasts work on the natural
sugars in the must and convert
them to alcohol at a temperature
of 25–30°C. The wine is drawn
off and the remainder is PRESSED
by a hydraulic basket press to
extract the wine still held in the
pulp. The wine is rested, then
RACKED off the lees into a vessel
for the INITIAL AGEING. The wine
rests and undergoes a secondary
fermentation which lowers the
acid content and so softens the
wine. It is pumped into a clean
container, leaving the dross in
the barrel, and after this SECOND
RACKING the wine is FINED by the
addition of special clays to
remove any remaining solids. It is
then FILTERED and left to MATURE
before bottling.

Pauillac Contrôlée'. However, if the wine is not considered good enough for such a prestigious AC, then it can be labelled *'Haut Médoc'*, *'Bordeaux Supérieur'* or just *'Bordeaux'*.

Médoc

The Médoc is a strip of land that borders the south side of the Gironde estuary. The vines are only planted along the river on a narrow, gravelly, sandy strip of land that varies in width from 5 to 10 kilometres. Médoc wine is made with a high proportion of cabernet sauvignon grape which takes many years to mature, so the wines are very long lived. Most of the wine for the basic appellation *'Médoc'* comes from the north while wine from the southern part is entitled to be labelled *'Haut Médoc'*. Within the Haut Médoc there are six communes that have their own appellations:

St Estèphe These are robust full-bodied clarets with plenty of tannin so they need time to develop fully. The best known Chateaux are Cos-d'Estournel and Montrose, and the Cru Bourgeois from here are very good wines.

Pauillac This is the most prestigious commune as it contains three of the First Growth Châteaux: Lafite, Latour, Mouton-Rothschild. The wines have a powerful fruity bouquet and a rich velvety texture when mature.

St Julien The high gravel content of the soil means that virtually all vines grown here make good wine. It is gentle and supple wine when mature. The best known châteaux are Léoville-Lascases and Talbot.

Margaux In good years the wine is excellent but poor years can produce thin wine. At its best it has exceptional finesse and elegance with a perfumed bouquet. The famous châteaux Margaux and Palmer are in this commune.

Moulis and Listrac These two communes lie behind St Julien but are situated away from the river, so the wines are much heavier than those of St Julien. This is a good area for Bordeaux Supérieurs and Crus Bourgeois.

In the 1855 Classification, châteaux of the Médoc are listed as First, Second, Third, Fourth and Fifth Growths. These sixty-one châteaux were chosen from almost 2,000 vineyards so that even a Fifth Growth must be regarded as a very fine wine. They can be identified by the phrase *'Cru Classé'*, on the label. The Classification then listed Exceptional Growths – *Crus Exceptionnels* – followed by *Crus Bourgeois* and *Crus Artisans*. The major change to the Classification occurred in 1973 when Château Mouton-Rothschild was re-classified from a Second to a First Growth. The Crus Bourgeois were re-classified in 1978 and now include 123 vineyards that represent the 'middle class' wine of the Médoc.

GRANDS CRUS CLASSÉS OF THE MEDOC
The Official Classification of 1855

Property	Commune

First Growths

Property	Commune
Ch. Lafite-Rothschild	PAUILLAC
Ch. Latour	PAUILLAC
Ch. Margaux	MARGAUX
Ch. Mouton-Rothschild	PAUILLAC
Ch. Haut-Brion	PESSAC

Second Growths

Property	Commune
Ch. Rausan-Ségla	MARGAUX
Ch. Rauzan-Gassies	MARGAUX
Ch. Léoville-Lascases	SAINT-JULIEN
Ch. Léoville-Poyférré	SAINT-JULIEN
Ch. Léoville-Barton	SAINT-JULIEN
Ch. Durfort-Vivens	MARGAUX
Ch. Gruaud-Larose	SAINT-JULIEN
Ch. Lascombes	MARGAUX
Ch. Brane-Cantenac	CANTENAC
Ch. Pichon-Longueville-Baron	PAUILLAC LONGUEVILLE
Ch. Pichon-Longueville-Lalande	PAUILLAC LONGUEVILLE
Ch. Ducru-Beaucaillou	SAINT-JULIEN BEAUCAILLOU
Ch. Cos-d'Estournel	SAINT-ESTEPHE
Ch. Montrose	SAINT-ESTEPHE

Third Growths

Property	Commune
Ch. Kirwan	CANTENAC
Ch. d'Issan	CANTENAC
Ch. Lagrange	SAINT-JULIEN
Ch. Langoa Barton	SAINT-JULIEN
Ch. Giscours	LABARDE
Ch. Malescot-Saint-Expéry	MARGAUX
Ch. Boyd-Cantenac	CANTENAC
Ch. Palmer	CANTENAC
Ch. La Lagune	LUDON
Ch. Desmirail	MARGAUX
Ch. Cantenac-Brown	CANTENAC
Ch. Calon-Ségur	SAINT-ESTEPHE
Ch. Ferrière	MARGAUX
Ch. Marquis-d'Alesme-Becker	MARGAUX

Fourth Growths

Property	Commune
Ch. Saint-Pierre-Sevaistre	SAINT-JULIEN
Ch. Talbot	SAINT-JULIEN
Ch. Branaire-Ducru	SAINT-JULIEN
Ch. Duhart-Milon-Rothschild	PAUILLAC
Ch. Pouget	CANTENAC
Ch. La Tour-Carnet	SAINT-LAURENT
Ch. Lafon-Rochet	SAINT-ESTEPHE
Ch. Beychevelle	SAINT-JULIEN
Ch. Prieuré-Lichine	CANTENAC
Ch. Marquis-de-Terme	MARGAUX

Fifth Growths

Property	Commune
Ch. Pontet-Canet	PAUILLAC
Ch. Batailley	PAUILLAC
Ch. Haut-Batailley	PAUILLAC
Ch. Grand-Puy-Lacoste	PAUILLAC
Ch. Grand-Puy-Ducasse	PAUILLAC
Ch. Lynch-Bages	PAUILLAC
Ch. Lynch-Moussas	PAUILLAC
Ch. Dauzac	LABARDE
Ch. Mouton Baronne Philippe	PAUILLAC
Ch. du Tertre	ARSAC
Ch. Haut-Bages-Libéral	PAUILLAC
Ch. Pédesclaux	PAUILLAC
Ch. Belgrave	SAINT-LAURENT
Ch. Camensac	SAINT-LAURENT
Ch. Cos-Labory	SAINT-ESTEPHE
Ch. Clerc-Milon-Rothschild	PAUILLAC
Ch. Croizet-Bages	PAUILLAC
Ch. Cantemerle	MACAU

Graves

South of the Médoc and on the left bank of the Garonne River lies the region of Graves which takes its name from the coloured quartz pebbles that abound there. Red wines are produced in the north around the town of Bordeaux and are not unlike the wines of the Médoc, often being described as sandy. The wine of Château Haut Brion was so good even in 1855 that it was included as a First Growth even though Graves was not known as an area for fine wine. Dry white wines are made from the sauvignon blanc grape and the best are full-bodied smokey wines listed in the 1959 Classification. Sweeter white wines are made further south in the areas closer to Sauternes.

CLASSIFIED GROWTHS OF THE GRAVES

Red wines
(classified in 1953 and confirmed in 1959)

Ch. Bouscaut	CADAUJAC
Ch. Haut-Bailly	LEOGNAN
Ch. Carbonnieux	LEOGNAN
Domaine de Chevalier	LEOGNAN
Ch. Fieuzal	LEOGNAN
Ch. Olivier	LEOGNAN
Ch. Malartic-Lagravière	LEOGNAN
Ch. La Tour-Martillac	MARTILLAC
Ch. Smith-Haut-Lafitte	MARTILLAC
Ch. Haut-Brion	PESSAC
Ch. La Mission-Haut-Brion	PESSAC
Ch. Pape Clément	PESSAC
Ch. Latour-Haut-Brion	TALENCE

White wines
(classified in 1959)

Ch. Bouscaut	CADAUJAC
Ch. Carbonnieux	LEOGNAN
Domaine de Chevalier	LEOGNAN
Ch. Olivier	LEOGNAN
Ch. Malartic-Lagravière	LEOGNAN
Ch. L. Tour-Martillac	MARTILLAC
Ch. Laville-Haut-Brion	TALENCE
Ch. Couhins	VILLENAVE D'ORNON

Sauternes

The region of Sauternes lies south of Graves. The sémillon and sauvignon grapes are used to make naturally sweet white wine. In the autumn, morning mists give way to long sunny afternoons that allow the grapes to ripen fully. The humid mornings encourage the development of a fungus – botrytis cinerea – which settles on the grapes. This *noble rot* gradually dehydrates the fruit so that it shrivels and turns pinkish grey, but the few drops of juice that remain have a very high concentration of sugar. There is a great risk that the whole crop will be lost, because the fungus makes the skin porous and if it were to rain the grapes would quickly absorb the water which would dilute the sugar and might even explode them, making them useless. To reduce this risk the vineyards are hand picked to remove the grapes as soon as they become shrivelled. At Château d'Yquem the pickers may pick the crop ten times in a vintage lasting three months. When weather conditions are favourable the district makes excellent wine but in some years it is thin and lifeless. In 1964, 1972 and 1974 Château d'Yqeum made no wine at all under its own label and the standard of winemaking is so high that each vine produces only about one glass of wine a year. When wine is made from these grapes the slow fermentation stops spontaneously once the alcohol level reaches 14°–17° and the remaining sugar gives the Sauternes its natural richness. Then the wine is matured in oak. The production of Sauternes is labour-intensive and time-consuming and its cost is reflected in the price of the wine. In a good year it has a magnificent full luscious flavour that continues to develop for many years. Château d'Yquem has long been acknowledged the finest of the Sauternes although many of the Premier Crus represent excellent value in a good year.

Barsac

This region just north of Sauternes produces similar wine but the bouquet is more intense and the finish a little drier. The best known châteaux are Climens and Coutet.

SAUTERNES AND BARSAC
The 1855 classification

First Great Growth (Premier Grand Cru)	
Ch. d'Yquem	SAUTERNES

First Growths (Premiers Crus)	
Ch. La Tour-Blanche	BOMMES
Ch. Lafaurie-Peyraguey	BOMMES
Clos Haut-Peyraguey	BOMMES
Ch. Rayne-Vigneau	BOMMES
Ch. Suduiraut	PREIGNAC
Ch. Coutet	BARSAC
Ch. Climens	BARSAC
Ch. Guiraud	SAUTERNES
Ch. Rieussec	FARGUES
Ch. Rabaud-Promis	BOMMES
Ch. Sigalas-Rabaud	BOMMES

Second Growths (Deuxièmes Crus)	
Ch. de Myrat	BARSAC*
Ch. Doisy-Däene	BARSAC
Ch. Doisy-Vedrines	BARSAC
Ch. d'Arche	SAUTERNES
Ch. Filhot	SAUTERNES
Ch. Broustet	BARSAC
Ch. Nairac	BARSAC
Ch. Caillou	BARSAC
Ch. Suau	BARSAC
Ch. de Malle	PREIGNAC
Ch. Romer	FARGUES
Ch. Lamothe	SAUTERNES

* No longer in production

Cérons, St Croix-du-Mont, Loupiac
Cérons lies on the south bank of the Garonne river within the Sauternes region. St Croix-du-Mont and Loupiac lie along the north bank of the same river. These three areas are entitled to their own appellations and all produce white wines similar to Sauternes although not as rich; they represent good value for money.

Premières Côtes de Bordeaux
The strip of land running along the north bank of the Garonne produces red and white wines entitled to this appellation contrôllée. Traditionally the wines have been sold in bulk to the négociants in Bordeaux but many of these wines are now bottled under their own vineyard names.

Entre-Deux-Mers
This area stretches between the two rivers and is the largest region of Bordeaux. Only the white wines are authorized to bear the AC 'Entre-deux-Mers' and reds from this region are sold under the AC 'Bordeaux'. There are fifteen large co-operatives and much of the dry white wine produced is used for blending purposes.

St Émilion
Situated on the north bank of the Dordogne River, this is one of the oldest wine regions of France. The high proportion of merlot grapes produces soft full wines that are easy to drink as they contain less tannin. They will mature before the wines of the Médoc. The most famous châteaux are Cheval Blanc, Ausone, Canon and Bel-Air. The 1955 official classification lists twelve Premiers Grands Crus and seventy-two Grand Crus.

THE 1955 CLASSIFICATION

First Great Growths (Premiers Grands Crus)

Ch. Ausone
Ch. Cheval-Blanc
Ch. Beauséjour-Duffau-Lagarrosse
Ch. Beauséjour-Becot
Ch. Bel-Air
Ch. Canon
Ch. Figeac
Clos Fourtet
Ch. La Gaffelière
Ch. La Magdelaine
Ch. Pavie
Ch. Trottevieille

Pomerol

This region, adjoining *St Emilion* on the north bank of the Dordogne River, is becoming very well known for its gentle rich clarets made predominantly from the merlot grape. Although there is no official classification the wines command high prices because production is limited and demand is high. Chateau Pétrus is highly regarded and many consider it the equal of the fine Médoc wines.

Fronsac

This small region to the west of Pomerol produces red wine that can be sold under the appellations *'Côtes de Fronsac'* or *'Côtes Canon Fronsac'*. These big fruity wines resemble those of St Émilion although they lack the finesse of their neighbours; the Fronsac wines are well worth drinking.

Bourg and Blaye

Facing the Médoc across the Gironde estuary are the two old towns of Bourg and Blaye. Quality can vary and much of the white wine is sold for blending purposes. However, as the prices of well-known clarets escalate these red wines can represent good value and many of the petits chateaux sold abroad come from these regions.

BURGUNDY

This beautiful part of central France noted for its gourmet food and superb wines stretches for about 200 kilometres although it is no more than a few kilometres in width. In the Middle Ages the wines of the region were highly regarded at Court but during the French Revolution the great vineyards, most of which had been owned by the Church, were broken up into small holdings for local citizens. Thus there are no great châteaux in Burgundy and the pattern of small ownership has persisted so that although the great vineyards still exist they are divided amongst several owners; for example the fifty-hectare Clos de Vougeot vineyard has fifty-six owners. Not all growers are good winemakers so it is possible to get wines of the same year from the same vineyard that vary in character, quality and price. Most growers sell their wine to négociants who blend, mature and market

WINES OF FRANCE

GENERIC WINES

VDQS

BORDEAUX

BURGUNDY

the wine. A reputable négociant will buy quality wine to sell under his own label. The area available for the production of Burgundy is limited and the recent increase in demand has caused severe price rises. Here is a brief explanation of the appellations of Burgundy.

General Appellations Wine from grapes harvested anywhere within the authorized Burgundy area may be sold under the appellation *'Bourgogne'* or *'Bourgogne Grand Ordinaire'*. Wine made from a mixture of pinot noir and gamay grapes is entitled to the AC *'Passe-tout-grains'* whilst wine from the aligoté grape bears the AC *'Bourgogne Aligoté'*.

Village Appellations Villages may legally give their names to wine from grapes harvested within their local area known as the commune. Vineyards near the town of Beaune may label their wine as *'Appellation Beaune Controlée'*. Some villages have hyphenated the name of the nearest most famous vineyard to the village name, as in *Gevrey-Chambertin*. This does not mean that wine bearing this appellation has any connection with the famous vineyard; it simply comes from the same local area.

Climats Certain plots – *climats* – of the vineyards produce superior wines. Their names may appear on the labels after the name of the commune as in *'Beaune Grèves'*. The very best of these may use the words *'Premier Cru'*.

Vineyard Names Some climats are so highly regarded for their top quality wines that their names alone have become the appellation. There are about twenty of these Grand Crus of Burgundy and their wines will simply be labelled with the vineyard name such as *'Chambertin'*.

Chablis
The most northerly area produces fine dry white wines from the chardonnay grape. Good chablis is a pale straw colour and possesses a flavour often described as *'flinty'* which makes it the perfect accompaniment to seafood. Frost is a real danger in late spring and a small crop will mean higher prices for this sought-after wine. A label will bear one of the following appellations:
Petit Chablis The basic wine of the area.
Chablis A blend of wines from several vineyards.
Chablis Premier Cru Wine from the superior climats.
Chablis Grand Cru Wine from the climats of: Vaudésir, Bougros, Les Preuses, Valmur, Les Clos, Blanchots, Grenouilles.

Côte de Nuits
This area stretches on either side of the Route National 74 from Dijon to Nuits-St-Georges. The fruity red wines are noted for their perfumed bouquet and great elegance. They command exceptionally high prices and mature more slowly than the wines of the Côte de Beaune. These

two areas together are known as the Côte d'Or and contain most of the Premier Cru climats for red wine. The Grand Cru climats are:

Chambertin	La Tâche
Chambertin Clos-de-Bèze	Romanée-Saint-Vivant
Musigny	Grands-Échézeaux
Bonnes Mares	Echézeaux
Clos-de-Vougeot	Clos-Saint-Denis
Romanée-Conti	Clos-de-la-Roche
Richebourg	Clos-de-Tart
Romanée	

Côte de Beaune
The town of Beaune is the centre of the Burgundy wine trade and the surrounding area is dotted with wine villages. Red wines are generally softer and lighter than those from further north. The communes of Aloxe-Corton, Meursault, Puligny-Montrachet and Chassagne-Montrachet produce the powerful white wines full of flavour and perfume that are amongst the world's finest wines. The Grand Cru climats are:

Corton	Montrachet
Corton-Charlemagne	Chevalier-Montrachet
Charlemagne	Bâtard-Montrachet

Côte Chalonnaise
This area lies south of the Côte de Beaune. The communes of Rully and Montagny make fresh white wine and Mercurey and Givry produce light-bodied fruity reds that are best drunk young. Sparkling wine is made by the méthode champenoise and is entitled to the appellation *'Crémant de Bourgogne'*.

Mâconnais
The Mâconnais lies on the left bank of the River Saône and makes pleasant red wines from gamay grape. It is better known for its fresh young white wines made from the chardonnay grape. The best known of these are Pouilly-Fuissé and St Véran although good quality whites also come from Lugny, Clessé and Viré.

Beaujolais
The gamay grape and the granite soil of the area south of Mâcon combine well to produce the fresh fruity red wines known as Beaujolais. In a good vintage year the best of them will continue to develop into well balanced flavoursome wines for a few years. Some of it is ready to be released for sale by 15 November each year and this wine is known as Beaujolais Nouveau. It is very lively fruity wine that begins to fade by the new year. Some thirty villages producing superior Beaujolais are entitled to the appellation *'Beaujolais Villages'*. Premium quality Beaujolais comes from the following communes which all have their own appellation:

St Amour	Moulin-à-Vent	Morgon
Juliénas	Fleurie	Brouilly
Chenas	Chiroubles	Côte de Brouilly

CHAMPAGNE

Many wine-producing areas in the world have tried to emulate the success of Champagne by producing good quality sparkling wine, but only vines from this small region just north of Paris are able to make wine of inimitable finesse. This is possible because of the area's geological composition and micro-climate, the use of superior grape varieties and a special method of production. Whilst each of these factors occurs elsewhere, only in Champagne do they coincide to produce the unique wine.

Some seventy million years ago what is now northern France and southern England was part of a sea that dried up leaving a sediment of chalk up to 1,000 feet deep and violent upheavals since then have forced great outcrops of it up to the surface. The chalk slopes of Champagne and the white cliffs of Dover are part of this phenomenon. The chalk provides effective drainage whilst retaining enough moisture to nourish plants, and it holds the sun's warmth for a much longer period than most subsoils, thus supplying the vital ingredient for vine cultivation in this very northerly region. Champagne has a continental climate with very cold winters and short hot summers so that the vines must get as much heat as is possible to ripen the fruit. The gravelly top soil is only about one foot thick and it is rich in minerals. The best vineyard sites are situated between 137 and 165 metres above the plain, where the vines are exposed to the maximum amount of sun and light but are protected from the winds and severe spring frosts.

Although there are five grape varieties authorized for the region, most champagnes are made from a mixture of two of these. The purple black pinot noir has a colourless sugary juice that gives body and long life to the wine whilst the small gold chardonnay contributes the finesse and perfume. Each vineyard is classified on a percentage scale with the best growths being rated as 100 per cent and the fruit from these vineyards being bought for 100 per cent of each year's declared grape price. The Champagne region is divided into three areas of production:

Montagne de Reims Pinot noir vines are planted on the gentle slopes near Reims.

Vallée de la Marne The vineyards lie on either side of the River Marne and grapes from here are said to contribute a particularly fine bouquet.

Côte des Blancs This area south of the River Marne is principally devoted to growing chardonnay grapes.

Champagne is a blended wine and the general pattern is for the big houses – 'grandes maisons' – to buy grapes or still wines which are then blended in their cellars in Ay, Reims or Épernay to their own specifications, so providing continuity of style from year to year. Recently, however, growers have been grouping together to form co-operatives that now make champagne to be sold under the co-operative label, whilst some particularly independent growers are making their own champagne from their own grapes. There is a ready market within France for these wines and the trend has severely reduced the quantity of grapes available to the champagne houses. Champagne is expensive; it is a labour-intensive product, large stocks must be held in reserve, and the méthode champenoise is a costly procedure even requiring special bottles and corks to package the wine safely. Many of the houses are modifying techniques in an attempt to curb increasing costs. One factor beyond their control is the weather and a late spring frost or wet summer can have a devastating effect on the quantity and quality of grapes. Thus the balance between supply and demand is always a delicate one with champagne and any imbalance is immediately reflected in the price. France is the largest consumer of champagne, and Britain is the most important export market.

THE PRODUCTION OF CHAMPAGNE

Picking It is critical that the graps be picked at the correct ripeness. *Épluchage* is the name given to the procedure of removing rotten grapes in order to improve the quality of the wine; this practice, however, is fast disappearing because of labour costs. Immense care must be taken in the handling of grapes to avoid damaging them.

Pressing The more rapidly the grapes are pressed, the less danger there is of the skins of the red grapes colouring the juice. They are put into a wooden press known as a Marc which holds 4,000 kilos of grapes and can produce 3,000 litres of juice, although the law only allows 2,666 litres of juice to be known as the 'vin de cuvée', and all the best champagne is made from it. The next 666 litres are known as the 'vin de taille' and most Buyers Own Brands are from this pressing. The remainder is the 'rebêche' and is distilled for Marc de Champagne or consumed locally.

Débourbage It is essential that all impurities in the must be given time to fall to the bottom of the cask, so that the clean must may be drawn off. In very hot weather, the must may be passed through refrigerated pipes to prevent premature fermentation.

First Fermentation For about two weeks the must bubbles violently as the yeasts begin converting the sugars to alcohol. From then on, if a fine bouquet and real finesse are to be obtained, the fermentation has to be slow, regular and complete. The ideal temperature is 12–20°C. Some firms are now using stainless steel or glass-lined cement vats to give better temperature control, and others have air conditioned their above-ground celliers.

Topping Up Casks or vats must be frequently topped up to prevent bacteria altering the character of the wine.

Racking and fining Two or three racks and a fining with bentonite or isinglass are carried out during winter to prevent the still wine from becoming cloudy.

Preparation of the Cuvée Great skill is required when blending the still wines together. The houses maintain large reserves of previous vintages to give character and flavour to wine. This is the most critical phase of the whole méthode champenoise. Even in a vintage year blending is necessary, because the wines from different vineyards and of different grape varieties must be added in varying proportions to achieve the desired balance of flavours.

Liqueur de Tirage A small amount of cane sugar and old wine is added along with special yeasts of a type that will fall easily, work in highly alcoholic surroundings and at low temperature. This ensures that every bottle will undergo a secondary fermentation.

Sealing The bottles are sealed by hand with corks and agrafe clips or mechanically with crown corks. The bottles are then stacked on their sides in underground chalk caves.

Second Fermentation This is best carried out at 10–12°C and will take 3–6 months. An inferior champagne fermented at 18°C would take only 8 days. The yeast turns the sugar into alcohol and carbon dioxide which dissolves into the wine thus creating the desired stream of bubbles known as the *mousse*. A long slow fermentation produces a very fine, lasting mousse. The gas exerts an extremely high pressure on the bottles and so the glass must be strong enough to resist it.

Ageing The best wines are aged for 3–5 years, but the legal minimum period for non-vintage wine is one year. During this time the alcohol reacts with the acids in the wine to produce the sweet-smelling esters which give fine champagne its exquisite bouquet, and a prolonged rest period results in a mellow well-balanced wine.

Rémuage The bottles are placed in a rack with oval holes – the 'pupitre' – their necks being tilted slightly downwards. The specialist worker, known as the *Rémueur*, grasps the bottom of the bottle and gives it a slight shake, turn and tilt. This happens to each bottle every three days for about six weeks and at the end of this time the bottles will be standing vertically with necks downwards. The purpose of this is to drive the sediment down on to the cork. This is a highly skilled art as the finer, more easily disturbed sediment has to be moved down on to the cork first so that the heavier, granular sediment can fall on top of it and so prevent clouding of the wine.

Resting Bottles are stacked upside down in the cellar, with the neck of one resting in the bottom of another. The champagne can remain like this for many years, continuing its slow ageing process. The very best vintage champagnes stay like this until ready for consumption, when the rest of the process is carried out.

After the second fermentation the bottles are placed in racks known as *pupitres*, and shaken, tilted and given an eighth of a turn every three days until the bottles are standing vertically with neck downwards, with the sediment resting on the cork.

Dégorgement The neck of the bottle is dipped in a freezing brine solution, so forming a small block of ice which contains the deposit inside the neck. The pressure built up in the wine expels the ice when the cap is removed. This process is done mechanically in most houses nowadays.

Dosage The *liqueur d'expédition* is wine of the same blend with a mixture of cane sugar and old wine added to it. A small proportion of high-class grape brandy may be included to stop further fermentation. This dosage is added to top up each bottle and give the champagne the desired sweetness. It also serves to mask any flaws in wine made from cheaper grapes.

Recorking A compounded cork of three sections is wired down to resist the pressure of the carbon dioxide contained in the wine.

Shaking Bottles are given a good shake up, either by hand or machine, to distribute the dosage evenly.

Resting The wine is rested for 4–6 months to allow it to marry and settle down.

Packaging The bottles are cleaned, labelled and despatched. Most houses only ferment in magnums, bottles and halves and all other sizes are decanted from bottles under pressure. The names of the large bottle sizes are:

Magnum	2 bottles
Jeroboam	4 bottles
Rehoboam	6 bottles
Methuselah	8 bottles
Salmanazar	12 bottles
Balthazar	16 bottles
Nebuchadnezzar	20 bottles

STYLES OF CHAMPAGNE

Brut or Nature Only a minute amount of sweetening is added in the dosage to remove the astringency of complete dryness.

Extra Sec or Goût Anglais Dry champagne.

Sec or Goût Américain Medium sweet champagne.

Demi Sec Sweet champagne.

Doux or Rich Exceptionally sweet champagne.

Non-Vintage The aim of each house is to maintain a consistent style of unvarying quality. Among the dozen or so well-known non-vintage champagnes there are soft feminine wines, some drier and more austere ones and others sweeter or full bodied. The quality of the grapes is the major factor determining the price of a champagne – if these come from 100 per cent Grand Cru vineyards, then they will be more expensive than if they come from a lesser vineyard.

Vintage When good weather conditions allow the production of top quality wine, a *'vintage'* year is declared by the Champagne authorities. Each house aims to produce a champagne unique in style to that vintage year and only the highest quality wines are used although up to twenty per cent of the wine in the bottle may come from other years.

Rosé Most rosé is made by blending some of the still red wine of the Champagne region with the white wine. It is more full-bodied but not necessarily sweeter than golden champagne, as the red wine provides a touch of astringency. This style was popular in late-Victorian times and some houses still produce a vintage rosé as a prestige product.

Crémant These champagnes have less mousse, because less sugar is added in the liqueur de tirage. Consequently not as much carbon dioxide is created as a result of the secondary fermentation in bottle. The term is now being used for sparkling wines of other regions.

Blanc de Blancs This champagne is made entirely from white grapes. It is a particularly elegant wine noted for its delicacy and finesse, and is marketed as a premium quality vintage champagne.

Blanc de Noirs Some champagne made entirely from black grapes is produced but most of it is consumed locally.

De Luxe Most houses market a premium champagne that is beautifully packaged and highly priced. Some are made solely from grapes from 100 per cent Grand Cru vineyards, others are made entirely of wine from the first pressing and most are vintaged. There are no legal requirements for these wines so there is much variation in style, quality and age of the wines marketed as de luxe champagnes.

Still Champagne The appellation for still wines from the Champagne region is *'côteaux champenois'*. Previously known as *'vins natures'* these red and white still wines have been made in this part of France from the third century AD. The most widely available reds come from Bouzy and Sillery.

Storage and Service

Champagne is a delicate wine that must be stored correctly if it is to be served in prime condition. All fine champagnes will repay keeping; non-vintage wine laid down for a few years will develop to flavoursome maturity. Even six months quiet rest at home before consumption will benefit champagne, providing the following conditions are available: a temperature of around 11°C (a few degrees on either side of this is acceptable but it is important to avoid seasonal and daily fluctuations); horizontal storage in a dark place away from vibration (light will seriously damage the wine).

Champagne should be served at a temperature of 6–8°C. If it is too cold it loses its taste, if too warm it is heavy and the sparkle does not keep. Champagne should be cooled as gradually as possible. The least cold parts of the refrigerator may be used but the best method is to put a bottle in an ice bucket in a mixture of water and ice. It will take about twenty-five minutes to reach the ideal drinking temperature. Tulip-shaped glasses will preserve the bouquet and allow the mousse to rise in a fine long-lasting stream; the glasses must be dry, as any dampness will flatten the champagne. The cork is best covered with a napkin and twisted gently before being eased from the bottle.

LOIRE

The valley of the Loire is one of the most picturesque regions of Europe as its natural rural beauty is enhanced by the graceful châteaux built by French royalty on the banks of the river. The wines of the Loire valley have always been in demand in France and there is a world-wide market for the fresh dry white wines. The valley can be divided into four main vineyard areas which stretch across northern France from west to east.

Nantais District The area surrounding the city of Nantes in Brittany is the home of Muscadet. A few decades ago this wine was unknown outside the local area but is now one of the most popular wines of France. The best wine is entitled to the appellation *'Muscadet de Sèvre-et-Maine'* and its clean crisp acidity complements seafood. The wine comes from the muscadet grape and is invariably sold young. It must be bottled quickly to keep the pale gold colour and some of the wine is sold *'sur lie'*. This means it has gone straight from the cask to the bottle without being filtered, so that it possesses freshness and pétillance.

Anjou-Saumur District Anjou produces rosé wine, the most flavoursome of which is made from the cabernet grape and marketed as *'Cabernet d'Anjou Rosé'*. The best wines of the region are white and the appellations *'Anjou'* and *'Saumur'* signify the generic wines. Côteaux du Layon and Côteaux de l'Aubance produce quality sweet white wines from botrytis-affected chenin blanc grapes, whilst in Savennières the same grape makes perfumed dry white wine. The Saumur area has a deep chalky soil and is the centre of a fine sparkling-wine industry. Still wine from the chenin blanc grape is fermented in bottle in exactly the same way as champagne and marketed as *'Crémant de la Loire'*.

Touraine District The vineyards surround the city of Tours. Around the wine villages of Chinon and Bourgueil the cabernet franc grape produces soft, light-bodied red wines. The most interesting wines of this district are those of Vouvray – these light white wines have a honeyed character whether they are made dry, sweet or sparkling and the best of them have the unusual ability to improve in bottle for up to fifty years.

Central Vineyards This district is located in the centre of France and has a continental climate so that in some years the crop is very small or highly acid because of unfavourable weather. Sancerre and Pouilly-Fumé both come from here. These wines made from the sauvignon blanc grape have a distinctive aroma and are essentially straight-forward wines best drunk whilst young.

RHÔNE

The valley of the Rhône river, running as it does from north to south has been a natural route into Europe for over 3,000 years. Greek traders first brought the vine to Marseille about 600 BC; cultivation spread along the Rhône and was encouraged centuries later by the Roman invaders. Today the vineyards stretch for about 200 kilometres from Vienne to Avignon along the main route to the famous Mediterranean beaches. This is also the land of olives, herbs and garlic for the magnificent cuisine which complements the excellent wine. Much of the wine is sold under the general appellation 'Côtes-du-Rhône' and some villages are entitled to market their produce as 'Côtes-du-Rhône Villages'. The following areas have their own appellations.

Côte Rotie This small district has some of the steepest slopes in France so that vines must be cultivated entirely by hand. The wine is made from a mixture of black syrah and white viognier grapes which produces a perfumed red wine of great elegance that is somewhat softer than the wines of Hermitage.

Condrieu and Château Grillet The viognier grape is used to make dry white wine with a delicate flowery bouquet. Output is limited because the yield is small. Château Grillet has the distinction of being the only single estate to have its own appellation; it is also the smallest in France.

Hermitage The hill of Hermitage is one of the landmarks of the Rhône and the granite subsoil allows the syrah grape to produce strong rich red wines that need years to develop and in a good year must rate among the finest wines of France. There is also a golden dry white Hermitage noted for its longevity.

Crozes-Hermitage and St Joseph The communes at the foot of the hill of Hermitage and around the town of Tournon make light red wines using modern methods of production so that wine can be bottled and sold within a year of the vintage.

Cornas Red wine from the syrah is made by traditional methods and given two years in cask so that the best are similar to the wines of Hermitage.

St Péray This is the best sparkling wine of the Rhône valley and is made by the méthode champenoise from the marsanne grape, producing a full-bodied wine. Sparkling wine is also made near Die from the clairette grape.

Châteauneuf du Pape This district is named after the ruined castle that stands above the village. In the fourteenth century this was the summer residence of the schismatic Popes who lived in Avignon rather than Rome. The vineyards are covered with cream-coloured boulders about the size of a clenched fist. These absorb the heat of the sun through the day and then reflect it back on to the vines at night so that the grapes ripen thoroughly. Thirteen different grape varieties may be used for the wine. Made by the traditional methods it is big, alcoholic, tannic wine but some estates now use modern methods to produce a lighter, well-rounded wine which matures earlier. Quality wine that is bottled locally, rather than sold in bulk to a négociant, is marketed in a burgundy-shaped bottle with the old Papal arms embossed on the glass.

Gigondas and Lirac These two areas on the southern Rhône produce good red wine of a similar style to Châteauneuf. Lirac also makes a rosé.

Tavel Tavel, with its sandy soil, makes very good rosé by bottling early to keep plenty of fruit in the wine. It is meant to be drunk within two years of the vintage and most of the wine is made by the local co-operative.

Beaumes de Venise The co-operative in Beaumes de Venise makes a sweet fortified wine from the muscat grape. It is known as a *Vin Doux Naturel*. The grapes are harvested late to concentrate the sugar and brandy is added to stop fermentation and retain the natural sweetness. These wines are meant to be drunk whilst young and are best served chilled with dessert.

OTHER REGIONS OF FRANCE

Jura and Savoie This region is in eastern France near the Swiss border. *'Vin jaune'* is made by leaving white wine untouched in wooden casks for six years. During this time a *'flor'* or veil of yeasts spreads across the surface of the wine. Louis Pasteur's discovery of bacteria was a result of his research into this phenomenon. The strong, very dry, gold wine is best served chilled as an aperitif. The dessert wine *'vin de paille'* or straw wine comes from fruit that is laid out on straw mats after picking so that the moisture evaporates leaving shrivelled grapes full of sugar.

South-West France The red wines of Bergerac, Madiran, Buzet and Gaillac resemble to some degree those of Bordeaux and as the prices of the latter increase there is much interest in the nearby appellations. The 'Black Wine' of Cahors is no longer as meaty as it was in previous decades but it is still a deep-coloured, rich, tannic wine. The best sweet white wines come from Monbazillac near Bordeaux and from Jurançon in the foothills of the Pyrenees.

The Midi The region known to the French as Le Midi stretches around the Mediterranean coast from the Spanish border to Nice and falls naturally into two winemaking areas. The vineyards of Provence are in the hinterland of the French Riviera and seventy per cent of the vintage is made into rosé wine. The only areas entitled to their own appellations are Bellet, Palette, Cassis and Bandol. Most of the wine is consumed by the influx of holidaymakers. The western parts of the coast to the Rhône river is known as Languedoc-Roussillon and this is the largest wine region in France. Much of the wine is produced and marketed by co-operatives as simple *'vin de table'*. The full rich red wine of Fitou is entitled to its own appellation and good VDQS red wine comes from Corbières, Minervois and Costières du Gard. The sweet fortified wines known as *Vin Doux Naturel* come from Banyuls and Rivesaltes and the same style of wine is made from the muscat grape in Frontignan.

GERMANY

The River Rhine rises in the Swiss Alps just a few miles away from the source of the Rhône. The Rhine flows north to become Western Europe's major waterway and the lifeblood of Germany for agriculture and industry. Along its banks old fortress-castles guard the crests of the vine-covered hill slopes that are capable of producing some of the world's finest sweet white wines.

The cultivation of the vine in these parts spread up the valley of the Rhône from Marseilles into the valleys of the rivers Rhine and Mosel in very early times. In the third century AD, the Roman Emperor ordered the destruction of the vineyards of these areas, but fortunately the Emperor Probus who ruled in AD 276–282 gave an order for them to be replanted.

Some of the more important vineyards were laid out in the twelfth century. Quite a number of them belonged to various religious bodies but have since passed into other hands.

In an afternoon or early evening, many Germans will share a bottle or two of wine before tucking in to a hearty meal, because the quality wines are meant to be drunk by themselves. The chief quality of the best of German wine, whether from the Rhine or its tributary the Mosel, is balance. The amount of acid must be just enough to heighten the taste of grape sugar and flavouring substances and leave a long lingering spicy finish. Too much sugar makes flat uninteresting wine, too much acid can mean tart, almost sour wine. The Rhine is as far north as the vine can be profitably cultivated, so the grower has a constant battle with the weather to produce ripe enough grapes. In many years the German winemaker has to add sugar to the must while it is fermenting so that the yeasts have enough to work on to produce alcohol. This process does not sweeten the wine, but many of the cheaper whites do have sugar added at a later stage as a sweetener. The riesling grape is widely planted in areas where high quality wine can be produced, because it gives character and longevity. However, it is difficult to cultivate, so many growers plant other varieties and blend a proportion of riesling into their wine, although wine that bears the name of a grape must be made from eighty-five per cent of this variety. The müller-thurgau is a cross variety developed in Germany especially for local conditions. It produces a heavy crop that ripens two weeks earlier than the riesling and makes flowery, fruity wine ready for early drinking. The sylvaner variety makes good blending wine whilst the spätburgunder, a relation of the French pinot noir, produces Germany's red wines. Both the riesling and müller-thurgau are very suitable for developing the fungus botrytis which dehydrates the grapes, concentrating the natural sugars in the shrivelled fruit.

German wines are traditionally referred to as Hocks or Moselles. The latter name is the French spelling for the name of the river. Hock is an abbreviation of Hochheim, a town on the Rhine which for centuries was the port for shipping the Rhine wines to other parts of Europe, especially England. The term is generally used for all wine produced along the Rhine and marketed in brown bottles. Germany imports huge quantities of wine from other countries in the EEC,

142

especially Italy and France, which is then blended, bottled and packaged for sale on the home and export markets as Tafelwein or Sekt.

Mosel-Saar-Ruwer Along the river Mosel with its tributaries the Saar and Ruwer, the vines cling to every available square metre of the steep-sided valleys and the villages are dotted along the river bank. High quality wine comes from this region because the slate covering the hillsides holds in moisture and reflects the heat it has absorbed through the day back on to the vines. The riesling grape is a difficult one to cultivate as it ripens late and bears a small crop but it is widely planted here to produce very elegant wine. The pale green-gold whites of the Mosel, marketed in green bottles, are gentle wines with low alcohol and a refreshing acidity, often producing a tingle or *spritzig* on the tongue. Wine from the Saar is a little more austere whilst the Ruwer produces some of Germany's finest most delicate wines.

Rheingau This pocket of land on the right bank of the Rhine has a micro-climate that affords it the most sunshine and least frost of any part of west Germany. Here the aristocratic riesling grape produces firm steely wine with an intensely fragrant bouquet and a richness that lingers in the mouth. The very best vineyards face south on to the river and benefit from the sunshine reflected from its surface. Morning river mists rise through the vines providing humid conditions ideal for development of the *noble rot* that is so necessary to produce the great sweet wines.

The best of the Rheingau single vineyards make wine of such high quality that they are marketed under their own names and referred to as 'Estates' – Schloss Vollrads, Schloss Johannisberg and Schloss Rheinharthausen command very high prices for their wines. Up on the hill behind the town of Hattenheim is the State-owned estate known simply as the *'Steinberg'*. The government owns vineyards in many wine-producing areas but this is the undisputed jewel of the State Domain. The nearby Kloster Eberbach is an old monastery that has been converted to a winery and cellars for the Steinberger wine. It is also the home of the German Wine Academy which holds wine courses for anyone from any part of the world interested in learning about German wine. The Research Station at Geisenheim is acknowledged to be one of the world's foremost authorities in viticultural studies.

Nahe The area around Bad Kreuznach on the River Nahe has a great range of soils and the riesling, sylvaner and müller-thurgau grape varieties are all planted here. The crisp clean wines have plenty of fruit and are sometimes described as a bridge between the delicate Mosels and the spicy Rheingaus.

Rheinhessen The undulating country between the Nahe and Rhine rivers has rich soil suited to market gardening and the sylvaner grape. This is a fairly bland variety, so plantings of müller-thurgau have increased in recent years to give the wines more character. Co-operatives bottle most of the wine to be exported as Liebfraumilch. This must not be confused with a wine called *'Liebfrauenstift'* which comes from the vineyards around the Liebfrauenkirch – 'The Church of Our Dear Lady' – in Worms.

Rheinpfalz The dry sunny climate of this area situated just north of Alsace produces full-bodied grapey wines. Modern techniques are used by the co-operatives to make wine for early drinking and most is sold under grosslage names.

Hessische-Bergstrasse Most of the vineyards in this very small region near Worms are owned by the State. They produce bland wine meant for immediate consumption.

Baden The Baden vineyards stretch along the Rhine facing Alsace. The müller-thurgau grape produces agreeable fruity whites and the spätburgunder makes a good red wine. This area has some of the most modern and largest co-operatives in Europe and ninety per cent of the wine is produced by them mainly for the local market. The best vineyards are in *'Kaiserstuhl'* and *'Ortenau'*.

Ahr This is the most northern red wine district in the world. These light red wines are low in alcohol and are made from the spät-burgunder grape.

Wurttemberg Situated around the city of Stuttgart, this region produces more red than white wine. They are mixed together to make the pink Schillerwein which the locals consume in great quantity.

Mittelrhein The area around Bonn and Koblenz provides much of the wine for Sekt. It is particularly difficult land to cultivate because of steep slopes and high winds.

Franken Würzburg is the centre of the Franken region. The sylvaner grape makes fine dry steely whites that still have a Germanic fruiti-ness. Franconian wine is marketed in the squat *Bocksbeutel* and is sometimes referred to as *Steinwein*.

CLASSIFICATION OF GERMAN WINES

German Wines

Table wine		Quality wine	
Tafelwein	Deutscher Tafelwein	Qualitätswein bestimmer An-baugebiete (QbA)	Qualitätswein mit Prädikat (QmP)

144

Tafelwein Wine marketed as Tafelwein may come from anywhere within the EEC. Germany imports large quantities of wine which is blended, bottled and packaged for local consumption and export. The label must show a phrase similar to 'Produce of EEC' which is usually in very small print.

Deutscher Tafelwein Ordinary table wine made exclusively from grapes harvested in Germany with a minimum alcohol content of 8.5°. It may carry the name of a district (*Bereich*) or village.

Quality Wines A *Qualitätswein* must originate in one of the eleven authorized regions and be made from approved grape varieties grown in approved vineyards. Every year a tasting panel in each area checks a grower's wine to ensure its authenticity of style and allocate it one of the grades of Qualitätswein:

(a) **Qualitätswein bestimmer Anbaugebiete or QbA**
(Quality wine from an authorized region). These everyday drinking wines must show on the label the name of the authorized region and the term '*Qualitätswein*'. The label may show a vineyard – *Einzellage* or *Grosslage* – name if eighty-five per cent of the grapes come from there.

(b) **Qualitätswein mit Prädikat or QmP**
(Quality wine with predicate). The predicate is one of the five categories listed below. These are the fine German wines. For a wine to be awarded this classification it must come from a single district in one of the authorized regions. The label must show the term '*Qualitätswein mit Prädikat*' and the name of the authorized region. Prädikat wines are divided into these five styles depending on the degree of sweetness:
Kabinett light fairly dry white wine.
Spätlese wine from late harvested grapes with the resulting high sugar content.
Auslese superior rich wine from fully ripe or botrytis affected grapes which give a full ripe bouquet.
Beerenauslese finest quality wine made from individually picked overripe grapes that have usually been botrytis affected. This amber coloured wine can keep for almost a century.
Trockenbeerenauslese very expensive luscious wine, made from hand-picked shrivelled grapes, showing excellent balance and a full scented bouquet. The word 'trocken' means dry and refers to the dried-up grapes in this case.
Eiswein rare sweet wine made from hand-picked fully ripe grapes that have been left on the vines into early winter, then picked once the water content has frozen to ice. They are pressed immediately so that only the sugar, aromatic and flavouring substances are obtained thus producing intensely sweet fragrant wine. An Eiswein must be labelled as one of the last three categories – for example 'Auslese Eiswein'.

TERMS USED ON THE LABELS

Anbaugebiete These are the eleven authorized regions of wine production discussed above and each has its own particular characteristics.

Bereich Each region is divided into large districts. The Rhinegau has only one district but the Mosel has three. The basic QbA wine is sold under this district name, for example 'Bereich Nierstein'.

Grosslage This is a collection of vineyards with the same climatic conditions, soil and terrain. Wine from one vineyard can be blended with wine from other vineyards within the same grosslage. The 'middle class' wines of the district are sold with this name, for example 'Niersteiner Gutes Domtal'.

Village Names The village amidst a collection of vineyards (Grosslage) is a centre for the local winemaking community and so a village name is attached to the grosslage name, as in 'Piesporter Michelsberg' – Piesport being a village amongst the Michelsberg vineyards.

Einzellage This is an individual vineyard. One vineyard may have several owners, so the quality and character of wine from one einzellage may vary considerably depending on the skill and care of the producer. The finest wine is marketed under the einzellage name but it is also entitled to use the grosslage name. As the name of the grosslage is often the same as the most famous individual vineyard in it, it is difficult to tell whether a wine is from an einzellage or grosslage just by looking at the label.

AP Number This number is awarded by the inspection board of the region after tasting the wine and consists of a series of codes. All quality wine must carry its AP number on the label. Here is an example:

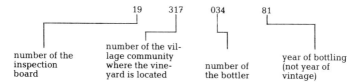

Erzeugerabfüllung This term means the wine has been bottled by its grower rather than sold in bulk to a shipper.

Weinkellerei This is a wine cellar or winery. A large-scale wine estate is known as a Weingut.

Liebfraumilch The name can only be used for a QbA wine made from grapes grown in the Rheinhessen, Rheinpfalz, Rheingau and Nahe. Most of these mild fairly sweet wines are sold under brand names.

Sekt The highest quality sparkling wine made in Germany is QbA Sekt which must be made from sixty per cent German wine. Much wine is imported and made into sparkling wine by the Charmat method and marketed as Schaumwein or Sekt.

Trocken or Diabetiker-Wein These are dry wines from which the sugar has been allowed to ferment out completely. They contain a maximum of 4 grammes of residual sugar and are therefore suitable for diabetics.

Picturesque script and unfamiliar words make German wine labels something of a mystery to many people, which makes them wary of the product. The name given to quality wines has up to four parts to it. The first word is the village name which always has the suffix 'er'; the second is either the einzellage or grosslage name which is the vital clue as to whether the wine is from a prestigious single vineyard or from the local collection of vineyards; the grape variety is third and if this is not stated it means that the wine is a blend with no particular outstanding character; the last word is the grading of quality wine that has been awarded to it. In this example the quality and price of one of these wines would be much higher than the other.

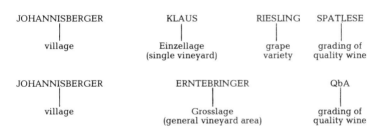

JOHANNISBERGER	KLAUS	RIESLING	SPATLESE
village	Einzellage (single vineyard)	grape variety	grading of quality wine

JOHANNISBERGER	ERNTEBRINGER	QbA
village	Grosslage (general vineyard area)	grading of quality wine

There are over 3,000 registered single vineyards in Germany. The names of the better known are included here to help the reader interpret the labels of the German wines most often seen outside the country.

BEREICH District name	GROSSLAGE Collection of vineyards	VILLAGE	EINZELLAGE Single quality vineyard within the Grosslage
Mosel-Saar-Ruwer			
Bernkastel	Badstube	Bernkastel	Doktor
	Kurfürstlay	Bernkastel	
	Michelsberg	Piesport	Goldtröpfchen
		Trittenheim	Altärchen
	Munzlay	Graach	Domprobst
		Zeltingen	Sonnenuhr
	Nacktarsch	Kröv	
	Schwarzlay	Erden	Treppchen
Saar-Ruwer	Römerley	Kasel	Hitzlay
	Scharzberg	Wiltingen	Hölle
		Ockfen	Bockstein
Zell-Mosel	Schwarze Katz	Zell	
Rheingau			
Johannisberg	Burgweg	Rüdesheim	Rosengarten
		Geisenheim	Rothenberg
	Daubhaus	Hochheim	Hölle
	Deutelberg	Erbach	Marcobrunn
		Hattenheim	Wisselbrunnen
	Erntebringer	Johannisberg	Klaus
	Honigberg	Winkel	Hasensprung
	Steinmacher	Eltville	Sonnenberg
		Kiedrich	Grafenberg
Nahe			
Kreuznach	Kronenberg	Bad Kreuznach	Kauzenberg
Schloss Bockelheim	Burgweg	Schlossbockelheim	Kupfergrube
Rheinhessen			
Nierstein	Auflangen	Nierstein	Olberg
	Gutes Domtal	Nierstein	
	Krötenbrunnen	Oppenheim	
	Rehbach	Nierstein	Pettenthal
Rheinpfalz			
Mittelhaardt-Deutsche	Honigsackel	Ungstein	
Weinstrasse	Mariengarten	Deidesheim	Herrgottsacker
		Forst	Pechstein
		Wachenheim	Gerümpel

QUALITY WINES FROM GERMANY

ITALY

The early inhabitants of Italy were drinking wine in the tenth century BC, well before the founding of Rome, although the Greeks brought 'modern' viticulture to Naples about three centuries later. Wine was such an integral part of daily life that Bacchus in Rome and Dionysus in Sicily were worshipped as gods of wine. Although Italians do not hold wine in such reverence as the French, they are now the world's biggest producers and consumers of wine. The range of wines is enormous and many styles, made from a number of grape varieties, are not seen outside their local areas. Until recently there was no uniform control over any aspect of winemaking, but in 1963 the Government passed a law controlling the names of origins of the wines to align Italy with the new EEC regulations.

The *Denominazione di Origine Controllata* – DOC – is only awarded once growers have supplied proof that a genuine typical wine style exists within a specified boundary and that grape varieties, yield per hectare, annual production and winemaking methods are all of a sufficiently high standard to warrant the DOC. A National Committee supervises over 200 DOC wines to ensure that they are grown, produced, aged, bottled and labelled according to regulations. Growers in some areas have organized themselves into consortiums to help maintain standards and promote their wine. A *Consorzio* issues an individual seal that can be found on the neck of a bottle guaranteeing the quality of the wine. There is one grading above that of DOC entitled DOCG, but the standard required is so high that very few wines have been awarded it. Ordinary table wines are known as Vini da Pasto and a DOC wine may be named after a grape variety or its region of origin. Generally the best wines come from Northern Italy, especially the provinces of Piedmont and Tuscany. Certain communes within a region are allowed to use the word *'classico'*, and *'superiore'* indicates that the wine has a slightly higher alcoholic content and has been allowed to age before release. *'Amabile'* refers to a semi-sweet style and *'abboccato'* to sweet wine.

Piedmont The province of Piedmont lies in the north-west of Italy and borders France. The most highly regarded red wine is 'Barolo' a full-bodied flavoursome red wine which will mature for many years. 'Barbaresco' is similar but slightly softer, whilst 'Gattinara' is reckoned by many to be more elegant than Barolo in a good year and demand exceeds its production. These wines are all made from the nebbiolo grape and are named after places. The Consorzio of Barolo growers issues a neck seal with a picture of a golden lion or a helmeted head. The barbera grape makes dark tannic wines which vary in quality and may be *'frizzante'* which is the Italian word for the tingling sensation on the tongue. The best are named after the grape with place name attached as in 'Barbera d'Alba' and will soften with bottle age. Asti is the centre of Italy's sparkling wine industry which uses the moscato grape to produce the sweetish fragrant wine by the Charmat and transfer methods. The best is sold as 'Asti Spumante and carries a neck label of the patron saint of Asti in blue and gold, while 'Moscato d'Asti' is cheaper and sweeter. Many of the big firms produce a dry sparkling wine by the méthode champenoise which is marketed under a prestigious brand name.

Tuscany The large area around Florence and Siena is the home of 'Chianti'. This, the most famous of all Italian wines, is made from a mixture of red and white grapes and there are two styles. The Chianti usually seen in the straw-covered flasks is fresh and grapey. A mixture of dried grapes is added to the young wine to encourage a slight secondary fermentation in bottle, softening the wine and giving the characteristic frizzante quality. Wine made like this is meant to be drunk young. Chianti made by the usual method and matured in oak casks for at least three years will develop into fine full-bodied wine with bottle age. This wine is known as Riserva and marketed in claret-shaped bottles. Unfortunately some Chiantis are quite bland as they contain too high a proportion of wine from the south of Italy or are of the first style and are dying of old age. The growers are divided into two main consorzii: Chianti Classico from the heart of the region bears the neck label insignia of a black cock; the Chianti Putto emblem of a cherub indicates quality wine from other vineyards. 'Brunello di Montalcino' is a very big aromatic red wine made from the brunello grape in the town of Montalcino. It is one of the most prestigious of Italian wines and is aged in cask for at least five years then in bottle for another two before it is sold. It then needs many more years before it is ready to drink.

Veneto From the area around the town of Verona in the north-east of Italy come three much exported wines. 'Valpolicella' and 'Bardolino' are red wines with a fruity bitterness and 'Soave' is a pale dry white with a slight floweriness. These wines are all meant to be drunk young and served chilled. 'Recioto' is a sweet red or white wine made from late picked grapes and Recioto Amarone is the popular medium dry version. 'Gambellara' is a light fresh white wine. The merlot grape provides other good drinking reds such as 'Merlot del Piave'.

Trentino-Alto Adige The vines in this region bordering Austria are set against a background of the Dolomites, creating one of the most picturesque sights in Italy. The Italian-speaking Trentino growers produce wines named for the classic grape varieties from which they are produced – cabernet, merlot, riesling, traminer and moscato. The German-speaking Alto Adige produces the finer red wines which are exported to Germany, Switzerland and Austria, the best known being 'Caldaro' and 'Santa Maddalena'.

Emilia-Romagna The area around Bologna, Parma and Modena is noted for the excellence of its cuisine and its large wine production. 'Sangiovese' is a dry, ruby red wine of excellent balance, 'Albana di Romagna' is a golden, fresh white wine (either dry or semi-sweet) and good 'Trebbiano' is a dry fairly acid wine which goes well with fish. 'Lambrusco' is a semi-sparkling red which froths in the glass when poured and has a pronounced prickle in the mouth. At its best this clean, fresh, dry wine goes well with rich meat and there is a sweeter version.

Lombardy The far north of Italy is a heavily industrialized region but some wines are grown on the steep terraces leading to the Alps. The red wines 'Sassellas', 'Grumello' and 'Inferno' are highly esteemed but most of them are drunk locally or exported to Switzerland.

Friuli-Venezia Wines from the environs of Trieste near the Yugoslav border are named after the pinot, cabernet and riesling grape varieties. The best-known wine is Tocai, a pale dry wine with a slightly bitter taste which complements the local seafood. This grape variety is in no way connected to the Hungarian grape of the same name which makes a dessert wine.

The Marches On this part of the Adriatic coast the Verdecchio grape produces pale straw-coloured wine with a pronounced lemony dryness. The best known is 'Verdecchio dei Castelli di Jesi' and is marketed in an elongated curved bottle.

Umbria This small region in central Italy is the home of the light delicate white wine named after the town of Orvieto. The grapes, mainly of the trebbiano variety, remain in open casks in the underground cellars until they begin to rot, so concentrating the sugar to produce amabile and abboccato 'Orvieto'. Good dry Orvieto is crisp and flowery with an underlying sharpness. Orvieto is always marketed in a flask-shaped bottle.

Latium The hills around Rome produce the clear, golden 'Frascati' wines. The juice is left in contact with the skins of the grapes for a longer period than most Italian whites so that frascati has a good grapey aroma and flavour. It is made in secco, amabile and abboccato styles. 'Est! Est! Est!', more notable for its name than for its quality, is light white wine made dry or sweet and marketed in a flat flask-shaped bottle.

Campania, Basilicata, Apulia, Calabria These regions in southern Italy produce vast quantities of highly alcoholic red wine, much of which is exported to strengthen the blended 'table wines' of Europe. The equally vast quantities of white wine are transported to Turin to become the base for vermouth. The best-known wine is 'Lacrima Christi' from the slopes of Mount Vesuvius near Naples. However, there is no protection for this name and it usually indicates cheaper red, white or rosé wine that may be dry or sweet.

Sicily Wine has been made on the island of Sicily for over three thousand years. Vines are grown on the slopes of Mount Etna. The red is a fine velvety wine while the full-bodied white has a fresh grapiness.

Marsala is a dessert wine from north-west Sicily. It is made from a blend of aromatic white wine, brandy and heated must which is matured in a solera system. It is probably best known as an ingredient of zabaglione, the frothy sweet made from egg and Marsala wine. Marsala Fine varies in style from dry to sweet and requires a minimum of four months ageing and must be no less than 17% alcohol by volume. Marsala Superiore styles range from dry to sweet. They must be a minimum of two years old and no less than 18% alcohol by volume. The name Marsala Speciale is given to Marsala with added flavours such as almond, coffee or fruit. Marsala Vergine is much drier than the others and is normally served lightly chilled as an aperitif. It is aged for a minimum of five years and must contain at least 18% alcohol by volume.

PORTUGAL

The wine of Portugal comes from north of the River Tagus. The climate is moderate with long sunny summers, and Atlantic breezes bring enough rain to ensure that there is a good harvest virtually every year. There are seven regions authorized by the Government and wine from these regions has an official paper seal on the neck of the bottle. However, the accent is on non-regional wine, because much of the wine is sold to big firms who blend it for marketing under brand names. Consequently the everyday drinking wines of Portugal have more character than most of their European counterparts.

Minhao The region of Minhao is in the far north of Portugal. The land here is vital for food production and so the local people train their vines on trees or granite posts, well above the vegetable crops below. This also protects the grapes against mildew in the damp climate although they have to be harvested from ladders. Wines from here are known as 'vinhos verdes' which means 'green wines', because of their faint underripe taste. The wines cause a slight tingling sensation on the tongue known as pétillance. This happens because the wine has a very high acid content. A few weeks after bottling a spontaneous secondary fermentation in the bottle softens the acid and a small amount of carbon dioxide is given off in the process which is absorbed into the wine to give the tingling sensation. White vinho verde, best known abroad, is very pale with a flowery bouquet and delicate lemony flavour. Red vinho verde is quite a hard dry wine and constitutes seventy per cent of the local production.

Dao The mountainous inland region around the Dao river is planted with a number of grape varieties. The continental climate and granite soil combine to produce quality wine which is made by co-operatives. There are few single estate wines as most of it is sold in bulk to the big firms who blend and mature it into wine known as *vinho maduro*. Some firms do market a well aged wine as a Dao Reserva.

Douro The Douro River is best known for port but it also produces red, white and rosé wines. Vila Real is the centre of the mighty empire of Mateus Rosé. This is made from black grapes with white pulp, which are fermented in refrigerated tanks then impregnated with a little carbon dioxide to give the rosé its characteristic sparkle.

Lisbon The vines that grow in the beach area around Lisbon are ungrafted stock because they are safe from the phylloxera which is unable to penetrate the sand. These vines are not pruned but allowed to re-root themselves in the traditional Roman method of cultivation. The red grapes produce dark tannic wine which needs many years to mature fully and Bucellas and Carcavelos are the straw-coloured fresh dry white wines. The red and white moscatel grapes grown around Setúbal are used to make dessert wines. Partly fermented wine and grape spirit are put into casks with fresh grape skins so that the full flavoured aroma of muscat penetrates the wine. It is matured in wood for up to twenty-five years and marketed as Moscatel de Setúbal.

Land is so precious in northern Portugal that vines are trained high above the ground and the grapes must be harvested from ladders.

SOUTH AFRICA

Vines were first planted in South Africa over three hundred years ago by Jan van Riebeeck, commander of the first Dutch settlement at the Cape of Good Hope. Many of the settlers were French Huguenots who had fled Europe to escape religious persecution. They extended the vineyards and improved the quality of winemaking so that by 1711 South African wines were becoming known abroad, especially the wines of Constantia. In 1805 the Cape became British territory and export to Britain flourished under the protection of trade agreements. However, the abolition of these preferential tariffs in 1861 and the decimation of the vineyards by phylloxera caused the collapse of the export trade. The vines were grafted on to American rootstock to safeguard them from the disease and within a few years the vineyards were flourishing to such an extent that by 1917 overproduction presented an even greater threat to the industry. To protect their interests the growers formed a central organization known as the Co-operative Wine Growers' Association – the KWV. The South African government gave this body the authority to fix minimum prices and under its guidance winemaking was established as a modern industry and export was resumed to Britain and Holland. The South African Wine Farmers' Association Limited was established in Britain to market South African wines abroad on behalf of the KWV. One of the main functions of the KWV is to absorb the surplus wine produced in the Cape, so countering the effects of overproduction. The KWV fixes annually the unsaleable percentage of the vintage on the local market and each grower delivers this portion of his crop to the KWV. This guarantees a stable local market price and the KWV is able to dispose of the surplus by exporting it under the KWV label or distilling it for brandy and neutral spirit.

In 1972 a system of control of origin was instituted to ensure that wines actually derive from the place stated on the label, and to maintain quality levels. The Cape wine-growing area is divided into five main regions and each region consists of a number of districts. For example, the Coastal Region includes the districts of Stellenbosch, Paarl and Swartland.

There are twelve of these districts and some of the farms within a district may be grouped together to form a ward. Thus a ward is a collection of several farms that have a similar style of viticulture and there are eighteen of these. There are also about fifty-three single estates which are recognized as producing fine wines. The Wine and Spirit Board is responsible for ensuring that a wine states correctly its origin, grape variety and vintage. Every bottle of wine passed by the board carries a seal which includes up to three coloured bands on the neck of the bottle. A blue band guarantees the wine comes from the place of origin stated on the label, the red band guarantees the vintage year and the green band guarantees the grape varieties are as stated on the label. Each seal carries an identification number. If the word 'Estate' is printed on the label it means that the wine is solely from one of the recognized estates whilst the word 'Superior' indicates wine of superior quality according to standards laid down by the Wine and Spirit Board.

The wine-producing districts are in the south-west corner of South Africa and are grouped in a sweeping curve that follows the coastline from the Olifants River in the north around to the Breede River in the south. The vines are harvested from late January to early March which is the end of summer in the southern hemisphere.

Constantia This district is located close to Cape Town and the suburbs of the city are encroaching on the vineyards. The warm dry summers and sea influence allow the production of fine quality wines from chenin blanc – known locally as steen – pinotage, cabernet sauvignon and shiraz grapes. The pinotage is a grape variety of South African origin, a cross of pinot noir and cinsaut varieties. It makes assertive, full-bodied wine which ages well. Groot Constantia, the estate which first made wine in 1679, is now state-owned and noted for its quality red wine.

Durbanville This district is located in the hills to the north of Cape Town and the city is also expanding in this direction. The mild climate and red granite soil mean that this district is particularly suited to the production of quality red wine and liqueurs. The two properties defined as wine estates are Meerendal and Diemersdal.

Stellenbosch This is a small district around the towns of Stellenbosch and Strand. White wines are produced on the sandy soil in the west whilst quality red wines come from the mountain slopes in the east. Twenty-six estates produce wine of origin and there are six co-operatives. Many of these estates export their fine wines including Goede Hoop, Jacobsdal, Meerlust, Middelvlei, Simonsig and Uitkyk.

Paarl This district lies some sixty kilometres from the coast and is centred around the inland town of Paarl in the Berg River valley. The French settlers first made wine here in the seventeenth century and the district is well known for its white wine. The KWV has its administrative headquarters and winery in Paarl and many growers deliver their grapes straight to this winery or to one of the ten co-operatives. The nine estates which produce wine of origin are Backsberg, De Zoete Inval, Fairview, Johann Graue, Landskroon, Boschendal, Villiera, Welgemeend and Laborie.

Little Karoo This is a large inland district that stretches from the town of Montague in the west to De Rust in the far east and is separated from the Indian Ocean by a mountain range. Rainfall is low because of the mountains and so the vineyards are irrigated. The district is known for its muscadel wines. Most wines are made by co-operatives and the one estate producing wine of origin is Die Krans.

Overberg This district surrounds the town of Caledon and is devoted mainly to the production of white table wines and dessert wines made from the muscat grape, known locally as hanepoot. Wine production is in the hands of one local co-operative.

Piquetberg This district is on the west coast and has a low rainfall and high temperatures. The local co-operative takes the harvest and produces dry white and dessert wines.

Robertson This district surrounds the inland town of Robertson which is situated in the Breede River valley. Vines have only been planted here for fifty years and it is best known for its muscat dessert wines. The largest brandy distiller in South Africa is in Robertson and the seven estates producing wine of origin are De Westhof, Excelsior, Goedverwacht, Mont Blois, Rietvallei, Weltevrede, Zandvliet.

Swartland This district is on the west coast, centred on the town of Malmesbury. The Atlantic breezes moderate the naturally warm climate and irrigation is only used when necessary. Swartland is a relatively new wine-producing area and the local co-operatives make dry white wine and distilling wine. There is one estate, Allesverloren, which produces wine of origin.

Swellendam This district stretches from the south coast inland to the town of Bonnievale. The rainfall is low and the local co-operatives produce white wines and distilling wine.

Tulbagh This is a small area surrounding the town of Tulbagh. It is well known for high quality white wines and sherries. The three estates are Montpellier, Theuniskraal and Twee Jonge Gezellen.

Worcester This district is located inland around the town of Worcester. There are seventeen co-operatives in the area, producing dry white and dessert wines. The three wines estates are Opstal, Lebensraum and Bergsig.

Modern technology enables the big wine firms to meet the world-wide demand for white wine. These *horizontal presses* extract the juice from the grapes within a few minutes.

ARGENTINA

Argentina ranks fifth among the world's wine producers and almost all of the output is consumed within the country. Vine cuttings were taken to Argentina by the Spanish conquistadors but it was the Italian immigrants of the nineteenth century who were responsible for cultivating and developing the vineyard areas so that by the turn of the century winemaking was a profitable industry. The most widely planted variety is the red and white criolla grape which is grown in California, where it is known as the mission grape. Plantings of the noble grape varieties are increasing because Argentina is interested in establishing an export market.

The wine region is in the west of the country in the foothills of the Andes mountains and stretches from the Salta province in the north through the provinces of Catamarca, La Rioja, San Juan, Mendoza to Rio Negro in the south. MENDOZA, which borders Chile, used to be a huge inland desert, but canals now irrigate the vineyards with water from the melting snows of the Andes. This province provides ninety per cent of Argentina's table wine and includes some huge wineries. The SAN JUAN province is also irrigated and the hot climate is particularly suited to the production of base wine for vermouth. Most of the country's enormous raisin crop comes from this area. RIO NEGRO, to the south of Mendoza, is much cooler and produces quality white wine and sparkling wine.

BRAZIL

Although Brazil was settled by the Portuguese, it was not until the Italian immigrants arrived after 1870 that viticulture became a local industry. The European vine cuttings they took with them did not flourish in the tropical climate and so the native American vine labrusca was widely planted. The characteristic 'foxy' taste of this grape flavours the wine, and it is used to make most of the everyday drinking wine. Brazil makes a full range of table, fortified and sparkling wines and imports wine to make enough vermouth to satisfy the local demand. Most of the country is too humid to permit viticulture and it is mainly confined to RIO GRANDE DO SUL which is in the southern area bordering Uruguay.

CHILE

Chile occupies the long narrow strip of land between the Pacific Ocean and the Andes mountains. Climatically the country is well suited to agriculture, because the cold offshore current moderates the temperature, creating ideal conditions for many crops including grapes. Chilean wine was well known in Europe during the period of Spanish colonization; the country has made wine for over 400 years and has never suffered from phylloxera. The person responsible for modernizing the industry was Silvestre Ochagavia who employed a French viticulturalist in 1851 and planted cuttings of the noble grape varieties of Europe. His success led to a great expansion of the area under vine and strict adherance to the French method of winemaking, so that the accent has remained on quality. The Chilean government actively promotes the wines abroad and although Brazil, Columbia and Venezuela are the main importers, the USA is an important market for fine wine and there is an increasing demand in Europe for the bulk wine.

There are three main wine-producing regions in Chile. The northern-most vineyards are in ATACAMA and COQUIMBO provinces, where there is virtually no rainfall. All vineyards are irrigated and most of the wine from them is distilled to make pisco, the Chilean equivalent of brandy. The region from ACONCAGUA to TALCA is ideally suited to viticulture, especially in the Maipo valley. Most of Chile's table wine is grown here and the cabernet grape makes particularly fine red wine. Some of the private estates are so large that they may have over 2,000 people living on them. The southern provinces from MAULE to BIO BIO have a very high rainfall and most of the wine from here is sold in bulk.

SPAIN

Spain is mentioned as an exporter of wine in the early records of civilization and her vines were bearing so prolifically by the first century BC that the Roman conquerors limited new plantings in Spain to protect Italian wine growers. Spanish wine was imported by Britain as early as the fourteenth century and the dark fruit wine was used to give body to the wines of Bordeaux until French regulations prohibited the practice. Today Spain has more land devoted to viticulture than any other country in Europe and is the third largest wine producer. Most of the Spanish sparkling wines, vermouths and brandies are consumed locally, and large quantities of wine are exported in bulk for sale as branded wine. The best wines bear the names of their regions of origin with the most highly prized coming from Rioja. Wines are made from a mixture of grape varieties fermented together and the warm spicy flavour noticeable in many Spanish wines comes from long maturation in oak casks. In 1970 the Government broadly defined the regions of wine production and set up a local authority, the Consejo Regulador, responsible for enforcing the new quality regulations in each area.

Rioja The region is located in the mountainous centre of northern Spain and is divided for the purposes of wine production into three areas. The Rioja Alta in the west has a fairly mild climate and there are numerous pockets of vineyards in the hills, with their own microclimates, producing excellent quality grapes to make the light-bodied wines. The Rioja Alavesa can experience the winds of the Pyrenees to the north, and the wines are stronger with more body. The Rioja Baja in the east has long, hot, dry summers contributing the high alcohol content to the local wine, most of which is used for blending with cheaper wines. Four major grape varieties are mixed to make the best Riojas which are aged for a minimum of two years in American oak casks. 'Reserva' wines are aged for about five years whilst 'Gran Reserva' wines may stay in cask for ten years. Wine that has been matured this way loses its fresh red fruitiness to become tawny coloured with a distinctive vanilla bouquet and silky texture. White wines are also aged in cask. Unfortunately some wines have too much oak character and the modern trend is to bottle a little earlier to retain more fruit flavour. Only a very good year is stated as a vintage (*consecha*) usually on Reservas, but much good Rioja is sold as non-vintage wine. Production plants are responsible for most of the bulk wine but there are about thirty large respected cellars (*bodegas*) which make and sell their own wines. Most of them have vineyards but they also buy grapes and blend the wines to produce house styles. The official seal of the Consejo is a symbol in the shape of a postage stamp with the word Rioja across it.

Catalonia The Alella area, just north of Barcelona, produces pale, light-bodied white wine and the Penedes area, south of the city, makes good quality red and white wines. This region has a thriving sparkling wine industry and the best of it is made by the méthode champenoise and labelled Espumoso.

Navarre This is situated just north of Rioja. The best wines of this region are made from the same grape varieties and have a similar style to those of the Rioja Baja.

Valencia and Alicante The coast of Spain produces huge quantities of ordinary blended red, white and rosé table wine for export and local consumption.

La Mancha This large inland plateau experiences long, very hot summers so that its wines are high in alcohol but lack the acid needed for good balance. Much of the wine is blended for local consumption and the rest distilled for brandy.

Malaga The region produces unusual wine from grapes dried in the sun on straw mats then blended with concentrated grape juice after fermentation. It is matured in a solera system resulting in rich dark sweet wine.

Galicia Situated in the extreme north-west of Spain just across the border from Minhao, the best of the Galician wines are 'vinos verdes' – green-tasting wines similar to those of Portugal.

SWITZERLAND

Switzerland's geographical location bordering France, Germany and Italy gives the Swiss easy access to Europe's fine wines. Although producing a reasonable amount of wine locally, it is a big importer. The wines of Burgundy, Alsace and Piedmont are sold from the 'cellar door' to a constant stream of Swiss in search of wine. Swiss vineyards must have high yields to remain economic and so the heavy-bearing grape varieties are planted, fertilized and irrigated. There is not enough natural sugar in the grapes of this cold climate and so fermentation is encouraged by the addition of sugar to the must to raise the alcohol level.

Lake Geneva The area around the lake and along the Rhône valley is an important wine region. The chasselas grape is widely planted and produces fresh white wine known variously as 'Dorin', 'Dézaley' or 'Perlan'. The canton of Vaud, which borders France, is a centre for red wine production from the classic gamay and pinot noir grapes; the wine is labelled 'Savagnin'.

Valais The canton of Valais stretches along the Rhone valley at the foot of the Swiss Alps. In this region the chasselas grape is used to make 'Fendant' and the sylvaner for 'Johannisberg'. 'Dôle' is made from a mixture of pinot noir and gamay grapes, and is regarded as Switzerland's best red wine.

Ticino The merlot grape is widely planted in this canton bordering Italy to make soft round wines. The best of them are labelled as 'Viti'.

Neuchâtel Red wine from the pinot noir grape and white wine from the chasselas grape are both named after the town – 'Neuchâtel'. The white wine is often pétillant and there is a sparkling Neuchâtel.

USA

The early settlers found that America had an abundance of native vines 'Vitis labrusca' so these were used to make the first local wine. However, it had a very unusual taste and eventually European vines 'Vitis vinifera' were shipped across to make wines which tasted similar to those of France and Germany. Unfortunately the European vines were not hardy enough to resist the 'foreign' diseases that attacked them. Most succumbed to mildew and those that survived it fell victim to phylloxera. This microscopic louse feeds on the vine roots by piercing the bark with its snout and drawing out the sap. It secretes a poisonous saliva which infects the wound and prevents it from healing so that the plant eventually withers and dies. This louse had lived among the American vines for centuries without doing any apparent harm but the European vines had tenderer roots and were highly susceptible.

Unfortunately, in about 1863 American vines carrying the louse were taken to France for experimental planting and within thirty years the devastating phylloxera had invaded almost every wine-growing area in the world from Germany to Australia. Ironically it reached California around 1873 as a passenger on European vines imported fro experimental planting, seriously damaging the vineyards. This tiny louse virtually brought world wine production to a standstill because the sick vines had to be ripped out in an attempt to stop the spread of the disease. The solution to the problem was the grafting of European vines on to the American rootstock, so that the louse could not damage the roots but the grapes could be those of the European varieties. Extensive replanting of grafted vines took place all over the world at the end of the nineteenth century and American wines were just beginning to gain recognition when Prohibition delivered an even more devastating blow to the industry. Most commercial growers ripped out the vines once again, this time to plant table grapes or other fruit. Amateur winemaking was still legal but lack of knowledge meant that most people used table grapes so that after Prohibition was repealed the commercial wine industry had to be almost entirely rebuilt. It takes many years for a vine to mature enough to produce quality wine, but by the 1960s the industry was functioning on a serious commercial basis. The next decade was a period of consolidation and in the late 1970s the world became aware once again that the USA was a quality producer.

The size of the population means that the USA consumes a huge quantity of wine, even though the individual citizen is not a big drinker. In California, some of the largest wineries in the world produce millions of litres of everyday drinking wine, known as jug wine, and vast quantities of wine are imported from Europe.

American wines can be grouped broadly into three categories: branded wines; generic wines which have such names as California Burgundy; and varietal wines which are named after the grape variety. The wines come either from the western region dominated by California or the eastern region centred around New York. If the word 'American' is on a label it means the wine is a blend from different states.

California This area has always had the climate and soil suitable for vine cultivation and when the Franciscan missionaries introduced one of the European *'Vitis vinifera'* vines around 1769 it thrived so well that it became known as the mission grape. Many of the settlers who moved west were from wine-producing regions of Europe and possessed the skills necessary to found the wine industry. One such immigrant was Colonel Harászthy, a Hungarian refugee who opened the Buena Vista winery in 1857 in the Sonoma Valley. This was probably the largest winery in the world at that time, and its wine was even sold in London. Harászthy is thought to have brought the mysterious zinfandel grape variety back from Europe on one of his research trips although now it is grown exclusively in California. Today California has more land under vine than Germany and provides seventy per cent of the total American wine production, including all the quality wine. It is also the home of the research department of the University of California at Davis which has been responsible for many of the advances made in the post-war wine industry that have changed winemaking from a cottage industry into a technological science largely funded by big business interests.

Growers use mechanization wherever possible to assist in vine cultivation, harvesting and transportation. Many of the vineyards are mechanically planted five rows at a time. Sprinkler systems are used not only to irrigate the vines but to provide protection against spring frost (a thin layer of water sprayed over the bud quickly turns to ice which acts as a shield). At vintage time much of the work is done at night; the mechanical harvesters shake the grapes off the vine and tumble them on to a conveyor belt which empties them into tanker lorries. At most wineries fermentation takes place in large temperature-controlled stainless steel vats and much American wine never sees any oak casks at all but is stored outside in stainless steel tanks which are virtually refrigerators.

Classic grape varieties are used for quality wines which may be all of one variety or a traditional blend such as cabernet and merlot. California's own grape, the zinfandel, makes full-bodied inky wine that was used for years to give backbone to the blended California Clarets. Some makers are able to produce a much lighter style of wine which is marketed under the grape name; these wines have a raspberry-like aroma. Many experimental techniques are employed and one of the more unusual aspects of winemaking in California is the novel method used to produce rich sweet wines from the 'noble rot' botrytis. In Sauternes and Germany this fungus spreads over the vineyards in late autumn dehydrating the berries and leaving shrivelled grapes full of concentrated sugar. In the Sonoma area one grower cultivates botrytis spores on tomato juice under laboratory conditions, then sprays them on grapes laid out on trays which are then covered with polythene sheeting. The humid conditions under the sheeting cause the spores to incubate within twenty-four hours and the grapes are then dried as quickly as possible. The maker is able to produce the equivalent of a German Auslese after five days, and although this method is not in widespread use it does serve to show the level of technology operating in the Californian wine industry.

The wine regions can be divided into those vineyards north of San Francisco in the Mendocino, Sonoma and Napa areas and those that stretch south of San Francisco through Santa Clara, Monterey and San Benito. The wineries themselves range from factory-sized concerns supplied by thousands of hectares of vines to small 'boutique' wineries set amidst equally tiny vineyards. The most important quality area is the NAPA VALLEY. It is about one hour's drive from San Francisco and this thirty mile valley is strictly wine country. Most styles of wines can be made here because grapes requiring cooler weather can be planted on the slopes whilst those on the flat valley bed receive full sunshine. The acknowledged champion of the Napa is Robert Mondavi whose own fine wines are of impeccable quality made from the classic cabernet sauvignon, pinot noir and chardonnay grapes. His faith in the Napa as a place capable of producing fine wine through a combination of the knowledge of the New and Old Worlds has been vindicated by the present high prices the best wines command and the land boom now evident in the valley. Small producers of fine wines include 'Heitz', 'Stags Leap', 'Spring Mountain', 'Freemark Abbey' and 'Phelps'. The 'Schramsberg' winery is entirely devoted to its excellent sparkling wine and the French house of Moët and Chandon have been producing sparkling wine at 'Domaine Chandon' since 1977. The 'Christian Brothers' owned by the Catholic Order of the same name makes particularly good brandy. Large-scale quality producers active in the valley include Heublin's 'Inglenook' and Coca Cola's 'Sterling' wineries.

The sparkling wine firm of Korbell is in the SONOMA area along with the Souverain, Sebastiani, Dry Creek and Buena Vista wineries. The Gallo winery in the San Joaquin valley was established in 1933 by two brothers and is now the largest winery in the world producing forty per cent of California's total wine output. Other giant concerns making a full range of about forty wine styles are Almadén and Paul Masson.

On the east coast, vines are grown in New England, New Jersey and Pennsylvania but the most important areas are in **New York State** around the Finger Lakes and Hudson River Valley. Most of the wines are made from the native grape varieties and their odd 'foxy' taste means that their distribution is not widespread. The concord grape is also used to make most of the commercial grape juice and kosher wine of the USA. The native catawba and delaware varieties are used in the making of local 'champagne' and the sparkling 'Cold Duck', although in the Finger Lakes district French hybrid grapes are now being included more frequently in the blend for sparkling wine.

SPIRITS
AND BEERS

BRANDY

Brandy is a spirit distilled from wine. Spirit from distilled fruits other than grapes is referred to by the name of the fruit coupled with the word 'brandy'. These fruit brandies are classified as *eaux-de-vie*. The word 'brandy' is a generic term and so can be made anywhere. Cognac and armagnac are examples of French brandies but there are a host of other brandies in France and every wine growing country in the world produces brandy.

COGNAC

Some seventy miles north of Bordeaux in western France lie the Charente and Charente-Maritime departments. Almost in the centre of their combined area is the town of Cognac which has given its name to the world's finest brandy. For centuries trade has been the main activity of this region because of its ports and navigable waterways. In Roman times the people of the Charente mastered the arts of viticulture and extraction of salt from seawater, so that by the Middle Ages the Dutch, Norwegian and English traders were shipping wheat, salt and wine from Charente to the rest of Europe.

The wine itself was highly acidic and light bodied which meant it did not travel well. Sometime in the mid-sixteenth century the wine was boiled down to strengthen it. There were added advantages to this practice as it saved space on ships and helped avoid taxation which was then levied on bulk. This *Brandewijn*, a Dutch word meaning 'burnt wine', was regarded as a wine concentrate to be drunk diluted with water.

By the end of the eighteenth century, the superiority of older brandies was recognized because of the quality of the wines in barrel that had made the long sea voyage to the colonies. Unfortunately in 1880 phylloxera completely destroyed the vineyards and cognac has only regained a substantial share of the world's brandy market in the past thirty years. The growers are not allowed to distil their wine into spirit unless they have a licence. There are only about 2,000 who are licensed to make brandy, and they must only use their own wine. Most growers sell their wine to one of the 25 co-operatives or 250 professional distillers. These firms then sell the newly distilled spirit to one of the cognac houses which uses the spirit in its blend, matures the cognac and eventually markets it. These cognac houses make the registered brands, many of which are household names in France and abroad. Very few cognac houses own vineyards and although most do buy wine and distil their own spirit they also have to purchase spirit to meet their requirements. The essential art in cognac production is the blending process which is the domain of these houses. Although there are about 250 cognac houses, four or five of them control the major part of the market. Exports account for eighty per cent of cognac sales with the UK, USA, Germany and Hong Kong being the most important outlets.

The Vineyards
The area permitted to make cognac has been legally defined since 1909. It is classified into six regions of descending quality, the determining factors being the soil, climate and light. A high proportion of chalk in the soil produces fine spirit and as the chalk content is reduced so is the quality of the brandy. The best vineyards are sheltered from the harsh sea winds while being close enough to the coast to escape the extreme temperature range of the inland continental climate.

Grande Champagne The French word 'champagne' is derived from the Latin 'campania', meaning 'open countryside' and in this context must not be confused with the region of the same name. The area surrounding the town of Cognac has crumbly chalky soil which is a major factor in producing spirit with exceptional delicacy and finesse that takes many years to mature.

Petite Champagne There is little difference in the soil of this area but there is a slight variation in the micro-climate. Consequently the spirit is very similar in style to that of Grande Champagne, but it matures more quickly.

Borderies This is quite a small area to the north-west of Cognac with deep clay soil although the climate is the same as the Champagne areas. Borderies spirit is highly regarded as blending material because of its tendency to firmness.

Fins Bois This large area contains much farming land and forest. The soil is gravelly and the spirit matures early.

Bons Bois The proximity to the sea and clay soil of this region produce a broad-tasting spirit. Only a small percentage of the land in the area is planted with cognac vines and most of the grapes are used in the production of cheap cognac.

Bois Ordinaires Parts of this area border the coast and the soil contains sandstone. Exposure to this maritime influence results in a fairly coarse spirit used in cheaper blends.

PRODUCTION OF COGNAC

The Base Wine About ninety-eight per cent of distilling wine comes from the St Emilion grape although Folle Blanche and Columbard are authorized. The wine is allowed to ferment in huge vats for three to five weeks and neither additional yeasts nor sulphur dioxide is permitted. This produces a sour high-acid wine with a low alcohol content. The wine must be distilled before the spring as a secondary fermentation which occurs naturally around that time would reduce the acid content. Although nine litres of base wine are required for every one litre of cognac, only about half of the wine actually produced in the Charente is distilled.

The Still A square brick furnace acts as a base for a small copper still known as the *Charente*, the capacity of which does not exceed thirty hectolitres. A curve of copper tubing known as the *swan throat* connects the still to a condenser which is a copper coil encased in a cold water tank.

First Distillation It takes about three hours for the wine to boil; the heat is kept steady as the steam and brandy elements pass up the swan throat and are condensed by the cooled piping. The resulting milky liquid, known as *brouillis*, is 26–32% alcohol.

Second Distillation The brouillis are then returned to the still and reheated. The first liquid to appear – the *heads* – is added to the next lot of brouillis for a further recycling. The *heart* fraction (*bonne chauffe*) is 70% alcohol whilst the *tails* are returned to the next brouillis to be heated in order to remove any remaining alcohol.

Ageing The infant cognacs are matured in Limousin or Tronçais oak casks. These are made from staves that have been weathered for four years to remove excess tannin from the wood. In many cognac houses new casks are used for new brandy as the raw spirit can stand the impact of strong tannin and draws colour from the new wood. After a year the spirit is racked into a slightly older cask and to stop it absorbing too much wood character it is eventually transferred to an older larger cask. The paler light-bodied cognacs will have been matured only in old casks which produce a more delicate spirit.

Casks must be topped up and sampled to ensure that a drinkable product is developing and small amounts of cane sugar or caramel may be added. As the brandy is absorbed by the wood of the cask, oxygen is absorbed by the spirit through the pores of the wood. The brandy becomes a beautiful amber colour, from contact with the wood, and assumes a perfumed vanilla bouquet.

There is, however, some loss from this process. In fact the French Excise authorities allow for a loss of 5% pure alcohol per year, but the loss usually averages 2–3%. The loss can be affected by dampness or dyness for if the warehouses (*chais*) are kept too damp, the brandy will lose strength, but if they are kept too dry it will evaporate too quickly. This is the reason for the great care taken in looking after the brandy. Huge capital is involved, for the older a brandy gets, the greater the financial risk. The oldest and most precious cognacs are kept in a special part of the chais known as the *paradis*. Each house holds its reserve in cask until it is between fifty and seventy years old when it is transferred to glass demijohns, because further ageing might make the spirit too woody. It is then rested quietly until it is needed for blending into the finest quality cognac.

Blending The cellar master (*maître de chai*) is responsible for producing a consistent style of cognac that can be immediately identified as the product of a particular house. He is constantly sampling the different casks to check on colour, bouquet and flavour and to determine which casks should be blended together. Any one brand contains many brandies of varying ages and types, and blending is done one stage at a time with long rest periods in between to allow the brandies to marry together.

Once the first distillation for *cognac* has begun it continues uninterrupted for eight hours and must be carefully tended at all times.

Bottling Distilled water is used to reduce the cognac to the required strength; it is then filtered, rested and bottled, the corks having been dipped in cognac.

STYLES OF COGNAC

Three Star By French law the youngest brandy in a cognac need only be eighteen months old although many countries to which it is exported, including Britain, require that it be a minimum of three years old. The stars or the term VS indicate a firm's standard blend.

VSOP The initials stand for Very Superior Old Pale. Cognac bearing this term is at least four and a half years old although many houses include much older spirit in the blend.

Vintage In 1963 the cognac houses were prohibited from marketing vintage cognac, i.e. the brandy of a single year. Until 1973 a few vintage cognacs were matured in Britain but entry into the EEC meant this was discontinued there also.

Early Landed This is a very young cognac that has been shipped specifically to Britain and matured in cask in a British bond. In the damp climate the cognac develops a different flavour and is paler because the spirit takes on less colour from the wood.

Late Bottled This is cognac that has remained in cask for a much longer period and the date of bottling will be shown on the label. Many of the cognacs that have matured in British bonds are late bottled because the damp air slows the maturation rate.

Luxury Cognacs Most houses produce a top quality cognac which is a blend of very old fine brandies. These cognacs carry prestigious names such as VVSOP, Vielle Réserve, Grand Réserve, Napoleon, XO, Extra, Cordon Bleu, Cordon Argent, Paradis and Antique. Many of them are only available in small quantity.

Fine Champagne This term may be used for cognac blended from brandies produced in the Grande and Petite Champagne areas but must contain a minimum of fifty per cent Grande Champagne brandy.

ARMAGNAC

The Armagnac region has long been known for its fine brandy; the first written reference to it was in 1411, about two centuries before any mention of cognac. Although the grape varieties are the same, there is little similarity between the two spirits in methods of production, maturation or final product. Armagnac experiences bone-chilling winds in winter and burning summer heat. For the purposes of brandy production it is divided into three sub-regions:

Bas-Armagnac The area to the west of Auch has a predominantly sandy soil and the finest brandies are produced from here.

Ténarèze The central area has clay soil which results in light early maturing brandies.

Haut-Armagnac The south-eastern area, which has the highest proportion of chalky soil, produces the lowest quality brandy.

The wine is distilled while on the lees so that more flavour passes into the spirit. This is heightened by distilling at a much lower strength, usually about 53% by volume, which allows retention of more of these flavouring elements, thus creating a pungent spirit. Armagnac is only distilled once, in a form of continuous copper still developed locally during the nineteenth century, which bubbles the spirit vapour through the base wine before it passes into the condenser. Mobile stills are used by some of the small growers and are

Mobile stills such as this one used to be wheeled from farm to farm in *Armagnac* to distill the raw spirit for the small producers.

drawn from farm to farm on little carts. Also, a distiller often sells his product direct to the public from the cellar door.

The infant spirit is matured in Monlezun oak. The high concentration of sap and tannin in this black oak adds flavour and colour to the Armagnac which ages much faster than it would in lighter oak. Good Armagnac is a deep nutty brown with golden lights and a dark heart; it is very very dry on the finish.

If a label bears the name of any of the three regions, then the brandy must come only from that region. The word *'armagnac'* indicates a blend, a three-year-old brandy will be Three Star; VO and VSOP indicate at least four years wood maturation; Extra, Napoleon and XO brandies have spent at least five years in wood casks. The phrase *'hors d'age'* is used for brandies over twenty-five years old. The label of a blend may carry a date which must be that of the youngest brandy in the blend, although vintage armagnacs are available. Most armagnac is marketed in a flat-faced bottle known as a *basquaise*.

GRAPE BRANDY

France In France a grape brandy is called *une fine*, and it is gaining an increasing share of the world market at the expense of cognac. This is the result of rising cognac prices supplemented by the versatility of brandy as a mixer. There are few restrictions on brandy production in France and consequently most of the commercial grape brandies are of indefinite origin. Surplus wine is often sent to the French government monopoly for distillation. The brandy is then sold to a firm for blending and bottling. Many of the grape brandies are packaged so that they bear a strong resemblance to good cognacs and most use the same terms such as VSOP and Napoleon, but this is simply a marketing exercise. Some of the major cognac houses have accepted the presence of grape brandy and are marketing their own.

Germany The Rhineland is the centre of the brandy industry. After 1918 German brandy was not allowed to use the word cognac, therefore it is now officially known as *weinbrand*. Distillers are permitted to purchase wine from anywhere in Europe, which is then pot stilled and aged in Limousin oak, developing a slightly sweet taste and flowery nose.

Greece Known locally as *koniak*, Greek brandy is distilled around Piraeus. The spirit is aged for three years and the temperature is allowed to rise in the maturing rooms. There is a particular nose and flavour to a Greek brandy that comes from the species of grapes used for the base wine. Unfortunately musty grapes in inferior brands give an obnoxious odour. Most of the wineries in Cyprus also produce a brandy.

Italy Italian law insists that brandies are matured for three years and both pot still and continuous still brandies are produced for domestic and export markets. Italian brandy has a good clean flavour with a touch of sweetness.

Spain The Jerez district is the major brandy producing area and most of the sherry shippers market a brandy. Spanish brandy was used as raw material for Dutch gins and liqueurs from the eighteenth century. Today much of the dark sweet brandy is exported to South America.

Australia The local demand is chiefly for mixing brandy as Australians are not particularly spirit drinkers. The base wine is made from white grapes that do not show marked varietal characteristics and only the fermented juice of fresh grapes is allowed as a base, so that purity levels are very high. Most of the brandy comes from the irrigated riverland of South Australia.

South Africa This is a spirit oriented country with about half of its wine harvest being distilled for brandy. It is made by pot still and matured for a minimum of three years although finer brandies are about five years old.

USA Brandy was first made on the Spanish missions in California about two hundred years ago and today this state is the major brandy producer. It may be made in either a pot still or continuous still and the California Brandy Advisory Board insists the spirit be wood aged – often in American oak – for a minimum of two years. The base wine has a strong grape flavour and sweetening, flavouring and colouring additives may be used subject to strict control, so that the end product is usually fruitier and lighter than its European equivalent.

GIN

Today gin is a flavoured spirit obtained by the distillation and rectification of grain, usually malted barley, rye or maize, but this was not always the case. Of all the popular spirits today, gin has probably the most interesting history.

The spirit originated in Holland over 300 years ago when a doctor successfully combined the juniper berry and alcohol to produce a cheap remedy for kidney complaints. The word 'gin' is a corruption of the French word for juniper – *genièvre*. English soldiers returning from the religious wars of Tudor times took with them a liking for the drink which gave them 'Dutch courage' in times of stress. From this time it became the Englishman's spirit and was politely referred to as Hollands.

In the eighteenth century gin was a cheap solace for London's poor, but there was no control over production and the concoctions could contain aniseed, turpentine and even sulphuric acid, for those were the days of the notorious 'Gin Lane'. The invention of the continuous still in 1831 meant that a better quality spirit could be made. Gradually it became more respectable to drink gin, although it was still known as 'Mother's Ruin' because of the juniper berry's supposed ability to induce abortion.

In the USA, too, gin had to weather a period of notoriety before it gained respectability. Prohibition in the 1920s saw vast quantities of 'bath tub' gin produced with just about anything from deadly wood alcohol to eau-de-cologne as its base. With the lifting of Prohibition, the sales of London Dry gin escalated, mainly due to the demand for that most famous of all cocktails, the Dry Martini.

London Dry Gin
In the production of London Dry gin the first distillation is by continuous still, so as to eliminate the fusel oil and other impurities. This produces a very high quality neutral spirit that forms the base for gin. The second step is to distil a flavouring into the neutral spirit and the resulting distillate is known as gin. Each firm has its own secret recipe for flavouring the gin but all distillers use juniper berries and coriander seeds. Other ingredients include angelica root, orris root, cassia bark, liquorice, orange and lemon peel, fennel, calamus root, cardamom seeds and almond. The collection of berries, spices, roots and bark used as flavouring is known as the *botanicals*.

Traditionally these are just added to the neutral spirit in a pot still and heated so that the vapours rise up the neck of the still into the condenser which cools them and they precipitate into the receiver as gin. The botanicals may be suspended in a cage in the neck of the still so that the vapours pass through them and absorb the flavour. Some firms use what is referred to within the trade as the *two shot* method of making gin. A much higher proportion of botanicals is added to the neutral spirit so that after distillation the gin has a very high concentration of flavour. This is then mixed with cold neutral spirit to reduce the flavour to drinking strength.

The art of the gin distiller is to determine which part of the distillate is suitable for the gin. The first part of the vapour – the heads – is unsuitable but when the flavouring has built up to the required strength the spirit is run into a gin receiver. The distillate is constantly *nosed* and sampled until a change in the character of the output can be noted and it is no longer suitable for gin. London Dry gin does not have to be made in London to be so called, although it is recognized that the best gins are made in London.

Plymouth Gin
This is made only in Plymouth by one distiller. It is wholly unsweetened and is the traditional gin of the British Navy; it is also the correct ingredient for a Pink Gin.

Old Tom Gin
This gin was originally used in preparing a Tom Collins. It was sweetened and of a distinctive character. Since 1939, however, production has almost ceased and there is little on the market at the present time.

Dutch Gin
This gin is also known as Hollands or Genever. The name Genever has nothing to do with the Swiss city or lake of that name but is again a corruption of the French word *'genièvre'*. The spirit is made in Holland, mostly in the cities of Amsterdam and Schiedam and the two main styles are *oude genever* and *jonge genever* – old and young gin. Genever is made from a neutral alcohol referred to as malt wine because the malted barley is fermented for a few days before being distilled. The malt wine and botanicals are distilled once to produce oude genever. However, malt wine is expensive and many distillers stretch it by blending it with grain spirit then distilling in a continuous still. Jonge genever is produced in much larger quantities and contains even less malt wine. Distillation at a low proof gives Dutch gin a distinctive grain flavour and for this reason it is rarely used in mixed drinks but is taken neat. The oude genever is probably much nearer to the original recipe than any other gin.

Lemon and Orange Gin
A very limited amount of flavoured gin is made by steeping the peel of the fruit in gin for eight to ten weeks.

Sloe Gin
This is made by steeping sloes in gin and is more properly accepted as a liqueur.

Cold Compounded Gin
Much of the gin available in many parts of the world is made by an entirely different method from distilled gin and is simply a juniper flavoured essence that has been added to alcohol and stirred to distribute the flavour. This gin essence can be produced in a chemical laboratory so there is no need to use a still at all. The base spirit is often a low grade of alcohol so the manufacture of *cold mix* gin is a simple and cheap procedure.

RUM

Sugar cane was introduced into the West Indies by Columbus and its cultivation spread rapidly through the Caribbean. By the seventeenth century cane was being distilled to produce a cheap spirit that served as a stimulant, disinfectant and all-purpose medicinal aid. The name of rum was probably originally used to describe the product of the British West Indies. A raw spirit was produced in the British West Indies as early as 1647 and was chiefly the drink of the slaves of the plantations at that time. This 'rumbullion', or 'Kill-Devil' as it was known, was developed into the drink we know today. It was consumed in vast quantities by the American settlers and in the early days of Australia's history, rum was so highly valued that it was used as currency. The Royal Navy issued it to warm those at sea, combat scurvy and act as an anaesthetic. One Admiral, nicknamed Old Grog, decided that the heavy consumption of rum was affecting his crew's working capacity and he had the rum watered down; even today 'grog' indicates a mixture of spirit and water.

Many French households keep rum in the kitchen as a culinary aid and its ability to heighten the flavour of fruit drinks makes it the traditional base of punch. The best-known rum drinks are the Daiquiri, Cuba Libre and Planter's Punch.

PRODUCTION

To make the spirit, the sugar cane is stripped of its leaves and crushed, and the juice produced from this process collected in vacuum pans, where the water of the juice is evaporated, to leave behind a syrup which eventually granulates. When this is sufficiently granulated it is placed in huge drums which revolve rapidly, thus extracting a thick sticky substance known as molasses from the sugar, which it leaves behind. The molasses is again reboiled producing a lower grade of sugar, and the extract of this second processing is used for the distillation of rum.

It is first mixed with water and fermenting agents, which depend on the area of production. Some areas use the yeasts produced from previous production. This *wash*, as it is known, is fermented out and distilled, producing rum.

Rum differs according to the strain of the yeast used in the wash, as well as to the method of distillation and the type and amount of caramel used in colouring. Rum needs maturation in the same way as whisky or brandy and since 1917, it has been illegal to sell rum in Britain which is under three years of age.

Puerto Rican Rum Generally these are dry light-bodied rums. The molasses is fermented in gigantic vats together with some of the mash from a previous fermentation. After about four days the wash contains 7% alcohol and goes into a column still, consisting of six connecting columns. The first is the purifying column which cleans the wash, the second is the analysing column where the alcohol is vaporized from the wash. The vapour passes into the rectifying column but the residue goes to the aldehyde column for reprocessing. The liquid passing over from the rectifying column is the rum, but two more columns are available for the production of neutral spirit.

If the rum is only matured for a year in uncharred oak casks, it is light bodied and fairly neutral in flavour and is known as white rum. Three years in charred barrels and the addition of caramel results in gold rum. Some rum is aged for over six years, acquiring a dry mellowness. Often referred to as *vieux* or *liqueur* rum, it bears comparison with matured brandy or de luxe whisky. The Virgin Islands and Cuba also produce light-bodied rum.

Jamaican Rum Traditional Jamaican rum is full bodied with a pungent aroma and assertive flavour. The molasses is allowed to ferment naturally. This can take up to three weeks but allows the development of more flavouring elements which eventually add dimension to the spirit. The wash is double distilled in a pot still and only the middle fraction is taken off as an infant rum. It is aged in oak for at least five years but the very dark colour comes from the added caramel. Much of it is aged and blended in the UK which is the largest customer for Jamaican rum.

Martinique Rum This rum is distilled from the concentrated juice of the sugar cane, rather than from molasses. It is produced by pot still and takes on colour from oak maturation. Haitian rum is similarly produced.

Demeraran Rum The Demerara River flows through Guyana and the individual flavour of the dark-coloured local rum results from the soil character. Some Demeraran rum is marketed with a very high alcoholic content and is the traditional rum for grog and the Zombie. If a rum is labelled 'Demeraran style' it usually indicates a dark-coloured rum with less pungency than Jamaican rum.

Batavia Arrack This is rum produced in Java, Indonesia. Little red rice cakes are put into the molasses which ferments naturally from wild yeasts. After some ageing in Java, the arrack is shipped to Holland where it is further aged for up to six years before blending and bottling. It is the base for Swedish Punsch.

Aguardente de Cana This sugar-cane spirit is the South American equivalent of rum. It is known as Cachaca in Brazil, where its annual consumption figures surpass the combined world sales of white, dark and golden rums.

Flavoured Rums In rum producing areas tropical fruits are macerated in white rum to create fruit-flavoured rums. The more sophisticated of these are distilled, resulting in a rum liqueur and the most popular flavours are banana, pineapple and coconut.

TEQUILA

Until recently tequila was little known outside its native Mexico, but it is enjoying a vogue at the moment, undoubtedly because of the success of such tequila-based cocktails as the Tequila Sunrise, Margarita and Silk Stockings.

PRODUCTION
Tequila is made from a species of agave plant, the blue-green *Agave tequilana weber*, known as maguey or blue mezcal in Mexico, or as century plant in the USA. It resembles a cactus with spiky leaves, but is in fact not a cactus, but a near relative of the Yucca or Amaryllis plants.

It grows slowly, taking eight to ten years to reach maturity. The spiky leaves are removed and the heart – called the pina because of its strong resemblance to a pineapple – and weighing between 23 and 115 kilos, is roughly chopped and steam cooked in ovens, or autoclaves, for seven hours.

After cooling, the pinas are washed, shredded and pressed between rollers to extract all the juice. Sugar and yeast are added to this juice, which is then fermented for two or three days in tanks, before double distillation in a pot still.

The tequila is allowed to mature for a minimum of three years in huge 40,000-litre vats before bottling.

Mezcal
Tequila and mezcal are produced by the same method, but the distinction between them is similar to the distinction between cognac and brandy. Tequila is a mezcal, but not all mezcal is tequila. By Mexican law, only mezcals made in the officially sanctioned regions – the area around the village of Tequila, and a secondary area around Tepatitlan – and reaching certain rigid quality standards, may be called tequila.

It is this inferior mezcal, which is produced in many parts of Mexico, that gives rise to the myth associated with tequila that it is only top grade if it has a bloated worm lying in the bottle – a long standing tradition of some mezcal, but of dubious attraction.

STYLES OF TEQUILA

White or Silver This tequila has been allowed to mature in vats that are wax lined and therefore remains colourless.

Gold or Anejo (aged) This tequila is matured in white oak vats which give it a golden hue and mellow taste.

Drinking Tequila
To drink tequila in the way the Mexicans do, place a small amount of salt in the join between thumb and forefinger. Lick the salt, drink the tequila cold and neat from a small glass and squeeze the juice of a quarter of a lemon or lime straight down the throat – do not suck the fruit. The expert holds the fruit with the hand that contains the salt, and takes only a few seconds to complete the manoeuvre.

Vodka, like gin, is distilled from a base of grain and is highly rectified, but no flavourings of any kind are added. Indeed, the finest vodkas are filtered through activated charcoal and even fine quartz sand to ensure absolute purity. This would be an accurate description of what the western world today calls vodka; history, however, tells us a different story.

The origins of vodka – the word means literally 'little water' – lie in twelfth-century Russia and Poland, where 'vodka' was the generic name for any spirit drink whether it was distilled from grape, grain or potato. These potions were frequently highly flavoured and aromatic.

In Russia, the Czar banned the production of vodka at the beginning of World War I, but a flourishing black-market trade continued and to control this a state monopoly was established in 1925.

Emigrés who fled from the Russian Revolution began to distil unflavoured vodkas in their new homelands but vodka did not became a fashionable drink in the western world until the late 1940s. The fashion started in the USA with such mixes as the Moscow Mule, Bloody Mary and Screwdriver. By 1975 vodka sales in the USA had the major share of the spirit market and it was the first spirit to outsell bourbon in its own homeland. There are now over 200 different brands on sale in the USA.

The advantage of *western* or neutral vodka which has contributed to its success is its complete lack of flavouring, which makes it such a good mixer with everything including a variety of fruit juices and minerals. It is, therefore, acceptable in cocktails, adding strength but not altering the taste. It is also odourless and is therefore more socially acceptable, particularly to women. It has good digestive and warming properties and it is said that its low volume of fusel oils means that it reduces unpleasant after-effects.

STYLES OF VODKA

Neutral Vodka This is distilled from grain – or sometimes molasses – then rectified, diluted to the required strength and filtered through activated charcoal. The source of the water and the choice of grain can have an effect on the quality – Polish vodka for instance is always made from rye.

Gold This has been cask matured, sometimes as long as ten years.

Green This is made by steeping Zubrowka grass in Polish vodka, and has a delicate aromatic bouquet. The bottle frequently contains a stem of the grass.

Other Flavourings Vodka is often flavoured with various herbs, chillies and peppercorns and these can be very aromatic. Various fruits can also be infused.

Serving Vodka
Iced vodka, straight from the refrigerator, served in small glasses is accepted as the traditional drink with caviar.

WHISKY

SCOTCH WHISKY

The earliest record of spirit being distilled in the British Isles is the barley-based 'Pot Ale' of the Irish religious establishments. It is likely that the art of distillation reached Ireland from Spain and it certainly travelled with the Irish monks when they settled in western Scotland. The Scots quickly developed a taste for the product and literature abounds with references to *uisge beatha*, the Gaelic for 'water of life'; *uisge* is pronounced 'whisky'.

Spirits were first taxed in 1643 and so began the long-running battle between the whisky makers and the Excise men. Up to the early nineteenth century illicit stills were operating on a massive scale protected where possible by the thirsty local citizens. Then in 1831 an Irish distiller, Aeneas Coffey, registered the patent for a new design of still. This was the continuous still which revolutionized the whisky-making process and turned distilling into big business.

Competition amongst distillers was intense, so that many turned to export. In the 1870s, when cognac production had virtually ceased because of phylloxera, the gap in the sales market was rapidly filled by Scotch.

Prohibition in the USA stopped the production of rye and bourbon, creating a new demand for Scotch. One British firm produced a blend specifically for the American public who clamoured for its soft light style that reminded them of rye. It was sold across the blockade by Captain McCoy, who guaranteed that this product was 'the real McCoy' and not a 'cut' spirit. Strangely enough, although there was a huge market for blends, single malts were not generally appreciated until after World War II. Italy is the largest importer of single malts although the USA, Japan and France are the most important export markets in terms of overall sales.

Many countries have tried to emulate the success of Scotland in producing this fine spirit, but Scotch whisky has a unique quality that defies imitation. This can be attributed in part to Scotland's soft spring water that begins as melting snow and flows through granite and peat which act as natural filters so that the water is of unquestionable purity but still contains the valuable minerals that add character to the whisky. The Scottish climate also allows the spirit to age slowly in cask without too high a rate of evaporation, so producing mature whisky with a complexity of flavours.

PRODUCTION OF MALT WHISKY

Conversion Barley is malted by soaking in water for about forty-eight hours; it is then spread out on a concrete floor where the warmth and moisture cause it to germinate. The barley secretes the enzyme diastase which makes the barley starch soluble and capable of producing sugars which can then be converted to alcohol. Germination is stopped by drying the *green malt* in a kiln over a peat fire, the smoke of which adds character and flavour to the final whisky.

Extraction The crushed dried malt is put into a mash tun with boiling water and churned violently, reactivating the enzyme and extracting the sugar. The resulting liquid is known as the *wort*.

Fermentation The wort goes into deep wooden or steel vessels and cultured yeast is added. This attacks the sugar and after about three days of violent action, converts it to crude alcohol of low strength known as the *wash*.

Distillation The liquid is put in the wash still and gently heated to a point where the alcohol vaporizes, rises up the still through the condenser which is kept water-cooled and precipitates as low wines of 30–40% alcohol.

The procedure is repeated in the smaller spirit still. Firstly the low alcohol *foreshots* pass over, then when the spirit has built to around 12% alcohol, the stillman who closely observes progress through the glass spirit safe, throws the tap to channel off the potable spirit. This is the critical stage as it determines how much of the congenerics are allowed to pass into the spirit contributing to the flavour. The undesirable last runnings – the *feints* – still contain alcohol, so both the feints and the foreshots are channelled into the wash still for further distillation. The shape of the still, the height of the head of the still and the angle of the pipe connecting the head to the condenser all affect the character of the whisky.

Maturation The spirit is reduced to 68.5% alcohol and piped into sherry casks or American oak casks. The minimum legal period of maturation is three years, but a period of five years is advisable. Highland malts are at their best at between fifteen and twenty years old, after which there is a danger of a slimy texture developing from prolonged contact with the wood. Some whisky buffs hold that it further improves in bottle.

Blending The blender's skill lies in his abilities to combine whiskies from different distilleries as well as the combination of malt and grain whiskies. The whiskies may be added to the blend because of colour, bouquet or flavour but the blender rarely tastes them; he makes his selection by colour comparison and nosing of the different spirits. There may be as many as seventy whiskies in one blend, the aim being to recreate a standard recognizable product. After blending, the new whisky is well mixed then rested for a few months to allow the components to marry. Caramel is added to give a tawny tinge to the colour, soft water is added to reduce the alcoholic content, then the whisky is filtered and bottled.

MALT WHISKY REGIONS

Highland Malts Light-bodied but full-flavoured malts are produced north of the line drawn from Greenock to Dundee and many of the single malts come from this prestigious region. The distilleries concentrated around the River Spey in the Glenlivet area produce

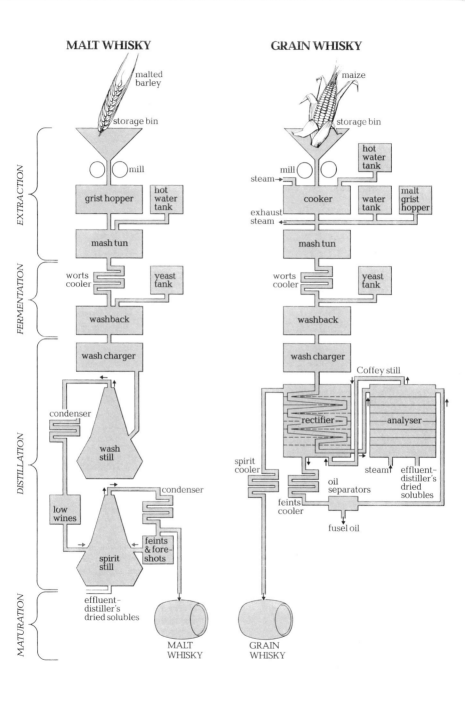

MALT WHISKY

malted barley

storage bin

EXTRACTION

mill

grist hopper

hot water tank

mash tun

FERMENTATION

worts cooler

yeast tank

washback

wash charger

DISTILLATION

condenser

wash still

low wines

condenser

spirit still

feints & fore-shots

MATURATION

effluent-distiller's dried solubles

MALT WHISKY

GRAIN WHISKY

maize

storage bin

mill

hot water tank

steam →

cooker

water tank

malt grist hopper

exhaust steam →

mash tun

worts cooler

yeast tank

washback

wash charger

Coffey still

rectifier

analyser

spirit cooler

steam

effluent-distiller's dried solubles

feints cooler

oil separators

fusel oil

GRAIN WHISKY

superior malts and the nearby Dufftown basin distilleries make smooth peaty malt whiskies.

Lowland Malts These are produced south of the Highland line and the majority of them are used for blending with Highland malts.

Campbeltown Malts The Mull of Kintyre is the original home of whisky. However, it produces a heavy smoky spirit that is not very adaptable in blending.

Islay The whiskies from the Isle of Islay are noticeably individual, being very sharp and pungent. Most blends have a little Islay whisky in them to provide extra depth of flavour.

PRODUCTION OF GRAIN WHISKY
The cereal, usually maize, is ground then cooked in a converter under steam pressure to burst the starch cells. It then goes into the wash tun with a little green malt and hot water. The origin of the water is immaterial and after fermentation the low wines have a lower alcoholic content than that produced for pot distillation.

The Coffey still employs the principle of distillation by steam and is a continuous process. It consists of two columns, an analyser which separates the constituent parts, and a rectifier which raises the strength of the spirit. Steam enters the base of the analyser, and when both columns are filled with steam, the cold wash is fed into the top of the rectifier and progresses through it inside a pipe. The body of the rectifier is filled with heated vapour which warms the wash so that it is almost at boiling point by the time it reaches the analyser. There the hot liquid wash meets the hot steam that has been injected under pressure, so that the alcohol vaporizes, mixes with the steam and is channeled back into the base of the rectifier. Inside the rectifier the vapour passes through a series of perforated plates. The tails – feints – are piped off into a cooler, the oil is separated out of them and the remainder is fed back into the analyser. About two-thirds of the way up the vapour hits a cold spirit plate and precipitates. It is immediately mixed with water to dilute it below flash point. The vapour that continues out of the top of the still is known as the heads or foreshots and is immediately re-distilled.

This process removes many of the congenerics of the original alcohol, making grain whisky much milder in flavour and aroma than malt whisky. However, it is also much purer and cheaper to produce and the recent demand for Scotch has meant an increase in the production of grain whisky.

STYLES OF WHISKY

Blended Whisky There are over 2,000 registered brands of blended whiskies and the best of them contain a good proportion of malt to give flavour to the more neutral grain whisky.

Single Malts A single malt is the unblended product of one distillery. Although there are over a hundred malt distilleries, relatively few of their whiskies are marketed as single malts. This is because of the strong demand for malts to make the branded whisky blends and the high cost of storing the malts which can take up to ten years to mature although they may be sold after three years.

Vatted Malts These are a blend of malt whiskies. Until the 1860s any blend consisted of malts but the advent of grain whisky meant vatted malts were rarely marketed until the recent revival of interest in this style of whisky.

IRISH WHISKEY

The process for making Irish whiskey differs from that used to make Scotch. The barley is dried and ground with a small proportion of green malt and other cereal, then mashed with boiling water in a kieve or mash tun that resembles a giant strainer. This mashing is repeated four times, producing the worts which are allowed to ferment. Once fermented the liquid is known as the wash and is distilled in enormous copper pot stills. A first distillation produces low wines, a second distillation produces feints which are then distilled a third time resulting in whiskey. It is matured in sherry casks for at least five years while the minimum age for whiskey used in a de luxe blend is twelve years. *Poteen* is an illicitly distilled Irish whiskey.

CANADIAN WHISKY

The early Scots and Irish settlers took the art of distillation with them to Canada over two hundred years ago. Although Canadian whisky is usually called 'rye', the main grain used is corn with some wheat and rye. The abundance of grain and soft fresh water provide the vital ingredients for excellent whisky and production is in a continuous still.

The law requires oak maturation for a minimum of three years and sometimes charred barrels or bourbon casks are used for ageing. Canadian whiskies are light bodied and well suited to mixed drinks.

US WHISKEY

The early Americans consumed large quantities of Cuban and West Indian rum until supplies were cut off by the British blockade during the American War of Independence. Then locally made spirit was at a premium for its medicinal value and as a stimulant, and many of the famous brands of whiskey date from the late eighteenth century. The present demand for whiskey is such that almost 3,000 brands are marketed in the US.

Bourbon Bourbon has been traced back to Bourbon County, Kentucky. In 1789 a Baptist minister, the Reverend Elijah Craig, set up a still beside a limestone creek in the desolate Bluegrass Country and distilled corn to produce his 'Kentucky Bourbon Whiskey'.

American regulations define bourbon whiskey as that produced from a mash of not less than 51% corn grain. It must be aged for a minimum of two years in new charred oak barrels that must not be re-used to make whiskey. Distillers hold that the natural wood caramel produced by charring gives the golden lights and particular flavour of bourbon.

Straight Bourbon is the product of one distillery and *Blended Straight Bourbon* is a blend from several distilleries. *Blended Bourbon* indicates a mixture of bourbon and other spirits, usually grain spirits or light whiskey. *Bottled in Bond Straight Bourbon* indicates that it has been matured in bond – and consequently tax free – for a minimum of four years and this extra ageing often produces a finer quality spirit. A whiskey can only be labelled 'Kentucky Bourbon' if it is distilled and matured in Kentucky for at least one year.

Sour Mash After the wort has been fermented and the low alcohol wash, also known as beer, has been drained off, the spent mash is left behind. Some of this is added to the next vessel of mash to be fermented, ensuring a continuity of flavour and style. This process is used in the making of some bourbons and *Tennessee Whiskey*.

Rye The word rye can only be used if the spirit is distilled from a mash of not less than 51% rye. Most rye whiskey comes from Pennsylvania and Maryland although there is wide variation in taste and quality between the numerous brands. There are some straight ryes and blended straight ryes but most are blended ryes indicating the inclusion of other whiskey or neutral spirit.

Light Whiskey A mixture of grains is distilled at a much higher proof than for other types of whiskey, thus producing a purer spirit which has a much lighter flavour and character. It is stored in used or uncharred oak, until required for blending purposes. This is a recent development in whiskey styles and a few straight light whiskeys are available, although most of it goes into blended whiskey.

Corn Whiskey Spirit distilled from a minimum of 80% corn mash is known as corn whiskey. It is frequently immature when marketed which has contributed to its low reputation.

JAPANESE WHISKY

The Western art of distillation was introduced to Japan in the second half of the nineteenth century. Distillers use pot stills for full-bodied malt whisky and continuous stills for lighter-bodied whisky for blending purposes. The top quality whiskies do contain some imported Scotch malt whisky to heighten the flavour. Most blended Japanese whisky is made from a combination of millet, corn and rice. It is aged in used charred oak before blending and maturation and has its own particular flavour and character.

Aquavit

All Northern European countries produce aquavit. The word derives from *aqua vitae*, the Latin for 'water of life'. This spirit is also known as schnapps. The Danes have been distilling it for over 400 years and the Danish spirit is still regarded as the finest aquavit. Grain or potato is distilled to produce a neutral spirit which is then redistilled with flavourings. Caraway is the main flavouring and citrus peel, cardamom or anise can be incorporated as well. Aquavit is served ice cold and as it is highly alcoholic it is usually served with food.

Arrack

Most Eastern countries produce an arrack which is a spirit that may be distilled from various bases such as grapes, milk, rice or cane. *Toddy* is the spirit distilled from the fermented sap of palm trees and *raki* is the favourite Turkish drink. It is an anise-flavoured spirit that turns milky when mixed with water. Batavia arrack is a rum. Most arrack is quite fiery and is rarely matured.

Grappa

This is the Italian spirit distilled from the residue of skins, pulp and stalks after the juice has been run off. It can be quite fiery but quality matured grappa is very flavoursome. *Invechiata* refers to aged grappa and *stravecchia* indicates extra maturation.

Marc

After grapes have been pressed to remove the juice suitable for winemaking, the *cake* that is left contains the grapeskins, pips and often the stalks. In France, the spirit distilled from this fermented pulpy residue is known as marc. It is highly pungent because of the flavouring elements that derive from the tannic pips and skins and so must be matured for many years. Marc de Bourgogne is quite well known and Marc de Champagne is one of the lightest available. Brandy made in Burgundy from wine lees or wine is known as Fine de Bourgogne.

Okolehao

This is the local spirit of Hawaii where it is known as *Oke*. The roots of the ti plant are fermented and the mash is then distilled in a column still. It is filtered through charcoal and sold unaged. There is a Crystal Clear and a Golden Oke and the spirit is used as a base for many of the local cocktails.

Ouzo

This aniseed-flavoured spirit is the local drink of Greece and Cyprus. Quality ouzo is made by double distilling the basic spirit then adding aniseed and other herbs for a redistillation. There are many styles of ouzo as most wineries produce their own. When water is added to ouzo it turns milky and quality ouzo becomes very milky. In Greece it is always served with some kind of food.

Pisco
In South America a spirit is distilled from the residue of muscat grapes and matured in clay jars. It is called after the town of Pisco in Peru. This spirit is the base of the Pisco Sour which is extremely popular in Chile and Peru.

Sake
A rice-based liquor that has been produced in Japan for over a thousand years, sake is actually a beer with a high alcoholic content because it is refermented to 17° GL, and cask matured for about a year. It has a delicate sweet flavour but a dry finish. It is traditionally served hot in a small porcelain pot with tiny cups.

Swedish Punsch
This is a blend of Batavia arrack (rum), aquavit and syrup. These ingredients are stirred together for a few months, wine is added and the blend is cask matured for a few more months. It can be drunk hot or cold or used in mixed drinks.

BEERS

About 6,000 years ago the ancient Egyptians were adept at brewing beer and virtually every civilization since has produced an alcoholic beverage from fermented cereal. Germanic tribes were brewing in the first century AD and in Roman Britain ale remained the national beverage despite the introduction of wine by the invaders. Farmers, lords and monks all brewed their own beer which was consumed in preference to the contaminated water supplies. The introduction of hops to fifteenth-century Britain meant that brewers were able to stop their beer going sour, but it took the 'ale' drinkers over a century to adapt to the lighter more bitter drink. The art of brewing was carried by the first settlers to the American colonies where most households also brewed their own beer until the rise of the commercial brewers.

PRODUCTION
The first step in beer production is *malting*. Barley is soaked in water which causes germination, thus converting the starch in the barley into sugar. The green malt is then heated in a kiln to stop germination and the temperature and length of time the malt is roasted determine the colour and sweetness of the beer. Then the *brewing* process begins. The kilned malt is ground into grist which goes into a mash tun with water and any other grain additives. The quality of the water is of the utmost importance in determining the character of the beer. The mash is heated for a few hours to extract the soluble materials from the grist. Much of this material is sugar but a proportion of non-fermentable substances also passes into the water. It is these which will give body to the beer. The sweet liquid known as the wort is run off from the mash and the residue is sprayed with hot water to remove any remaining sugar. The wort and dried hops go into a copper vessel known as the brew kettle, and are boiled for one to two and a half hours according to the style of beer being made. The hopped wort is then run into a vessel called a hop back. The spent hops settle on the screen base and the hot wort filters through them. It is then cooled and run into the fermenting vats where *fermentation* will take place in one of two ways depending on the strain of yeast that is added; the yeast also helps determine the flavour of the beer.

The 'lager' yeasts fall through the liquid and for a week or so they work on the sugars from the bottom of the vessel until the brewer decides it is time to slow down the fermentation rate. This is done by ice cooling or refrigerating the beer almost to zero temperature and storing it like this so that it continues to ferment very slowly. It may be kept this way for a few months although four or five weeks is more usual. Finally, the lager is carbonated, filtered and filled into kegs, bottles or cans. Most European beers are made by this method.

'Ale' yeasts stick together as they multiply and form a surface on the liquid so that ale results from top fermentation. British beers are made by this method. The liquid ferments for about a week at a much higher temperature than lager does; sugar is then added and the cask is sealed. The brew continues to ferment and the carbon dioxide that is released is trapped and so absorbed in the liquid. Sometimes a handful of hops is dropped into the cask before sealing, and this produces a 'bitter' beer. It may be filtered before use but much draught ale is not, so it must be left to settle before being consumed. Some draught beer and all bottled and canned beer is *pasteurized* by subjecting it to steam which sterilizes the beer and lengthens its shelf life but removes much of the flavour. Bottled beer reacts adversely to direct light and may develop a strange odour and become cloudy if exposed to the sun, so beer is best stored in cool dark places. Cask beer that is too cold is flat and cloudy and if it is too warm it becomes very gassy.

STYLES OF BEERS

ALES (top-fermented beers):

Barley wine A dark fruity beer with a very high alcoholic content.

Bitter A copper-coloured draught ale particularly favoured in Britain. It is bitter because of the high proportion of hops used in its production.

Brown Dark brown sweet beer.

Mild A faintly sweet beer that is slightly weaker and darker than bitter.

Stout A very dark beer made with a high proportion of malt and hops. Roasted barley adds colour and flavour. The less alcoholic milk stout is sweeter. The world's most famous stout is Guinness.

LAGERS (bottom-fermented beers):

Bock A strong beer of German origin. In the USA these are usually darker and sweeter beers. Belgian bock is much less alcoholic.

Doppelbock Extra strong beer especially popular in Germany.

Dortmunder A 'blonde' beer with a dry lightly-hopped flavour.

Munchener A dark brown malty beer.

Pilsner A pale gold beer that originated in Pilsen, Bohemia in 1842. The town is now in Czechoslovakia. This is the most imitated of all beer styles.

APERITIFS AND DIGESTIVES

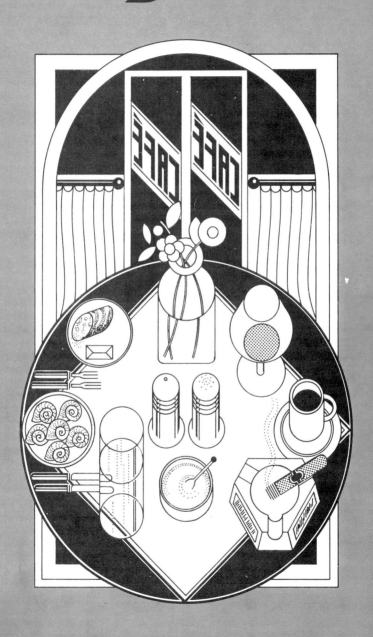

The principle of a drink before dinner is so widespread that some South American countries refer to that time as the 'vermouth hour', the Dutch call it the 'bitter hour', the Americans 'the cocktail hour' and in France it is the 'hour of l'Aperitif'. The word 'aperitif' is derived from the Latin *aperire*, to open – the inference being that an aperitif will stimulate the gastric juices and so sharpen the appetite in readiness for the evening meal. Each country has its own favourite beverage for this purpose, although what is consumed in one part of the world as an aperitif will raise many an eyebrow in another. Vermouths and bitters are widely regarded aperitifs as their tangy aftertaste primes the appetite. In parts of France, however, port or a kir may be offered before a meal; in Britain a chilled fino sherry is the time-honoured aperitif and Scandinavians will take schnapps. Spirit is still consumed before dinner in most parts of the USA, and the Spanish are partial to the local brandy with water. Chilled Sercial madeira is very palatable while the classic aperitif, accepted everywhere, is fine champagne.

A digestive is something that aids digestion and as such usually refers to an after-dinner drink. Most liqueurs fall into this category, and aniseed drinks are accepted as digestive aids although in many countries they are drunk before a meal. Europeans particularly enjoy a post-prandial eau-de-vie; port and madeira are often passed around after dinner and cognac is held in high esteem as a digestive.

EAUX DE VIE

These are true fruit brandies made by distilling the fermented mash of a fruit. They have a higher alcoholic content than most liqueurs and are dry to the taste. Many European countries distil eaux-de-vie but the most famous are from the Alsace region of France. The French also refer to them as *alcools blancs* – white alcohols – as they are aged in glass and therefore colourless. Eaux-de-vie are expensive because of the amount of fruit needed to produce them and they are best served chilled in chilled glasses with enough room to allow the liquid to be swirled, so releasing the bouquet.

Calvados
A brandy made from a mash of cider apples. Only apple brandy produced in the defined areas of the provinces of Brittany, Normandy and Maine is entitled to the name 'Calvados'. In the heart of this large defined area is the Pays d'Auge, and apple brandy from there can bear the appellation *Calvados du Pays d'Auge*. The fermented mash of apples is double distilled in a pot still and then matured in oak casks for up to twenty-five years, picking up colour and flavour from the wood. Some apple brandy is made in continuous stills and when cider is distilled the spirit is known as *eau-de-vie de cidre*.

Applejack
The New England brandy distilled from the fermented mash of cider apples. The best is made in pot stills and the minimum maturation period is two years in wood. It may be bottled as a straight brandy or combined with neutral spirits to be sold as a blended applejack.

Poire Williams
Eau-de-vie de poire distilled from the pear known as Williams or Bartlett. It is sometimes marketed in a pear-shaped bottle with a ripe pear inside. The Swiss product may be wood aged and in Germany it is known as Birnenwasser.

Stone Fruit Brandies
Stone fruits fermented with their kernels and then double distilled. The bitter almond tang comes from the essential oils contained in the crushed kernels. The brandies are bottled immediately, or stored in glass, to preserve the fragrance. The best-known are:

Barack Palinka Hungarian apricot brandy

Coing quince brandy

Kirsch cherry brandy

Kirschwasser German or Swiss cherry brandy

Mirabelle brandy from the small gold Mirabelle plum

Prune plum brandy

Prunelle sloe brandy

Quetsch brandy from the black Switzen plum

Slivovitz plum brandy from the Balkan countries

Soft Fruit Brandies
A distilled mixture of soft fruit macerated in alcohol. Wild berries produce the most delicate eaux-de-vie, although it takes as many as 30 kilos of fruit to produce one bottle of brandy. The best-known are:

Brombeergeist German or Swiss blackberry brandy

Erdbeergeist German or Swiss strawberry brandy

Fraises strawberry brandy;

Fraises de Bois wild strawberry brandy

Framboise raspberry brandy

Himbeergeist German or Swiss raspberry brandy

Houx Alsace holly berry brandy

Mûre blackberry brandy

Myrtille bilberry brandy

LIQUEURS

All liqueurs consist of a base spirit blended with a flavouring agent and sweetener. Herbs are the traditional flavouring, and it is probable that liqueurs developed from potions made from herbs steeped in alcohol to extract their medicinal properties.

In medieval Europe the resulting liquids were occasionally applied to wounds, but were more often taken internally. Some were sweetened to make them more palatable. People who could afford these liquors treasured them as protection against infection and plague, but many apothecaries fell foul of religious laws because of the claims they made for their potions.

Until the nineteenth century many households had their own blend, made from garden herbs and local spirit. Particular areas became famous for certain styles of liqueurs: the elixir of the monks at Fécamp in the fourteenth century was known as a preventive against malaria; the dark red liqueur made from Dijon blackcurrants was reputed to ward off physical diseases; and the bitter wormwood liquor of Marseilles dulled the senses of those in distress until 1915 when the government halted production.

The Spirit Base
To produce a fine liqueur the alcohol used must be as pure as possible. Constituents of alcohol such as aldehydes contribute to the aroma of wine but are undesirable in a liqueur base. The manner of distillation and the degree of rectification will determine the purity of the spirit. Whisky, rum, grape brandy, cognac, fruit spirit and rice spirit are all used although most liqueurs have a neutral or grain spirit base.

The Flavouring Agent
Some liqueurs are made with one flavour predominating whilst others have over seventy constituents. The most usual agents are:

herbs (herbal oils are extremely concentrated and used in minute amounts) such as: basil – preservative and tonic; hyssop – stimulant; peppermint and melissa – digestive; rosemary – clears the head; sage – tonic and lowers fever; thistle – encourages perspiration; thyme – antiseptic and stimulant; wormwood – depressant.

flowers such as camomile, lavender, lily, orange blossom, rose, saffron.

fruits such as citrus peel, edible fruits, raisins.

barks such as angostura, cinchona, cinnamon, myrrh, sandalwood, sassafras.

roots such as angelica, celery, gentian, ginger, henna, liquorice, orris root, turmeric.

seeds such as aniseed, apricot stones, almonds, caraway, clove, cocoa, coffee, coriander, dill, juniper berries, musk, peppers, star anis, vanilla.

Sweetener

Liqueurs are usually sweetened with a sugar syrup after the blending has been completed, but honey is used in some. The traditional classification of French liqueurs relates to the alcohol-sugar ratio. The higher the sugar content, the finer the liqueur as sugar gives the liqueur body and finesse.

PRODUCTION

Extraction

The flavouring agent must be extracted from the natural substance – the essential oil can then be used as an ingredient in the blending process. There are four methods used to extract the oil, depending on the solubility and chemical stability of the ingredient:

Pressure in which mechanical presses are used to extract the oil from citrus peel.

Maceration where the flavouring agents are soaked in cold spirit, then pulverized to gain maximum flavour. The mixture is filtered and the resulting liquid may be concentrated or used in distillation. This method is employed for natural products that do not react favourably to heat.

Infusion which is maceration in warm spirit maintained at a constant temperature for several days. More flavour can be extracted, much more rapidly, by infusion than any other method.

Percolation when the spirit is continuously bubbled through the flavouring agent. Alternatively, the spirit is boiled and the vapours pass up through the flavouring agent, condense and return to the boiling spirit.

Distillation

The natural products are steeped in the alcohol until it is well impregnated with flavour, then it is distilled – often under vacuum – to protect the delicate essences. As in all distillation, it is the middle fraction which is most useful, being a colourless dry distillate of high alcohol strength. This liquid is further purified by rectification (redistillation) to remove impurities which would change the flavour.

Compounding

Once the ingredients have been assembled, it is the function of the compounder to blend them in strict sequence to produce a desired flavour. Most liqueurs are made to secret recipes many of which are centuries old.

Maturing

As with other blended alcohols, liqueurs must be given time to allow the ingredients to marry together. The finest liqueurs are matured in oak casks, which aid in mellowing the liquid.

Fining
Vegetable matter is still suspended in the liquid and must be removed. The procedure is similar to fining wine.

Bottling
The liqueur is topped up with spirit to bring it to the correct alcoholic strength. Sometimes sugar syrup is also added to adjust sweetness and many liqueurs are coloured with harmless vegetable dyes. All liqueurs are given a final filtration to ensure starbright clarity before bottling.

GLOSSARY OF LIQUEURS

Absinthe A very dry bitter drink with high alcoholic content. Ingredients include aniseed, liquorice, fennel, hyssop, coriander and wormwood. Dr Ordinaire, the Frenchman who invented it, sold the recipe to the Pernod family in 1797 and the liquor was subsequently marketed as Pernod. The French Government legislated against the use of the depressant wormwood (*Artemisia absinthium*) in 1915 so that the ingredient was dropped from the Pernod recipe. Star anis, a plant native to China, then became the base of Pernod 45. It was fashionable for women to drip the bitter liqueur on to a lump of sugar which was cupped in a small long handled spoon with drain holes.

Advocaat A Dutch liqueur made from egg yolks and grape brandy. The alcoholic strength is only about 30° proof and it is generally used in mixed drinks. Imitations made from cornflour and raw spirit are marketed in some countries.

Aiguebelle A herb liqueur with over fifty ingredients produced near Valence, France. It is made in two colours and the green is stronger than the yellow.

Alchermes A red Italian liqueur made from rose and jasmine extract added to a nutmeg, cinnamon and coriander distillation.

Amaretto An Italian liqueur with an almond-apricot base. Amaretto was first made in Saronno near Lake Como in the sixteenth century.

Amourette A French liqueur, violet in colour.

Anesone A potent anise-liquorice liqueur produced in Italy and USA.

Angelica A sweet yellow Basque drink similar to Chartreuse.

Anisetta Stillata An Italian aniseed liqueur from Pescara.

Anis del Mono An aniseed liqueur from Barcelona, available in a sweet and dry form.

Anisette There are a number of sweetened aniseed liqueurs. Marie Brizard produced her anisette in Bordeaux around the middle of the eighteenth century and that is now regarded as the foundation of the French liqueur industry.

Apple Gin A colourless liqueur compounded at Leith, Scotland.

Apricot Liqueurs These are made by macerating apricots in brandy that is then sweetened. A true apricot brandy is an eau-de-vie but apricot liqueurs can be called Apricot Brandy as long as they have a required amount of fruit.

Atholl Brose A Scottish drink based on Highland malt whisky, uncooked oatmeal, honey and cream.

Aurum A pale gold Italian liqueur, highly aromatic with a delicate orange flavour.

Baerenfang A German liqueur which is predominantly honey flavoured with lime and mullein flowers.

Bahia A Brazilian blend of coffee and grain spirit.

Baska A French coffee liqueur from Angers.

Bénédictine One of the oldest – if not the oldest – and most widely renowned liqueurs in the world. It is distilled at Fécamp, in Normandy, and its origin has been traced to the Bénédictine monks of Fécamp, as far back as 1510. The liqueur is golden, highly aromatized and very sweet. The popular practice of drinking it with an equal portion of brandy has created the name B & B. The company now markets an official 'B & B'. The distinctively-shaped bottles bear the initials DOM (Deo Optimo Maximo – 'To God, most good, most great') although there is now no connection with any religious order.

Bescen A Dutch blackcurrant liqueur.

Blackberry Liqueur A liqueur made from blackberries macerated in brandy, which is sweetened; the resultant liquor is often topped up with eaux-de-vie to add finesse.

Bocksbeeren The Eastern European name for Blackcurrant Liqueur.

Brontë An English liqueur from Yorkshire. French grape brandy is blended with honey and herbs, then bottled in a squat pottery jug.

Cacao Mit Nuss A colourless German liqueur made from chocolate and hazelnuts.

Capricornia An Australian liqueur based on tropical fruit. It takes its name from the Tropic of Capricorn.

Carlsberg A bitter herbal liqueur from Czechoslovakia.

Casque An English honey-brandy liqueur.

Cayo Verde A lightweight American liqueur based on key limes.

Cédratine A sweet Corsican liqueur with good digestive properties.

Cerasella A red Italian liqueur with fine cherry flavour.

Chartreuse A liqueur which contains over 130 herbs and spices,

Tidal Wave   Champagne Napoléon   Brewer Street Rascal
Overleaf: Silk Stockings   Cool Banana   Blue Lady   Apricot Sour

manufactured at the Grande Chartreuse monastery, near Grenoble in France, by Carthusian monks from 1607 until 1901, when they were expelled from France. The monks set up a distillery in Tarragona, Spain and the liqueur was produced there until production resumed in France in 1931. After 1901 the French Government sold the trademark so that until 1932, when the monks regained the use of the name, there were French imitations. The original liqueur was the strong white Elixir, no longer produced; Green Chartreuse is 96° proof whilst the sweeter Yellow Chartreuse is 75° proof.

Cheri-Suisse A Swiss cherry chocolate liqueur.

Cherry Blossom Liqueur A delicate pink liqueur with a strong fragrance of Japanese cherry blossoms.

Cherry Brandy Liqueurs Most of these are labelled as cherry brandies but are produced by maceration of the fruit in spirit, sometimes with the addition of herbs. Some examples are Cherry Marnier, Peter Heering, Guignolet, Grants Morella, Cherry Karise and Rocher.

Cherry Nalivka A low-strength cherry liqueur of Baltic origin.

Cherry Whisky Cherry-flavoured whisky presents some blending problems because of the acid levels of both ingredients. The most well-known is Chesky, a French liqueur.

C.L.O.C. A Danish caraway liqueur, water-white and weaker than Dutch kummel.

Citronen – Eis A yellow German liqueur made from the juice and essential oil of lemon. The word *Eis* indicates that it is meant to be drunk over ice.

Coconut Liqueurs White rum, flavoured with essences from macerated coconuts. These are now widely available under such brand names as Malibu and Cocoribe.

Cointreau One of the best known French triple-sec curaçaos, sold in a distinctive square bottle under the name of Cointreau liqueur; it is colourless and has an orange flavour. The alcoholic strength of the liqueur is the same throughout the world; the liqueur itself is manufactured at Angers in the district of Anjou.

Cordial Campari A dessert liqueur of a light yellow colour, obtained from distillation of raspberries.

Cordial Médoc A dark red French liqueur. Something in the nature of a distilled claret flavoured with herbs.

Cordial Reby A liqueur with a cognac base, brown in colour.

Cream Liqueurs Cream, spirit and flavourings can now be combined successfully to produce thick, rich-textured liqueurs. Some Irish cream liqueurs are Baileys, Carolans, Waterford and O'Darby; two well-known names in the USA are Hereford Cows and Aberdeen Cows; the Australian version is called Contichinno.

Crème d'Amandes A sweet almond liqueur.

Crème de Banane A pungent liqueur made from a maceration of bananas in spirit. It was a particular pre-war favourite.

Crème de Cacao A very sweet liqueur with a strong cocoa-vanilla flavour. The name Chouao, which usually figures on Crème de Cacao labels, is that of a district in Venezuela reputed to produce the best cocoa beans in the world.

Crème de Cassis In Dijon, crème de cassis has been produced by maceration for centuries. The high vitamin C content of the blackcurrants means it is still regarded as a health-giving digestive.

Crème de Ciel A Dutch liqueur, after the style of curaçao, light blue in colour.

Crème de Fraises A sweet French liqueur flavoured with strawberries. Strawberry red in colour.

Crème de Fraises des Bois A French liqueur made from wild strawberries.

Crème de Framboise A sweet French liqueur flavoured with raspberries, a speciality of the Dordogne Valley, France.

Crème de Mandarine The general term used for tangerine liqueurs.

Crème de Menthe A very popular liqueur with digestive properties. It is made of grain spirit flavoured with peppermint and sweetened. When it leaves the still it is absolutely colourless, and some crème de menthe is sold in pure white form. As a rule, however, it is coloured green.

Crème de Mokka A French liqueur, light brown in colour with a coffee flavour.

Crème de Noisettes A sweet hazelnut liqueur.

Crème de Noix This sweet walnut-based liqueur is a local speciality in Périgord, France.

Crème de Noyeau A pink or white French liqueur made from the extracted oils of peach and apricot kernels. It has an almond flavour.

Crème de Pecco A Dutch liqueur with a tea flavour. Semi-sweet, colourless.

Crème de Prunelles A sweet liqueur plum-green in colour.

Crème de Roses A pink liqueur, flavoured with rose petals, vanilla and citrus oils.

Crème de Vanille A smooth, rich French liqueur made from vanilla beans.

Crème Yvette The best known of the crème de violettes. It is an old American liqueur, highly alcoholic, with the flavour, colour and perfume of Parma violets.

Cuarenta-y-Tres A sweet yellow liqueur from Cartagena, Spain, which is compounded from forty-three different herbs.

Curaçao A sweet digestive liqueur made from grape spirit, sugar and orange peel. The Dutch first used the bitter oranges from the island of Curaçao near Venezuela and some Dutch distillers still import the dried peel from there. The name is now applied to all orange liqueurs. After infusion the spirit is distilled. If the resulting liquor undergoes rectification it becomes triple-sec curaçao, a water-white, dry distillate which is then sweetened and coloured.

Drambuie The oldest of the whisky liqueurs. Scottish legend says the Mackinnon's had the recipe from Bonnie Prince Charlie, although it was not made commercially until 1906. Its basis is Scotch whisky and heather honey. The name Drambuie is from the Gaelic 'An Dram buidheach' meaning 'the drink that satisfies'.

Elixir d'Anvers A green-yellow liqueur with a bitter-sweet flavour. Made in Antwerp, it is extremely popular with the Belgian people.

Elixir di China A sweet Italian anise liqueur.

Enzian Calisay A sweet, pale gold liqueur based on Spanish herbs.

Escharchado A Portuguese aniseed liqueur containing sugar crystals.

Falernum An almond-flavoured liqueur from Barbados.

Filfar A Cypriot curaçao usually bottled in stone jugs.

Fior d'Alpi An Italian liqueur flavoured with alpine flowers and herbs. It is highly sweetened so that sugar crystals will collect on the branch inside the tall fluted bottle. Isolabella, Edelweiss and Mille Fiori are of this style.

Forbidden Fruit A highly alcoholic American liqueur. Extract of grapefruit and orange compounded with honey to give a bitter-sweet taste.

Frigola A thyme flavoured liqueur from the Balearic Isles.

Galliano A golden yellow herb liqueur. It is produced in Milan, Italy, and packaged in a tall fluted bottle. It is named after Major Galliano who distinguished himself during the Italian-Abyssinian war in 1896.

Gallweys An Irish liqueur based on whisky, honey, herbs and coffee.

Ginepy A white or green Italian liqueur with a predominantly anise flavour.

Glayva A Scottish herb and spice liqueur.

203

Glen Mist A dry Scottish liqueur on a whisky base. The spirit is compounded with herbs, spices and honey then matured in whisky casks.

Goldwasser Danzig Goldwasser is a white aniseed and caraway liqueur with gold flakes in the liquid. Produced in Danzig from 1598 by the Der Lachs, it is now made in West Berlin.

Gorny Doubnyak A bitter Russian liqueur compounded from ginger, galingale, angelica, clove, acorns and oak shavings.

Grand Cumberland A golden sweet Australian liqueur with a passion fruit flavour.

Grande Liqueur A French liqueur made in two colours, green and yellow, with a Chartreuse-type flavour.

Grand Marnier A French curaçao invented in 1880 with a cognac base; of the two versions, Cordon Jaune is of a lower alcoholic content than Cordon Rouge.

Greensleeves A green English liqueur from peppermint and brandy.

Guignolet A French cherry liqueur.

Gyokuro Rikyu A low-alcohol Japanese liqueur based on green tea and grape brandy.

Half-Om-Half A tawny coloured Dutch liqueur which is half curaçao and half orange bitters.

Irish Mist An Irish liqueur based on aged whiskies, herbal extracts and Irish heather honey. Its largest market is the USA.

Irish Velvet An Irish liqueur based on Irish whiskey, strong black coffee and sugar.

Izzara A Basque angelica and honey liqueur similar to Chartreuse with an armagnac base. The green version has a higher alcohol content than the yellow.

Jerzynowka A Polish liqueur made from maceration of blackberries.

Kahlua A Mexican coffee liqueur.

Kaiserbirnlikor An Austrian lemon liqueur.

Karpi A wild cranberry liqueur from Finland.

Karthauser A German version of Chartreuse.

Kirsberry A Danish cherry liqueur.

Kitron A Greek liqueur from the leaves of lemon trees distilled with grape brandy and sweetened.

Krambambuli An East German liqueur flavoured with angelica and violet extract.

Krupnick A Polish honey liqueur.

Kummel One of the most popular of all liqueurs with definite digestive properties. It has been made in Holland since 1575, but Kummel Allash and Riga, and Gilka Kummel from Berlin used to be even more universally popular than the Dutch kummel. Kummel has in its base some highly distilled or almost neutral spirit, sometimes distilled from grain, sometimes from potatoes. It is flavoured with caraway seeds to which it owes its digestive qualities. It is more or less sweetened, according to the formula used for different brands, but is always water-white. Normally served over ice.

Lakka A Finnish liqueur with a bitter-sweet tang from cloudberries grown only in the Arctic. Also known as Suomuurain.

Lapponia A Finnish liqueur made from Arctic liggonberries.

La Tintaine A French anise liqueur.

Liqueur d'Angélique A French liqueur produced from angelica and cognac.

Liqueur d'Or A sweet French liqueur with flakes of gold.

Lochan Ora A honeyed Scotch whisky liqueur.

Macvin A liqueur from the Jura region of France where newly-fermented red wine is mixed with marc, cinnamon and coriander.

Mandarine Napoléon A Belgian liqueur distilled from Andalusian tangerine peel macerated in eaux-de-vie then compounded with cognac.

Mandarinetto Tangerine liqueur produced in Italy.

Maraschino A white Italian liqueur produced from distillation of sour Marasca cherries including the crushed kernels. Sometimes a small amount of Kirsch is added to give extra finesse. Originally the cherries all came from Italian Dalmatia, now in Yugoslavia.

Marnique An Australian quince liqueur similar to Grand Marnier.

Masticha A Greek liqueur made on the island of Chios from aniseed and gum mastic on a brandy base.

Mazarin A light-brown French liqueur with a flavour similar to Bénédictine.

Melette Anisette produced in Ascoli Pinceno, Italy.

Mentuccia An Italian liqueur with a mint base which makes it an excellent digestive; there are supposed to be 100 herbs in the liqueur. Also known as Centerbe or Silvestro.

Mersin A Turkish triple-sec curaçao.

Mesimarja An aromatic Finnish liqueur made from Arctic brambles.

Mokka mit Sahne A German liqueur produced from coffee and cream.

Monte Aguila A bitter Jamaican liqueur based on pimento.

Mus A Turkish banana liqueur.

Nassau Orange A pale gold Dutch liqueur with the flavour of bitter oranges. Also known as Pimpeltjens Liqueur, it was served in 1652 at a banquet to mark the landing of the Dutch at what is now Cape Town, South Africa.

Nocino An Italian liqueur made by infusing nut husks in spirit. It imparts a delicate aroma to ice-cream.

Ocha A Japanese tea liqueur.

Oxygenée An aniseed-flavoured absinthe substitute.

Pasha A Turkish coffee liqueur.

Paradisi A Dutch grapefruit liqueur.

Parfait Amour A sweet pink or violet liqueur with a citrus base; it contains spices and flower petal extract.

Pastis A liquorice-based liqueur from Marseilles. The taste is not as pronounced as anis and it turns white when added to water. Some of its characteristics resemble those of absinthe but it contains no wormwood.

Pimento Dram A dark red liqueur made by steeping green and ripe pimento berries in rum.

Pineau des Charentes A liqueur from the Charentes region of France produced from fresh grape juice and one year old cognac blended together then matured in cask.

Pomeranzen German curaçao-type liqueur in green and gold made on a base of unripe Pomeranzen oranges.

Ponche A brown Spanish liqueur based on sherry.

Rabinowka A pink liqueur, dry or sweet, flavoured with rowanberry.

Raki An aniseed Turkish liqueur drunk with ice and water.

Raspail A yellow French liqueur compounded with herbs such as angelica, calamus, and myrrh. It is known for its digestive properties.

Ratafia Any sweetened liqueur on a spirit of wine base. The flavouring agents are usually almonds or the kernels of peaches or cherries.

Reishu A Japanese melon liqueur.

Riemerschmid A German fig liqueur.

Rock and Rye An American liqueur made from fruit flavouring, rock sugar candy and rye whisky. The sugar crystallizes inside the bottle.

Royal Cherry Chocolate A rich English liqueur with a cherry and chocolate base.

Royal Ginger Chocolate An English liqueur compounded from root ginger and cocoa beans.

Royal Mint Chocolate A recipe of English origin which is produced in France. It is based on milk chocolate and peppermint and has digestive properties.

Royal Orange Chocolate An English liqueur based on oil of orange, cocoa beans and pure milk.

Sabra An orange chocolate-flavoured liqueur from Israel.

Sacco A peppermint liqueur produced in Turin.

St Hallvard A bright yellow Norwegian liqueur on a potato spirit base.

Sambuca A highly alcoholic Italian liqueur made from an infusion of witch elderbush and liquorice. It is traditionally served ignited with three coffee beans floating in the glass.

San Michele A tangerine-based Danish liqueur.

Sapan d'Or A greenish liqueur not unlike Bénédictine.

Silverwasser (Danzig) A colourless sweet liqueur with flakes of silver, flavoured with aniseed and orange.

Sloe Gin A deep-red liqueur made by steeping sloe berries (wild plum) in gin, then maturing the liquor in wood. The traditional English name for it was Stirrup Cup.

Solbaerrom A fruity Danish liqueur.

Southern Comfort An American liqueur, 87.7° proof with an orange-peach flavour. There is some dispute as to whether it is a liqueur or a spirit but its adaptability makes it an excellent mixer.

Strega A yellow Italian liqueur compounded from over seventy herbs and barks.

Tamara An Israeli date liqueur.

Tangao A tangerine brandy liqueur.

Tangerinette A French liqueur, red in colour and with the flavour of tangerine oranges.

Tapio A dry water-white Finnish liqueur based on juniper berries.

Thitarine A sweet North African liqueur compounded from figs, herbs and liquorice.

Tia Maria A Jamaican liqueur based on rum flavoured with Blue Mountain coffee extract and spices.

Trappistine A pale yellow-green liqueur made with herbs and armagnac from the Abbayé de la Grâce de Dieu, Doubs, France.

Triple Sec A description of sweet white curaçao used for a number of brands of curaçao.

Tuica A liqueur made in Roumania, flavoured with plums.

Van der Hum An aromatic liqueur made in South Africa, its chief flavour comes from the *naartjie* or tangerine. The name translates as 'Mr What's his name'. When mixed with brandy it is referred to as Brandyhum.

Vandermint A Dutch chocolate and mint liqueur.

Verveine du Vélay A bitter French liqueur based on the herb vervain and available in green or yellow.

Vieille Cure A brown French liqueur of high strength with an aromatic flavour from its fifty herbs macerated in cognac and armagnac.

Wisniowka A sweet Polish liqueur made from cherries and vodka.

MADEIRA

This fine fortified wine comes from the island of Madeira in the Atlantic Ocean. It was discovered in 1419 by Portuguese mariners who found it covered by a dense impenetrable forest. Legend has it that the sailors set fire to the forest which burned for seven years, leaving the already fertile soil enriched with its ashes. In the eighteenth century, ships trading between Britain and her colonies stopped at Madeira for provisions and some of the local wine was always included, often as ballast. The wine was slowly heated during the sea voyage, developing a mellow burned flavour that became popular. In nineteenth-century households it was considered respectable to offer a glass of madeira with cake to both men and women. The wine is very long lived and, although essentially sweet, the finish of good madeira is very dry and never cloying. Germany and France are the major importers of madeira which they use as a culinary aid, but the quality madeiras go to Britain.

VITICULTURE AND VINIFICATION
The vines are trained on overhead pergolas to protect the grapes from the scorching sun. After pressing, the juice is transported as quickly as possible to Funchal the capital of the island and centre of manufacture. It is here that the juice is fermented. The fermented juice, known as *vinho claro*, is then fortified with local grape brandy. After resting, the cask of wine, known as a *pipe*, is put into the Estufa, a large central-heated store. The pipes of madeira are very gradually heated to a maximum of 50°C, held at this temperature for up to three months and then very slowly cooled to normal temperature. This process develops the same caramel-like flavour of wine that the long sea voyages used to produce. The madeira is now indifferent to heat and cold and is able to stand long exposure to air, for example in an opened bottle.

STYLES OF MADEIRA
There are four types of madeira named after the grapes from which they are produced:

Sercial A pale dry wine with a slight almond flavour. The very dry finish makes it an excellent aperitif served chilled. Sercial is quite harsh when young and takes a long time to mature.

Verdelho A golden wine with a smoky flavour. It is soft and sweet and benefits from even a few months bottle age. This can be the most elegant of the madeiras and is the classic wine to serve with soup.

Bual A velvet-brown coloured wine with a rich full flavour that complements many desserts.

Malmsey A dark rich wine with soft full flavour. The sharp tangy finish balances the sweetness and many consider it one of the world's finest wines.

Blends A few madeiras are blended and marketed under the shipper's trade name, e.g. Rainwater and London Particular.

PORT

Port is the name given to the fortified wine produced around the valley of the river Douro from a point near Barca d'Alva on the borders of Spain to within fifty miles of Oporto. The river is at the base of a narrow valley, between fifteen hundred and two thousand feet deep, the sides of which are layered rock. The vineyards have been hacked into the mountain side and walled terraces have been built like contour lines to prevent the earth from disappearing down into the river bed.

Until the eighteenth century the upper Douro valley produced coarse feeble wine. Elderberry juice was frequently used to improve the colour and various methods of stabilization were tried, one of which was the addition of local grape brandy to a cask during fermentation. This preserved the natural sugar of the grape and provided a more palatable wine. Portugal and Britain had been allies for many centuries and in 1703 the Methuen Treaty granted Portugal preferential trading terms. The winemakers began adapting their red table wine to the English palate by adding brandy to create a sweeter drink, and by the second half of the eighteenth century vintage port was being shipped to Britain. English merchants established headquarters in Oporto and purchased vineyards so that many of the port shippers now have British names.

It is from the port of Oporto and Oporto alone that this famous wine is shipped to the far corners of the world, but Oporto gives only its name to the wine for it is in the town of Vila Nova de Gaia, across the river from Oporto, that it is aged for many years in shade and silence. Most port was shipped in bulk and even vintage port was bottled in Britain until recently. Today France is the major market for non-vintage port which the French drink as an aperitif, although Britain is still the main buyer of vintage port.

VITICULTURE

In the deep river gorges of the upper Douro and its tributaries the winter air currents are icy and thick fog often develops. When summer comes the storms build up and their effects are felt over the entire region. The sun heats the stones and the valleys become ovens of up to 50°C without a breath of air. Vines are planted from water level to a height of one thousand feet, above which the grape would not ripen satisfactorily. When the vine shoots turn green and the grape bunches begin to lengthen, it is a perilous time for the vinegrower. He must watch for the morning frost and beware of the storms. Then comes the summer with its terrible dryness and burning winds. If the grapes can survive all this then the harvest takes place in September. At the ideal moment for each estate, known as a *quinta*, the women harvest the ripe grape bunches with scissors and baskets. The baskets are emptied into hods at the end of each row of vines and collected by *barracheiros*, stalwarts who can carry a 75 kilo load on their shoulders. The barracheiros are irreplaceable for no other method of transporting the grapes down the steep slopes has been found.

VINIFICATION

The practice of treading the grapes has become obsolete because of the lack of seasonal labour and the grapes now go into a gigantic centrifugal crusher. The juice is pumped into a concrete or stainless steel vat known as a *cuba* where fermentation takes place. The *autovinificator* is being used increasingly to aid fermentation. The cuba is enclosed and fitted with a system of valves which use the pressure built up by the carbon dioxide given off during fermentation to spray the must over the cap of skins, so extracting maximum colour in the minimum time. The new wine goes into tonneaus with one year old local grape brandy. The timing of the addition of the brandy is critical as it determines the sweetness of the wine for the rest of its life. The wine rests in the cellars of the quintas until the spring when it is transported by road tanker to the port lodges in Vila Nova de Gaia for blending and maturation. Traditionally a flat-bottomed boat known as a *barcos rabelos* was used for transportation to the port but there are now dams across the river.

Depending upon its early characteristic the new wine will be put into one of the two great port families: the blends or the rarer and more highly prized vintages. In the production of blends the wine is left in cask for two years, after which it is tasted and appraised. Other wines are then added, either to strengthen the port or enhance its bouquet and colour. This blending process is based on a successful formula which can be followed and maintained so that a trade product can be consistently marketed. The blends are put into enormous wooden casks in order to prevent oxidization and too-rapid an evaporation. As it takes on greater age the wine is enlivened and enriched with the careful addition of younger wine. No port wine may be drunk until it has aged five or six years in the wood. It reaches fullness after about thirty years but one can drink ports of sixty years or more which are still perfect.

STYLES OF PORT

Vintage Port In a very good year, a shipper will make a vintage port. This is still a blend but only of wines of the same year. Very few ports are the unblended product of one quinta. To preserve the fruit the wine must be bottled before all impurities have had time to settle out in cask, so a sediment will form in a bottle of vintage port. A white splash on the glass indicates the topside of the bottle during its early maturation in the lodge and so the crust will have formed on the opposite side. This crust will form again after the wine has been moved if it is left to rest for a few weeks. The port must be decanted off the crust before being served. The law requires that vintage port be bottled in Portugal and carry the seal of guarantee of the government authority. Each shipper makes his own decision on whether to declare a vintage and as there is more demand for good quality blends than for vintage port most shippers will declare about three times in a decade. Generally declared vintages have been 1945, 1947, 1948, 1950, 1955, 1960, 1963, 1966; five shippers declared 1967, 1970, 1975, 1977.

Late Bottled Vintage Port of a single year that has been in wood from four to six years before bottling. It is ready for immediate consumption. The label must bear the vintage date and the year of bottling.

Date of Harvest Port that has been in wood for at least seven years then bottled. It must bear the vintage date, year of bottling and an indication that the wine has been aged in cask, while descriptions such as 'Reserve' are permitted for this style.

Indication of Age Tawnies that have been aged for ten, twenty, thirty or over forty years. The label must carry an indication of age, the year of bottling and state that the port has been aged in cask.

Crusted Port A blended port that has been bottled after five or six years and then cellared until it throws a crust. This style is not sold in Portugal and needs at least seven years in bottle.

Tawny Port As port ages in oak, its colour changes from purple through ruby to a light tawny; a fine tawny port has usually been in wood for about ten years and has a velvety consistency. It can also be made by blending red and white ports.

Ruby Port A blend of old and young wine. The former contributes softness and character, the latter a fresh fruitiness. It is chilled before bottling to precipitate any sediment and so lengthen its shelf life.

White Port White grapes fermented out to make a dry wine which is then fortified. It is drunk as an aperitif.

Vintage Character A quality blended port ready for immediate drinking. These ports must not carry a date on the label.

SHERRY

The province of Cadiz in Spain has been producing wine since Roman times and began exporting to England as early as the fourteenth century. The word 'sherry' is the anglicized version of Jerez, the name of the town at the centre of the trade; the British originally referred to the wine as sherris sack. By the sixteenth century there was a thriving British community in Jerez because of the number of merchants who operated their sherry shipping businesses from there and many of the firms still have British names. Even today Britain is the largest market for sherry followed by Netherlands and West Germany. In 1967 a British court decreed that only wine from the Jerez District of Spain was entitled to be called sherry and all other wines of a similar style must clearly state their country of origin with the word sherry; so we have 'Cyprus sherry' and 'South African sherry' but only one sherry.

VITICULTURE AND VINIFICATION
Soil in the Jerez area is graded on the proportion of chalk contained in it. *Albariza* soil is about fifty per cent chalk and so is very absorbent. The dried hard surface reflects the heat and holds in the moisture thus producing superior sherry grapes; *barros* soil is clay with ten per cent chalk and the wines are coarser and heavier; *arenas* soil is sandy with ten per cent chalk resulting in much lower quality grapes. The Palomino de Jerez grape is widely planted in the albariza soil and the Pedro Ximinez (PX) and Moscatel grapes used in making sweet dessert sherries are grown elsewhere.

The traditional method of producing sherry is being modified by the introduction of modern machinery. Once harvested, grapes used to be placed on esparto mats to dry in the sun leaving a concentration of sugar. Now they are placed on asbestos sheets covered with tents of polythene sheeting which draw the moisture from the grapes. The harvest goes to efficient central wineries capable of handling immense volumes of fruit. The must is pumped into traditional wood butts open to the air or stainless steel fermenting tanks. Palomino must is fermented right out but PX and Moscatel musts have wine spirit added to stop fermentation and retain the sugar content.

It is at this stage that a strange scum called *flor* (flower) develops on top of the wine. In most wine other than sherry, this would be considered a disaster and the wine would soon turn to vinegar. It is the result of a natural yeast peculiar to Jerez and man has no say in whether the flor will develop or not. If it does, then the wine will be a fino; if it does not, the wine will become an oloroso, and if only a slight flor develops it will be an amontillado. A very close watch is kept on the wine and the olorosos receive a larger amount of fortification which prevents any late flor from developing. Eventually the flor drops through the wine to the bottom of the cask and after racking, fining and maturing the new sherry is put into the solera system.

In the lodges sherries are blended through the solera system to maintain the desired quality and style of each shipper's product. The system can best be understood by imagining an inverted pyramid of wine barrels known as butts. The word 'solera' refers to the butts nearest the ground, which contain fine old wine. On top of these is a row of butts of slightly younger wine and the butts continue in tiers with each tier, known as a *criadera*, containing progressively younger wine; the new wine goes into the last criadera. Each criadera is numbered and the solera butts may be backed up by six to twelve criaderas. When old wine is withdrawn from a solera butt, it is replaced with younger wine from the criadera above. The younger wine then takes on the quality of the old wine, and after a few months the wine in the solera butt is indistinguishable from what it was before. This systematic replacement from the criadera above is known as the solera system. It is impossible to produce a vintage sherry by this method, but a wine may bear the date the solera began. A brand of sherry can be a mixture of several soleras. After the blending, colour wine may be added before fining and refrigeration. The sherry is then bottled or shipped in bulk.

While olorosos are drunk at room temperature, the lighter amontillados and finos are best served chilled.

STYLES OF SHERRY

Fino A very pale light dry wine with a delicate aroma and clear refreshing taste.

Amontillado An aged fino with an amber colour and dry nutty flavour. Unfortunately many wines so labelled are just sweet blends and the word is often used to describe a 'medium' sherry.

Manzanilla A fino that has been aged at Sanlucar de Barrameda. This town is by the coast and the sea air affects the wine. It is pale, dry and very crisp with a faintly bitter aftertaste.

Oloroso A dark gold wine with plenty of body and a distinctly nutty flavour. Pure olorosos are dry but most are sweetened for export markets.

Cream, Brown and Amoroso Oloroso sherries with a high proportion of sweet wine added for export markets.

Palo Cortado
A rare oloroso, not produced every year, with the body and colour of an oloroso but the nose and dryness of an amontillado.

Montilla
The region of Montilla has the same albariza soil and produces a style of wine very similar to sherry. Fermentation takes place in traditional large earthenware jars or modern cement-lined vats and there is little need for fortification as the wines have a naturally high alcohol content.

British 'Sherry'
Much of the cheaper wine sold in Britain is actually made from dehydrated grape juice from Greece or Cyprus. Water and yeasts are added to the concentrate which then ferments in the usual manner until it is fortified and sweetened.

VERMOUTH

Vermouth is an aromatized wine. Its name is derived from the German 'wermut' (wormwood). This herb was added to wine as early as AD 78 for medicinal purposes, but there were further advantages in that it could mask the flavour of sour wine and act as a preservative. Vermouth was certainly made in Italy in the seventeenth century and probably earlier in Germany, but it is no accident that the best vermouths were produced on both the French and Italian sides of the Alps, for it was in the foothills of the mountains that many of the herbs and flowers which are used for flavourings were originally found.

The French traditionally produced the lighter, drier vermouths and the Italians the sweeter, heavier ones. Vermouths of all types are now produced in both areas, but some people still use the terms 'French' for a dry vermouth (as in 'Gin and French') and Italian for a sweet one (as in 'Gin and Italian'). Vermouth is essentially a wine and as such will deteriorate once opened; dry vermouths should be drunk within two weeks, the sweet versions within a month of opening the bottle.

PRODUCTION

Vermouth production is a complicated process and each producer jealously guards his exact recipe; the production sequence however is generally standard.

The wine base is usually white wine, never of a fine or distinctive quality for so many transformations will occur that this would be an unnecessary expense. The base is sweetened by an addition of *mistelle* – unfermented grape juice and brandy – followed by the flavoured alcohol.

The flavour is extracted from the aromatic ingredients by maceration, infusion or distillation or even a combination of these methods, depending on the maker's requirements. The ingredients can include hyssop, quinine, coriander, juniper, cloves, camomile, orange peel, calamus roots, gentian roots, oregano, cinnamon, sandalwood, sage, orris, mace and even violet and rose petals.

After thorough blending, alcohol and sugar are added to achieve the correct strength and sweetness. Caramel is added for red vermouth. Both types are then aged for up to six months to allow the flavours to marry, and refrigerated to precipitate any tartrate crystals. The vermouth is then filtered to ensure it is crystal clear and pasteurized to stabilize the flavours.

French Vermouth It takes almost four years to make a French vermouth and the centre of the industry is Marseilles. Here the base wine is stored in thick oak casks and spends some time outside to allow exposure to the sea air. Consequently, these vermouths – sweet or dry – have a distinctly spicy aroma.

Chambéry A particularly fine example of dry vermouth is made in the foothills of the Alps at Savoie. It was granted Appellation d'Origine Contrôlée status in 1932. Herbs found only in the Chambéry region are used as flavouring and pure sugar, rather than mistelle, is used as the sweetening agent.

Italian Vermouth Turin is the centre of the Italian vermouth industry, although most of the wine comes from southern Italy. It takes about two years to produce a vermouth and all styles have much broader flavour than the French counterparts.

Other Vermouths Virtually every country that produces wine also makes vermouth, most of which is consumed locally. The South American countries have a big market for vermouth, especially Argentina, and it is taken almost entirely as an aperitif – over ice or with soda and a dash of bitters.

STYLES OF VERMOUTH

Red Caramel and sugar are added to make a sweet red vermouth.

Bianco A vermouth of medium sweetness is usually a golden colour.

Dry The colour varies from water-white to light gold.

Rosé Vermouth made with a base of rosé wine flavoured with herbs and spices has a bitter-sweet flavour.

Fruit Flavoured This style is becoming more popular and some very fine examples include orange and strawberry flavours.

OTHER AROMATIZED WINES

There are a number of well-known proprietary brands that are aromatized wines produced in a manner similar to vermouth. Many of them contain quinine and gentian to heighten the bitter flavour. These are especially popular in France where they are served as aperitifs but their fairly low alcoholic content makes them suitable for drinking at any time. The most widely available are Ambassadeur, Amer Picon, Byrrh, Dubonnet, Lillet, Primavera, St Raphael and Suze.

BITTERS

Essences extracted from plants, bark, roots and stems are compounded with alcohol to form a tincture known as bitters. Some bitters are supposed to have a medicinal character such as acting as a stomach tonic or as a malaria preventative. In the USA the law distinguishes between ordinary commercial bitters and medicinal bitters, which are not subject to the regular Internal Revenue alcohol tax and may be sold by grocers, drug and department stores. This applied throughout Prohibition when vast quantities of bitters were sold through the drug stores and used to make palatable the bathtub brews. These bitters are used as 'pick-me-ups' or taken with soda and include Fernet Branca, Ferro China and Campari from Italy, Toni-Kola from France, and Underberg from Germany. Bitters used as flavourings are Angostura from Trinidad, Peychaud from New Orleans, Abbots Aged from Baltimore, and peach and orange are the most popular fruit-flavoured bitters.

CIGARS

A well-stocked bar will always carry a good selection of cigars of all types, for the smaller panatella, cheroot and whiff styles are always popular with pre-prandial cocktail drinkers.

The smaller cigars are usually machine made and the inner *filler* may be from a different part of the world than the outer *wrapper*. The leaf from which a cigar is made may be grown in places as far apart as Java, Borneo, Sumatra in the East Indies, the USA, India, Japan, Central and South Africa, and many others. There is a very fine leaf from the West Indies, particularly from Jamaica and Cuba.

The Havana Cigar

Although fine cigar leaf is grown, and cigars are made, in many parts of the world, indisputably the best cigars in the world come from Cuba and are called after its capital city, Havana. It is the climate, geology and skill of the people of Cuba that together produce the leaves of sun-cured tobacco from the red earth of this Caribbean island.

Tobacco is grown all over Cuba, the finest from the areas of Vuelta Abajo, Partidos, Remedios and Oriente. All four produce a fine quality cigar leaf but the best of all comes from the Vuelta Abajo which provides the all-important wrapper leaf. The Vuelta Abajo is a natural hot-house just as the whole island of Cuba is a natural humidor.

In this unique climate and soil the Cuban tobacco plants grow to about six feet in height with leaves of up to eighteen inches in length. The leaves are cut between February and March, strung over bamboo poles and hung out to dry in huge barns. They are then stacked in great heaps to dry in the sun. It is now that the mysterious fermentation begins to take place within the leaves as they turn to a rich golden brown. The cured leaves are tied in bundles of five, known as hands, put into bales and stored in warehouses to mature for eighteen months to two years when they are judged to be ready for the cigar maker.

A cigar is made of three constituent parts – the *filler*, the *binder* and the *wrapper*. The filler, as the name implies, forms the interior of the cigar and to a large extent determines its flavour. To make a cigar, two to four leaves of filler tobacco are laid end to end and rolled into the binder, a leaf with good tensile strength chosen from the lower half of the plant. Great skill is required to ensure that the filler is evenly distributed so that the cigar will draw properly.

The next step is the wrapper. A whole leaf of the finest quality is chosen for this, the outside of the cigar. It must be smooth, not too prominently veined and of a good colour. Above all it must give a noble flavour and aroma because the wrapper is a vital ingredient in the taste of a cigar. Once this important leaf has been selected, the stalk is stripped from it by hand; the top point is nipped out between thumb and fingernail and the stalk wound around the fingers to remove it completely. The half-shaped leaves are cut into two wrappers with hook-shaped tops facing opposite directions. This is why if you examine a number of cigars carefully you will find that some of them are wrapped left-handed, others right-handed. All the cigars in a top quality box of cigars should be wrapped in the same direction.

Finally, the cylinder of tobacco in its binder leaf is laid at an angle across the cut strip of wrapper. The wrapper is then wrapped carefully around the binder, overlapping at each turn until at the end of the hook it is stuck down with a pinhead of vegetable gum, forming the rounded closed head of the cigar which is then guillotined at the other end to the correct length.

The well-known names with which the brands are prefixed, such as Petit Corona, Corona and Corona Grande, describe the size and not the make. Corona, for example, simply means a cigar that is about 14 centimetres in length, straight-sided with a rounded end.

The leaf used for wrappers varies considerably in natural colouring and when cigars are packed they are sorted into colour groups and these are marked on the boxes as follows:

Claro or CCC blonde, light golden brown;
Colorado-Claro or CC darker tawny colour;
Colorado or C ripe dark brown;
Maduro or M mature, rich, very dark.

A colour known as candella is very popular in the United States and this is of a greenish-yellow tint, but it has been artificially produced and is seldom found in the rest of the world.

There are pressed and unpressed cigars. The pressed cigar is made with the tobacco in the filler packed more loosely so that when the cigars are put in boxes the pressure of the shut lid will compact the cigar into the correct smoking density making it almost square. Unpressed cigars are made at the time of manufacture as compact as they should be for perfect smoking. Whether cigars are pressed or unpressed is largely a matter of the tradition of individual factories. Havana cigars are normally packed in oblong, colourfully labelled cedar-wood boxes, but for the specialist there are also bundles of fifty tied with ribbon in square plain cedar boxes – these are known as *cabinet* selection. The idea is that cigars thus packed interact on each other so that their flavour improves as they mature.

For those who like their cigars green, that is to say fresh, moist and unmatured, there are the cigars from the humidor glass jars which preserve this condition.

Another way of packing a cigar is in an individual aluminium tube. This is a popular and safe way of carrying a cigar in a pocket to prevent it being damaged. It is also an advisable package for people who have to keep their cigars near odours which might affect the flavour or by the sea where salt air can damage the cigar.

Selecting a cigar
There are many elaborate rituals indulged in when selecting a cigar. One is holding the cigar up to the ear and twirling it between finger and thumb. This is known rather scathingly as 'listening to the band', and reveals absolutely nothing for a faint crackle can be heard even in a cigar that is immature. Sniffing is another popular practice which does no harm but which does no good either. If you sniff a cigar you will find it will smell, not surprisingly, of tobacco. Another pointless ritual is that of warming the length of the cigar before lighting it. This

was originally done to burn off a rather disagreeable gum used for sticking down the wrappers of certain cigars made a hundred or more years ago. The pinhead of gum used nowadays is odourless and tasteless and there is no point in carrying on such a practice.

For some it is part of the cigar-smoking ritual to remove the band. If you feel you must remove it, do so by pressing the cigar gently below the band and easing it off with delicate care. But the experts believe that the band should only be removed when the cigar has reached its 'cruising' temperature, when about one-fifth of it has been smoked, and the band should come off easily as the cigar will have shrunk slightly.

Before you can light a cigar you have to open the closed end to allow the smoke through. Biting it off is a favourite practice with fictional house detectives but it is not to be recommended as there are more elegant and efficient ways of achieving the same result. Piercing the closed end with a match or spike is also not to be recommended. The opening thus created is too small and draws the smoke and oils down on to the tongue in a hot concentration which can be very disagreeable. Make your cut with a V-shaped or flat cutter which makes a good sized but not too large clean-edged opening through which it is possible to draw cigar smoke at its fragrant best. After cutting, the cigar should be tapped lightly on the finger to remove particles of loose tobacco. Light a cigar with a wooden match, spill of wood or a gas lighter, but not with sulphur or wax matches, or a petrol lighter because they affect the flavour. Light it gently, holding the flame some little distance from the cigar. Rotate the cigar in the flame to make sure that the end surface glows and lights evenly.

Fine Havanas can live in the right conditions for up to fifteen years. The most satisfactory way to maintain the condition of a cigar is to keep it in a humidor, i.e. a cabinet with a tight-fitting lid in which there is a moisture pad. This will regulate the humidity by moistening dry air and, if the pad is kept dry, absorbing excess moisture in wet weather.

Should it be impossible to obtain a humidor, then cigars are best left in their original cedar-wood boxes, well away from any extremes of heat and cold and away from any strong-smelling substances. If cigars are stored in bulk, they should be kept in a cupboard used only for that purpose and kept at a constant temperature of 15°–18°C.

From the time they are packed, cigars may take up to several years to mature and during this time they may sweat slightly, depositing a fine grey powder on their surface – a natural and unharmful process – and it should be removed with a soft, camel-hair brush.

Cigars which have been allowed to become dry should never be moistened and those which, through excessive damp, have began to smell musty will have been spoilt irreparably and can only be thrown away. There is no remedy for a failure of this kind.

To give the care and attention which prevents such disasters is to understand the delicate nature of cigars and the immense pleasure they offer to those who treat them well.

GLOSSARY

Acetic – Term used to describe wine that has turned sour because bacteria has converted the ethyl alcohol into acetic acid.

Agave – (century plant) source of cocui, tequila pulque and mescal.

Agraf, Agraffe – (Fr) clamp which holds the pressure of the second fermentation in a champagne bottle.

Alcohol – Ethyl alcohol (C_2H_5OH) is a colourless liquid with a faint but pleasant smell. The ethyl alcohol level is measured to determine the alcoholic content of a beverage.

Methyl alcohol is a toxic substance produced by the breakdown of pectin in the skins of the fruit. A minute amount is permissible in wine as it adds to the bouquet but it must be distilled off when making a high grade spirit to render it odourless.

Amaro – 'Bitter' in Italian. It is a generic term applied to the hundreds of proprietary brands of bitter digestive drinks sold in Italy.

Apoplexy – Vine disease.

Appellation Contrôlée – Limited production of wine districts and protection of names under French Law. (AC)

Astringent – A mouth puckering sensation. The degree of astringency depends on the amount of tannin in a beverage.

Bacchus – Wine god, also American hybrid grape.

Balthazar – Bottle size (16 bottles) 12.80 litres.

Barrique – (Fr) barrel or hogshead.

Baumé – The measurement of sugar in wine. 1° baumé equals 18 grams of sugar.

Beeswing – The light film that occasionally clings to the glass. It occurs most frequently in port.

Bottle stink – A stale smell can come from wine for a few minutes after the cork has been pulled. This will dissipate if the wine is left for a few minutes or is decanted. Bottle stink must not be confused with corked wine.

Bouquet – The fragrant impression left after nosing a beverage.

Broyage – Crushing of grapes.

Bung – Stopper for wine or beer cask.

Bond – The store, vault or cellar in which wine and spirits are kept under Customs and Excise supervision before duty has been paid. The purchaser of wine or spirit in bond is liable for the payment of the duty thereon before he can take delivery of his purchase. To pay duty on and take delivery of wine and spirits in bond is to clear from bond.

Caramel – Burnt sugar for colouring.

Carbonated – Impregnated with carbonic acid gas (CO_2).

Carbon dioxide – CO_2 is a product of fermentation. For still wine it is allowed to escape into the air. If fermentation takes place in a closed container such as a tank or a bottle, the gas is trapped and the liquid absorbs it to produce a sparkling wine. When only a little CO_2 is absorbed into the wine it will give a faint prickling sensation on the tongue. The wine is then said to be 'spritzig', 'frizzante' or 'petillant'. The presence of CO_2 accelerates the absorption of alcohol into the blood stream.

Chambrer – To place a wine in a room where it will gradually acquire the temperature of the room.

Chaptalisation – The practice of adding sugar to the grape must. This occurs in Germany, Burgundy and other cold areas where the natural grape sugar level is not enough to produce sufficient alcohol. It must be strictly controlled to maintain high standards of winemaking.

Collage – Fining of wine.

Congenerics – The flavouring and aromatic elements that are retained in a spirit after distillation. The more highly distilled the spirit, the less congenerics there are in the beverage.

Co-operative – A cellar belonging jointly to a number of small producers.

Corkage – A fee paid to a restaurant when bringing one's own wine and having it served in the restaurant. (This does not apply in Australian BYOs).

Corked wine – Wine permanently tainted by a mouldy cork.

Cru – Growth.

Crystals – Tartrate crystals can appear in red and white wine. Tartaric acid is the principal acid in wine and it gradually precipitates as tartrate crystals as the wine matures. Sometimes they can be seen clinging to the bottom of the cork. The presence of tartrates is a sign of quality. However, most uninformed people object to their presence and modern winemaking practice is to refrigerate white wines to hasten this precipitation so that the bottled wine will remain free of them.

Decanting – Wine benefits from being poured into a special glass container. This separates the liquid from any deposits that may be in the bottle. It also exposes the wine to the atmosphere which allows it to 'open out' its bouquet and flavour.

Demijohn – A bulging, narrow-necked glass container holding from 3 to 10 gallons, used mostly for the storing of Madeira wine, and also for spirits. It is usually cased in wicker with wicker handles or lugs.

Demi-Sec – Half dry. It is applied to Champagne and also to other sparkling wines. Sometimes it can apply to certain rosé wines.

Deposit – The sediment which many red and some white wines throw while in bottle. In white wines this is tasteless and harmless but red wine deposit contains tannin and can be very bitter and unpleasant. It should be left in the bottle when decanting.

Distillation – The process whereby a liquid base is heated so that it vapourizes. The vapour is cooled and condenses as another liquid which has a higher alcoholic content. This is so because alcohol has a much lower boiling point than water so it vapourizes first.

Dosage – The final addition of sugar in Champagne process.

Fermentation – The process whereby yeasts break down the sugars in a substance and convert them to ethyl alcohol and carbon dioxide. By-products of this conversion are glycerine, volatile acids and higher alcohols such as fusel oils. Fermentation ceases when all the sugar has been converted which results in a dry wine. The process can be halted by the addition of brandy which raises the alcohol content above the level at which yeasts are able to work. This retains most of the natural grape sugar in the liquid which is known as a fortified wine.

Filtration – Most wine is filtered prior to bottling. It is pumped through a succession of asbestos and porous porcelain plates which remove any solids. Care must be taken to ensure the wine is not contaminated during this process.

Fining – The traditional method of clearing a wine is to mix a clay such as bentonite through the liquid. Any solid particles in the wine cling to the clay which eventually falls to the bottom of the container. However this process takes about eight days and many wineries now prefer to filter the wine or clarify it in a centrifuge.

Fortified – Wine is fortified by the addition of grape spirit. This raises the alcohol content and stops fermentation so that some sugar is retained in the beverage. It also acts as a preservative. Examples of fortified wines are port, sherry, madeira and marsala.

Frappé – A liqueur which is frappé is served over crushed ice. Any other beverage such as wine means very cold.

Frosting – A glass is frosted by wetting the rim with a wedge of lemon and dipping it in caster sugar.

Generic – A general name applied to a group of wines, which does not relate to their origin.

Hectare – One hectare equals 2·471 acres.

Hogshead – Cask containing about 56 gallons or 256 litres, half a pipe. This measurement may vary depending on content.

		Gallons	
	Litres	US	Imp.
Burgundy and Bordeaux	225	59·5	49·5
Beer and cider	246	64·8	54·1
Sherry	246	64·8	54·1
Whisky	250	66	55
Port	259	68·4	57
Brandy	273	72	60

Jeroboam – Bottle size (4 bottles) 3·20 litres.

Jigger – American bar measure 40 ml. or 1·5 imp ounces.

Lees – The sediment deposited by wine during maturation.

Maderisation – Wine that has been exposed to air (usually because of a faulty cork) will develop a brown hue. This will adversely affect the flavour of wines that are meant to be fresh and crisp. However white wine that has been aged in oak will be slightly maderised and this contributes to its soft round flavour.

Magnum – Bottle size (2 bottles) 1·60 litres.

Mash – Prepared ingredients before fermentation.

Mead – An alcoholic beverage made from fermented honey.

Methuselah – Bottle size (8 bottles) 6·40 litres.

Mousec – French term for sparkling.

Must – Grape juice before fermentation.

Nebuchadnezzar – Bottle size (20 bottles) 16 litres.

Nip – A quarter bottle.

Noggin – English measure equal to a quarter pint.

Oxidised – Wine that has been over-exposed to air will turn brown and have a burnt caramel smell.

Pipe – The standard cask for port in the British Isles; its gauge is 115 gallons, averaging 56 dozens (672) when bottled.

Posset – A drink of hot milk mixed with ale or wine and flavoured with honey and spices.

Punt – The hollow in the base of a wine bottle. The French term is 'pointe'.

Pupitre – Rack with oval holes in which Champagne bottles are placed for turning.

Racking – Wine is transferred from one container to another. This removes it from its lees and possible contact with bacteria. Red wine may be racked several times during its initial ageing period.

Rectification – (redistillation) of spirit.

Rehoboam – Bottle size (6 bottles) 4·80 litres.

Salmanazar – Bottle size (12 bottles) 9·60 litres.

Sediment – Fine wine is a living product and chemical changes continue as it matures in bottle. Thus the tannins and colourants gradually precipitate out and this is why old red wine is usually a tawny colour. The deposit can vary from a fine film to a heavy crust.

Shrub – A term used to describe a drink with a spirit base that contained orange or lemon juice. It was made in large quantities and left to mature for a few weeks before being consumed.

Soft wines – In the USA, wines that have a very low alcohol content are referred to as soft wines.

Sulphur – Sulphur dioxide is added to wine as a disinfectant. Sometimes it can be detected in recently bottled wine but the smell should dissipate after a few minutes contact with the air.

Syrups – High quality fruit syrups are essential ingredients in many mixed drinks. They are sweet non-alcoholic essences which give colour and/or flavour to the drink. The most readily available are grenadine (pomegranate), cassis (blackcurrant), fraise (strawberry), framboise (raspberry) and orgeat (almond). Falernum is a milky coloured syrup flavoured with lime, almond and ginger. Sugar syrup is the sweetener used most frequently in cocktails as it mixes readily. A simple sugar syrup is made by dissolving 2 cups of sugar in 1 cup water then simmering for 10 mins. This keeps indefinitely if refrigerated. A commercial preparation marketed as gomme syrup is a very acceptable alternative.

Tannin – Tannin is contained in the skins, stalks and pips of grapes. It is readily absorbed into the juice once the grapes are crushed. A red wine needs a high tannin content to age for a long period.

Ullage – The ullage is the amount of space between the wine and the cork. A large ullage may result from incomplete filling or may indicate that the bottle has leaked at some stage. Very old wine often has a large ullage. The term is also used for a barrel of beer which has been tapped.

Vinification – The process of making wine.

Viticulture – The science of grape growing.

VSEP – (Very Superior Extra Pale) cognac.

VSO – (Very Superior Old) cognac.

VSOP – (Very Superior Old Pale) Armagnac and cognac.

VVSOP – (Very Very Superior Old Pale) cognac.

Weeper – A bottle showing signs of a leaky cork.

XO – Designation of cognac.

TABLES OF MEASUREMENT

IMPERIAL MEASURES

160 fluid ounces	= 1 gallon
5 fluid ounces	= 1 gill
20 fluid ounces	= 1 pint
4 gills	= 1 pint
2 pints	= 1 quart
4 quarts	= 1 gallon

METRIC MEASURES

10 millilitres	= 1 centilitre
10 centilitres	= 1 decilitre
10 decilitres	= 1 litre
10 litres	= 1 decalitre
10 decalitres	= 1 hectolitre
10 hectolitres	= 1 kilolitre

CONVERSION TABLES

In the following table the key figure is printed in the centre column, this can be read as either the metric or Imperial measure, thus:

1 gallon = 4·544 litres or 1 litre = 0·220 gallons.

Gallons		Litres	Pints		Litres
0·220	1	4·544	1·761	1	0·568
0·440	2	9·087	3·521	2	1·136
0·660	3	13·631	5·282	3	1·704
0·880	4	18·174	7·043	4	2·272
1·101	5	22·718	8·804	5	2·840
1·321	6	27·262	10·564	6	3·408
1·541	7	31·805	12·325	7	3·976
1·761	8	36·349	14 068	8	4·544
1·981	9	40·892	15·846	9	5·112

Fluid Ounces		Millilitres
0·035	1	28·416
0·07	2	56·832
0·106	3	85·248
0·14	4	113·664
0·176	5	142·080
0·211	6	170·496
0·246	7	198·912
0·282	8	227·328
0·317	9	255·744

Fluid Ounces	Gills	Gallons	Cls.	Litres
1	·2	·00625	2·84	·0284
2	·4	·0125	5·68	·0568
4	·8	·025	11·36	·1136
5 (1 gill)	1·0	·0312	14·20	·1420
6	1·2	·0375	17·04	·1704
8	1·6	·050	22·72	·2272
10 (½ pint)	2·0	·0625	28·41	·2841
12	2·4	·075	34·09	·3409
14	2·8	·875	39·76	·3976
16	3·2	·1	45·43	·4543
18	3·6	·1125	51·11	·5111
20 (1 pint)	4·0	·125	56·82	·5682
22	4·4	·1375	62·48	·6248
24	4·8	·15	68·19	·6819
26	5·2	·1625	73·83	·7383
28	5·6	·175	79·51	·7951
30	6·0	·1875	85·23	·8523
32	6·4	·2	90·87	·9087
34	6·8	·2125	96·55	·9655
36	7·2	·225	102·20	1·022
38	7·6	·2375	107·96	1·079
40 (1 quart)	8·0	·25	113·64	1·136

1 Hectolitre = 100 litres = 22 gallons
To convert gallons to litres multiply by 4·546
To convert litres to gallons multiply by 0·22

The **standard spirit bottle** contains 26·4 fluid ounces (75 centilitres), except brandy, which contains 24 fluid ounces (68 centilitres).

No. of measures per gill	Ounces	No. of measures per standard bottle
1 out	5	5⅓
2 out	2·5	10⅔
3 out	1·67	16
4 out	1·25	21⅓
5 out	1·00	26⅔
6 out	0·835	32
7 out	0·715	37⅓
8 out	0·625	42⅔
9 out	0·556	48
10 out	0·500	53⅓

Imperial and American Gallon

There is a difference between the British and American gallon. The British Imperial gallon is equal to 1·20 American gallons. The British Imperial gallon contains 160 fluid ounces and the American gallon contains 128 American fluid ounces. From this it will be observed that, whilst the American gallon is smaller than the British gallon, the American fluid ounce is a larger measure than the British fluid ounce. 1 American fluid ounce = ·960 British fluid ounces. 1 British fluid ounce = 1·0416 American fluid ounces.

To convert American fluid ounces to British fluid ounces multiply by 1·0416. To convert British fluid ounces to American fluid ounces divide by 1·0416.

Hydrometer
An instrument for determining the specific gravity of liquids. Attributed to Archimedes, but not much used until re-invented by Robert Boyle.

It takes the form of a narrow sealed instrument of cylindrical section and consists of three parts – counterpoise at the bottom, a bulb containing air, and the scale at the top. It can be made of glass, poised with lead shot or mercury, or of gilt brass.

Sikes' hydrometer has an arbitrary scale and has to be used with a thermometer and book of tables.

The Gay-Lussac's Alcoholometer is for testing alcoholic solutions, and its scale reads percentage per volume, 0° to 100°.

SPIRIT STRENGTHS

Traditionally, there have been three main scales used in measuring alcoholic strength.

(1) The 'Sikes' scale as used in Britain and the Commonwealth;
(2) The 'Gay-Lussac' (GL) Scale as used in France and most of Europe;
(3) The American scale as used in the USA.

This has led to many misunderstandings in the past and has given producers some labelling problems.

However, under the new EEC regulations from 1st January 1983, alcoholic strength in Europe (and Britain) is expressed in % of alcohol by volume as on the Gay-Lussac scale.

During the lifetime of this book, however, labels will still be found with the old Sikes measurement and, as the American scale still exists, it is hoped that the following explanations, examples and scale will be of some assistance.

To understand the three scales used one must first accept that for all three scales water (no alcohol) is rated as 0 and that absolute (pure) alcohol is the top of each scale.

On the Sikes scale absolute alcohol is given as 175. On the Gay-Lussac scale it is 100 and, on the American scale, 200. Therefore it will be seen that 70° proof Sikes = 40° GL or 40% alcohol by volume = 80° US proof.

To convert GL to US proof one merely has to multiply by 2 and vice versa, but the formula for converting to and from Sikes is slightly more complicated.

To convert from Sikes to GL divide by 1·75 and from GL to Sikes multiply by 1·75.

For example:

(i) 70° Sikes	= 40° GL	= 80° US
70 ÷ 1·75	= 40 × 2	= 80
(ii) 100° US	= 50° GL	= 87·5° Sikes
100 ÷ 2	= 50 × 1·75	= 87·5

COMPARATIVE SCALES FOR ALCOHOLIC STRENGTHS

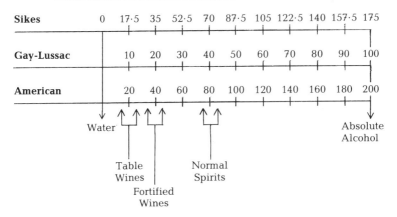

BIBLIOGRAPHY

GENERAL

GROSSMAN, Harold, *Grossman's Guide to Wines, Beers and Spirits*, 6th edition, Charles Scribner's Sons, New York; Frederick Muller, London, 1977

LICHINE, Alexis, *Alexis Lichine's Encyclopaedia of Wines & Spirits*, 3rd edition, Cassell, 1974

VANDYKE PRICE, Pamela, *Dictionary of Wines and Spirits*, Northwood, 1980

MIXED DRINKS

EMBURY, David, *The Fine Art of Mixing Drinks*, Faber, 1963

TRADER VIC, *Trader Vic's Bartender's Guide*, Doubleday, 1972

SPIRITS AND LIQUEURS

HALLGARTEN, Peter, *Spirits and Liqueurs*, Faber & Faber, 1979

LORD, Tony, *The World Guide to Spirits*, Macdonald & Jane's, 1979

McDOWALL, R. S. J., *The Whiskies of Scotland*, John Murray, 1975

RAY, Cyril, *Cognac*, Peter Davies, 1973

VANDYKE PRICE, Pamela, *The Penguin Book of Spirits and Liqueurs*, Penguin Books, 1980

WINES

CHIDGEY, Graham, *Guide to the Wines of Burgundy*, Pitman Publishing, 1977

EVANS, Len, *Complete Book of Australian Wine*, 3rd edition, Paul Hamlyn, 1978

FORBES, Patrick, *Champagne, the Wine, the Land and the People*, Victor Gollancz, 1967

GONZALEZ GORDON, Manuel, *Sherry*, Cassell & Co., 1972

HANNUM, H. and BLUMBERG, R., *The Fine Wines of California*, Dolphin, 1973

HALLGARTEN, S. F., *Alsace, its Wine Gardens, Cellars and Cuisine*, 3rd edition, Wine & Spirit Publications, 1978

HALLGARTEN, S. F. and F. L., *The Wines and Wine Gardens of Austria*, Argus Books, 1979

JOHNSON, Hugh, *The World Atlas of Wine*, Mitchell Beazley, 1977

KNOX, David, *Estate Wines of South Africa*, David Philip, Claremont, Cape Province, 1976

LIVINGSTONE-LEARMOUTH, John and MASTER, Melvyn, *The Wines of the Rhone*, Faber & Faber, 1978

READ, Jan, *Guide to the Wines of Spain and Portugal*, Pitman Publishing, 1977

ROBERTSON, George, *Port*, Faber & Faber, 1978

RONCARATI, Bruno, *Viva Vino, Doc Wine of Italy*, Wine & Spirit Publications, 1976

SIEGEL, Hans, *Guide to the Wines of Germany*, Pitman Publishing, 1978

SMITH, Joanna, *The New English Vineyard*, Sidgwick & Jackson, 1979

VANDYKE PRICE, Pamela, *Guide to the Wines of Bordeaux*, Pitman Publishing, 1977

BEER

JACKSON, Michael, *The World Guide to Beer*, Mitchell Beazley, 1979

REGISTER OF DRINKS

229

231

INDEX OF SPIRIT BASES

233

GENERAL INDEX

ACKNOWLEDGEMENTS

The United Kingdom Bartenders Guild would like to extend their gratitude to the following people and companies for their efforts towards making this book possible:

Atkinson, Baldwin & Co., Limited
Amaretto di Saronno, Drambuie, Galliano
Cinzano (UK) Limited
Gilbey, W. & A. Limited in conjunction with I.D.V., *Gilbey's Gin, J & B Rare Scotch Whisky, Smirnoff Vodka*
Hedges & Butler Limited and Fourcroy (UK) Limited, *Bacardi Rum, Mandarine Napoléon Liqueur*
Matthew Clark & Sons Limited, *Martell Cognac, Taittinger Champagne*
Reynier, J. B. Limited, *Exir Sirops*
Saccone & Speed Limited, *Bols Liqueurs*
Scovill, (US), *Hamilton Beach, Bar-blenders and Ice-crushers*

Also:

Heal & Son Limited (London), for furnishing the glassware throughout, Robert Dowling for the colour and equipment photograpy, and Ewing Paddock for the chapter illustrations.

A special thanks to Marilyn Harvey for the time and knowledge she has contributed to this book.